Building Web Apps with Spring 5 and Angular

Build modern end-to-end web applications using Spring and Angular

Ajitesh Shukla

BIRMINGHAM - MUMBAI

Building Web Apps with Spring 5 and Angular

First published: August 2017

Production reference: 1210817

Published by Packt Publishing Ltd.
Livery Place
35 Livery Street
Birmingham
B3 2PB, UK.

ISBN 978-1-78728-466-1

www.packtpub.com

Credits

Author
Ajitesh Shukla

Reviewer
Parth Ghiya

Commissioning Editor
Aaron Lazar

Acquisition Editor
Nitin Dasan

Content Development Editor
Zeeyan Pinheiro

Technical Editor
Pavan Ramchandani

Copy Editors
Sonia Mathur
Sameen Siddiqui

Project Coordinator
Vaidehi Sawant

Proofreader
Safis Editing

Indexer
Francy Puthiry

Graphics
Abhinash Sahu

Production Coordinator
Nilesh Mohite

About the Author

Ajitesh Shukla is an accomplished software engineer with over 18 years experience in the IT industry, taking up different roles and responsibilities in startups and bigger companies, including Infosys, Computer Associates, WaveCrest, Evoke Technologies, and Raksan Consulting. He has worked on several web and mobile app projects based on technologies such as Java, Spring, Hibernate, AngularJS/Angular, ReactJS, and Ionic framework. Currently, he's interested in building cloud-native apps, cloud platforms, blockchain, and cyber security.

Ajitesh is an avid blogger and writes for websites such as DZone and Vitalflux, among many others. His hobbies include playing musical instruments, writing, and attending and organizing meetups.

Currently, Ajitesh has been working with a startup, Raksan consulting, as a Technology Evangelist where he is leading their innovation team and carving out newer solutions in the area of cloud platforms such as AWS/Google cloud, cloud-native technologies, data analytics, and blockchain.

You can follow Ajitesh on LinkedIn (`/ajitesh`) and GitHub (`/eajitesh`). You can also follow Ajitesh on Stack Overflow (`/users/554132/ajitesh`).

I would like to dedicate this book to my wife, two lovely daughters, my parents and family members whose love, support and blessings have always been there with me, inspiring and supporting me in all endeavors I undertook, while also playing the role of critique and making sure I get the job done in best possible manner. I would like to convey my sincere thanks to my friends and colleagues who have always helped me achieve greater things in life while constantly inspiring me in take up newer challenges and give my best to each one of them. Special thanks to my current employer, Raksan consulting, who motivated me enough to cross over this milestone. Last but not the least, I would like to thank Packt Publishing for giving me the opportunity to author this book.

About the Reviewer

Parth Ghiya has a good experience in NodeJS, frontend technologies (Backbone JS, Angular JS, and others), portal frameworks (Liferay and EXO), and database technologies (MongoDB, MySQL, PostgreSQL, SQL, and others). He has quick adaptability to any technology and a keen desire for constant improvement.

Currently, Parth is associated with a leading open source enterprise development company, KNOWARTH Technologies, as a software consultant where he takes care of enterprise projects with regards to requirement analysis, architecture design, security design, high availability, deployment, and build processes to help customers along with leading the team.

Parth has led and delivered projects in health care, HIPAA-compliant health care portals, travel, HR, and payroll, and mobile applications.

Parth has proven skills in working with various of technologies such as Angular JS, Angular 2/4, Liferay, MySQL, Pentaho, NodeJS, Idempiere, Alfresco, MongoDB, Grunt, gulp, webpack, ionic, nativescript, Jenkins, SVN, GIT, and AWS Cloud, and is a capable full-stack developer.

Parth has been recognized with awards such as *Best Employee* and *Special Contribution Award* for his valuable contribution to the business. He is an active contributor in Stack Overflow and other forums. He is a good trainer and has mentored many people. He writes blogs and is a speaker, and he has actively organized webinars. He can be contacted at ghiya.parth@gmail.com.

You can follow him on Facebook (ghiya.parth), Twitter (@parthghiya), or add him on LinkedIn (parthghiya). You can also follow Parth on Stack Overflow (https://stackoverflow.com/users/2305149/parth-ghiya).

Thank you is the best prayer that anyone could say and I say that a lot. I would like to tender my humble thanks to my family, teachers, and my extended family (all my friends and colleagues) who have helped me constantly excel myself and be a humble person, and gave me their time--the most thoughtful gift of all. I would like to thank KNOWARTH for providing new opportunities to constantly enhance myself. I would also like to thank Packt Publishing for giving me the opportunity to review this book.

www.PacktPub.com

For support files and downloads related to your book, please visit www.PacktPub.com.

Did you know that Packt offers eBook versions of every book published, with PDF and ePub files available? You can upgrade to the eBook version at www.PacktPub.com and as a print book customer, you are entitled to a discount on the eBook copy. Get in touch with us at service@packtpub.com for more details.

At www.PacktPub.com, you can also read a collection of free technical articles, sign up for a range of free newsletters and receive exclusive discounts and offers on Packt books and eBooks.

https://www.packtpub.com/mapt

Get the most in-demand software skills with Mapt. Mapt gives you full access to all Packt books and video courses, as well as industry-leading tools to help you plan your personal development and advance your career.

Why subscribe?

- Fully searchable across every book published by Packt
- Copy and paste, print, and bookmark content
- On demand and accessible via a web browser

Customer Feedback

Thanks for purchasing this Packt book. At Packt, quality is at the heart of our editorial process. To help us improve, please leave us an honest review on this book's Amazon page at https://www.amazon.com/dp/1787284662.

If you'd like to join our team of regular reviewers, you can e-mail us at customerreviews@packtpub.com. We award our regular reviewers with free eBooks and videos in exchange for their valuable feedback. Help us be relentless in improving our products!

Table of Contents

Preface

The book covers topics related to creating an end-to-end modern web application by using Angular for building the web app frontend and Spring framework for the backend, while integrating the apps via REST APIs and securing the API transactions using Spring Security concepts. Traditionally, Java developers have been used to developing the backend of a web application, while the frontend (UI) has been left for UI developers. However, this book aims to enable and empower Spring web application developers to quickly get started with Angular and build frontend (UI) components as well along with the backend components.

The following are some of the key challenges that we will address in this book:

- Building Angular apps (especially for Spring web developers)
- Security
- Integration
- Deployment

Here are some of the key milestones that we will cover in this book:

- Preparing development environments, where we highlight the usage of Docker containers to create a development environment that is easy to spin up and decommission once done
- Creating Spring Boot web application backend components such as API endpoints, controllers, services, and data access components using the Spring Web MVC framework and Hibernate
- Creating web application frontend (UI) or rather single-page apps (SPAs) using Angular concepts such as Components, Services, Routing, and so on
- Unit testing both Spring and Angular apps
- Building and running both Spring and Angular apps
- Securing the API transactions using Spring security and also taking care of security aspects related to the content displayed on the frontend (Angular apps)
- Integrating Angular apps with Spring Web app REST endpoints
- Deploying web apps based on Continuous Delivery principles

What this book covers

Chapter 1, *Introduction to Spring Web Framework*, provides an introduction to the Spring and the Spring Web MVC framework along with code samples for configuring Spring MVC and creating Spring Boot web applications.

Chapter 2, *Preparing the Spring Web Development Environment*, provides information on the necessary tools (along with code samples) that may be required to be installed/configured for working with Spring web apps.

Chapter 3, *Data Access Layer with Spring and Hibernate*, covers the concepts and code samples related to setting up Hibernate with Spring.

Chapter 4, *Testing and Running Spring Web App*, describes concepts and code samples related to running a Spring web app and writing unit tests for different types of web app components such as controllers, services, DAOs, and so on.

Chapter 5, *Securing Web App with Spring Security*, explains the concepts related to Spring security such as authentication, CSRF protection, and so on API requests made by Angular single page apps (SPAs).

Chapter 6, *Getting Started with Angular*, covers Angular fundamentals along with code samples and instructions on how to set up the Angular app development environment.

Chapter 7, *Creating SPA with Angular and Spring 5*, explains the key concepts related with creating single page applications using Angular and Spring.

Chapter 8, *Unit Testing with Angular Apps*, takes you through the steps required to set up environment and write/execute unit tests with Angular components/services, and so on.

Chapter 9, *Securing Angular Apps*, describes concepts related to protecting the content displayed by Angular apps from common web vulnerabilities and attacks such as cross-site scripting (XSS), cross-site request forgery (CSRF), and cross-site script inclusion (XSSI).

Chapter 10, *Integrating Angular Apps with Spring Web APIs*, describes concepts related to how Angular apps can be integrated with Spring endpoints based on the REST protocol.

Chapter 11, *Deploying Web Applications*, describes concepts related to deploying web applications using continuous delivery principles.

What you need for this book

Developers will be required to work with some of the following software:

- Java
- A Java framework such as Spring or Hibernate
- The Eclipse IDE (optional)
- Angular
- The Javascript IDE (optional) for working with Angular code
- Jenkins
- GitLab
- Docker

Who this book is for

This book is targeted at Java web developers, with a basic knowledge of Spring, who want to build complete web applications in a fast and effective way. It will help those who want to gain a stronghold on both frontend and backend development to advance in their careers.

Conventions

In this book, you will find a number of text styles that distinguish between different kinds of information. Here are some examples of these styles and an explanation of their meaning.

Code words in text, database table names, folder names, filenames, file extensions, pathnames, dummy URLs, user input, and Twitter handles are shown as follows: "In order to bypass Angular built-in sanitization for the value passed in, Angular provides a class such as `DomSanitizer`."

A block of code is set as follows:

```
@RequestMapping("/")
String home() {
    return "Hello world. How are you?";
}

public static void main(String[] args) {
    SpringApplication.run(HelloWorldApplication.class, args);
}
```

When we wish to draw your attention to a particular part of a code block, the relevant lines or items are set in bold:

```
@Controller
@RequestMapping("/account/*")
public class UserAccountController {
    @RequestMapping
    public String login() {
        return "login";
    }
}
```

Any command-line input or output is written as follows:

```
docker pull gitlab/gitlab-ce
```

New terms and **important words** are shown in bold. Words that you see on the screen, for example, in menus or dialog boxes, appear in the text like this: "It is required to add GitLab username/password credentials which can be achieved by clicking on **Add** button"

Warnings or important notes appear like this.

Tips and tricks appear like this.

Reader feedback

Feedback from our readers is always welcome. Let us know what you think about this book-what you liked or disliked. Reader feedback is important for us as it helps us develop titles that you will really get the most out of.

To send us general feedback, simply e-mail feedback@packtpub.com, and mention the book's title in the subject of your message.

If there is a topic that you have expertise in and you are interested in either writing or contributing to a book, see our author guide at www.packtpub.com/authors.

Customer support

Now that you are the proud owner of a Packt book, we have a number of things to help you to get the most from your purchase.

Downloading the example code

You can download the example code files for this book from your account at `http://www.packtpub.com`. If you purchased this book elsewhere, you can visit `http://www.packtpub.com/support` and register to have the files e-mailed directly to you. You can download the code files by following these steps:

1. Log in or register to our website using your e-mail address and password.
2. Hover the mouse pointer on the **SUPPORT** tab at the top.
3. Click on **Code Downloads & Errata**.
4. Enter the name of the book in the **Search** box.
5. Select the book for which you're looking to download the code files.
6. Choose from the drop-down menu where you purchased this book from.
7. Click on **Code Download**.

Once the file is downloaded, please make sure that you unzip or extract the folder using the latest version of:

- WinRAR / 7-Zip for Windows
- Zipeg / iZip / UnRarX for Mac
- 7-Zip / PeaZip for Linux

The code bundle for the book is also hosted on GitHub at `https://github.com/PacktPublishing/Building-Web-Apps-with-Spring-5-and-Angular`. We also have other code bundles from our rich catalog of books and videos available at `;https://github.com/PacktPublishing/`. Check them out!

Downloading the color images of this book

We also provide you with a PDF file that has color images of the screenshots/diagrams used in this book. The color images will help you better understand the changes in the output. You can download this file from `https://www.packtpub.com/sites/default/files/downloads/BuildingWebAppswithSpring5andAngular_ColorImages.pdf`.

Errata

Although we have taken every care to ensure the accuracy of our content, mistakes do happen. If you find a mistake in one of our books-maybe a mistake in the text or the code-we would be grateful if you could report this to us. By doing so, you can save other readers from frustration and help us improve subsequent versions of this book. If you find any errata, please report them by visiting http://www.packtpub.com/submit-errata, selecting your book, clicking on the **Errata Submission Form** link, and entering the details of your errata. Once your errata are verified, your submission will be accepted and the errata will be uploaded to our website or added to any list of existing errata under the Errata section of that title.

To view the previously submitted errata, go to https://www.packtpub.com/books/content/support and enter the name of the book in the search field. The required information will appear under the **Errata** section.

Piracy

Piracy of copyrighted material on the Internet is an ongoing problem across all media. At Packt, we take the protection of our copyright and licenses very seriously. If you come across any illegal copies of our works in any form on the Internet, please provide us with the location address or website name immediately so that we can pursue a remedy.

Please contact us at copyright@packtpub.com with a link to the suspected pirated material.

We appreciate your help in protecting our authors and our ability to bring you valuable content.

Questions

If you have a problem with any aspect of this book, you can contact us at questions@packtpub.com, and we will do our best to address the problem.

1
Introduction to Spring Web Framework

In this chapter, you will learn about the key concepts of the Spring framework, and how we can use this framework to develop web applications. The following are some of the topics that will be dealt with:

- Introduction to the Spring IOC container
- Introduction to the Spring web MVC
- Building a `Hello World` web application with Spring Boot
- Implementing controllers
- Handling request parameters
- Handler interceptors
- Handling responses
- Creating a RESTful Web Service
- Dockerizing Spring Boot Application

Starting with the section, *Implementing controllers* in this chapter, we will start building a sample healthcare web application to demonstrate the key concepts. The following are some of the key functionalities of the sample app which will be covered as part of building the app:

- Signup for doctors and patients
- Logging into the app
- Searching for doctors based on their specialties
- Fixing an appointment
- Interacting with the doctor

Introduction to the Spring IOC container

As a primer to learning the Spring Web MVC framework, it is recommended to learn some of the following object-oriented design principles, which act as a basis for the Spring Web framework. Note that these principles form a part of the famous **Single responsibility, Open-closed, Liskov substitution, Interface segregation, and Dependency inversion (SOLID)** principle by Robert Martin (Uncle Bob):

- **Single Responsibility Principle (SIP)**: This principle states that a module, a class, or a method should have the responsibility of serving just one functionality of the underlying software. In other words, a module, a class or a method should have just one reason to change. Modules or classes following SIP have high cohesiveness, and thus, can be termed as reusable entities. Classes violating SIP are found to have high cyclomatic complexity, and thus, low testability.

- **Open-Closed Principle (OCP)**: This principle states that the classes are open for extension, but closed for modification. Based on this principle, the core classes of the Spring Web MVC consist of some methods which are marked as final, which, essentially, means that these final methods can not be overridden with custom behavior.

- **Liskov Substitution Principle (LSP)**: This principle states that if a class A (child class) is derived from class B (parent class), then the object of class B can be replaced by (or substituted with) an object of class A without changing any of the properties of class B. It can be inferred that the functions which use references of the base class must be able to use objects of the derived class without the need to know about the implementation of the base class. For example, let's consider the square and rectangle example. In the case where square derives from rectangle, then, as per LSP, an object of the class Rectangle can be substituted with an object of the class Square. However, in reality, this is not possible without doing appropriate implementation in the Square class setter methods, where setting either of length or breadth sets another side of equal length, and/or code using these classes do appropriate checks to find out whether the object is an instance of the class Square or Rectangle.

- **Interface Segregation Principle (ISP)**: This principle states that the fat interfaces having large number of API definitions should be split into smaller interfaces defining a set of cohesive APIs. Not following this principle leads to the client providing empty implementations for unwanted APIs.

- **Dependency Inversion Principle (DIP)**: This principle is pretty much related to the IOC principle, which is discussed in the next section. It states that the dependency relationship between higher-level modules with low-level modules is reversed, thus making these modules independent of each other's implementation details.

Before we get into understanding what is Spring IOC Container, let us quickly learn what is IOC.

What is IOC?

Many a times, the Hollywood principle of *Don't call us, we will call you* is used to explain the concept of Inversion of Control. In Hollywood, this is what one gets to hear after auditioning is done. If we apply this principle to the programming model, instead of the classes creating dependencies along with serving functionality, the dependencies are appropriately made available to the classes during runtime, and the classes just need to focus on delivering the functionality.

Simply speaking, **Inversion of Control** (IOC) is about inverting the flow of control that the traditional programming model used to have in terms of objects at the higher-level handling the creation and management of lower-level objects' (can also be termed as dependencies) life cycle. In the IOC programming model, higher-level objects rather receive one or more instances of these dependencies from the calling object or external framework. This is why IOC is also termed **Dependency Injection,** wherein the dependencies are injected appropriately, and, objects bother themselves solely with the program execution and not with the object creation. Inversion of Control is related to the object-oriented principle known as the **Dependency Inversion Principle** (DIP), coined by Robert Martin (Uncle Bob).

Let's take a look at the following code sample, which represents higher-level objects handling the creation of lower-level objects (dependencies):

```
/*
 * This class demonstrates the dependency of higher-level object
 * (DrawWithoutIOC)
 * onto lower level objects such as Rectangle, Square which are
 * created within
 * Shape class based on the value of shapeType which is passed as a
 * method
 * parameter to draw method.
 */

public class DrawWithoutIOC {
```

```
      Logger logger = Logger.getLogger(DrawWithoutIOC.class.getName());

  public void draw(String shapeType) {
    Shape shape = new Shape();
    try {
      shape.draw(shapeType);
    }
    catch (UndefinedShapeException e) {
      logger.log(Level.INFO, e.getMessage(), e);
    }
  }
/*
 * Note that Shape class creates instances of Rectangle or Square
   class
 * based on the value of shapeType. Any new value that needs to be
   supported requires change in the draw method of Shape class.
 */

  private class Shape {
    public void draw(String shapeType) throws
      UndefinedShapeException
    {
      if(shapeType.equals("rectangle")) {
        Rectangle rectangle = new Rectangle();
        rectangle.draw();
      } else if(shapeType.equals("square")) {
        Square square = new Square();
        square.draw();
      } else {
        String shapeNotSupportedMessage = "Shape " + shapeType + "
            not supported";
        logger.log(Level.INFO, shapeNotSupportedMessage);
        throw new UndefinedShapeException
          (shapeNotSupportedMessage);
      }
    }
  }

  public static void main(String[] args) {
    DrawWithoutIOC drawWithoutIOC = new DrawWithoutIOC();
    drawWithoutIOC.draw("circle");
  }
}
```

Let us take a look at the class DrawWithIOC, which accepts the implementation of the Shape object in its public constructor. Note that the dependencies, such as different implementations of the Shape object, are rather injected, and code just does the execution of business logic without bothering about creation of objects related to the different implementations of Shape. Other alternatives to injecting the dependencies are passing arguments to a factory method of the class, or through properties that are set on the object instance:

```
/**
 * In this class, the Shape is passed as parameter to DrawWithIOC
 * constructor.
 * draw method on a DrawWithIOC object just invokes the draw method
 * on Shape object.
 * It, no longer, manage the creation of Shape object based on
 * shapeType and there upon, invoke the draw method.
 **/

public class DrawWithIOC {
  Logger logger = Logger.getLogger(DrawWithIOC.class.getName());

  private Shape shape;

  public DrawWithIOC(Shape shape) {
    this.shape = shape;
  }

  public void draw() {
    this.shape.draw();
  }

  public static void main(String[] args) {
    Shape shape = new Rectangle();
    DrawWithIOC drawWithIOC = new DrawWithIOC(shape);
    drawWithIOC.draw();
  }
}
```

What is a Spring IOC container?

A Spring IOC container is a framework which, basically, manages the life cycle of **plain old Java objects (POJOs)**, and injects them into the application as required. Java objects define their dependencies using one of the following methods:

- Dependencies are passed as arguments to the `constructor` method of the object. See how the object is passed as an argument to the `constructor` method in the example cited in the previous section.
- Dependencies are passed as arguments to the `setter` method of the object.
- Dependencies are passed as arguments to a `factory` method of the object.

A Spring IOC container injects the dependencies after it creates the beans. Note the fact that dependencies are no longer managed by Java objects. They are rather managed and injected by the framework, and hence, Inversion of Control.

The following are the packages which are core to the IOC container:

- `org.springframework.beans`
- `org.springframework.context`

It is the interface, `org.springframework.context.ApplicationContext` (sub-interface of the interface, `BeanFactory`), which represents the Spring IOC container and is responsible for managing the life cycle of beans. The instructions related to creating, configuring, and assembling the objects is termed **Configuration Metadata**. The configuration metadata is often represented using Java annotations or XML. A Java application using **Spring IOC Container** is created by combining **Business POJOs** with the previously mentioned configuration metadata, and passing it on to the IOC Container (an instance of `ApplicationContext`). The same is represented using the following diagram:

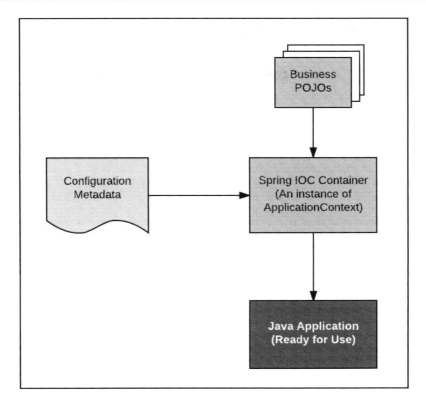

Figure 1: Java Application with Spring IOC Container

Let's illustrate the preceding diagram with an example. The following code represents how a service, namely, `UserService` is instantiated using Spring IOC container in a Spring Boot web application. Notice how the annotation-based autowiring feature has been used to have `ApplicationContext` autowired to the `userService` field in this code:

```
package com.example;

import org.springframework.beans.factory.annotation.Autowired;
import org.springframework.boot.SpringApplication;
import org.springframework.boot.autoconfigure.SpringBootApplication;
import org.springframework.stereotype.Controller;
import org.springframework.web.bind.annotation.RequestMapping;
import org.springframework.web.bind.annotation.ResponseBody;

import com.services.UserService;
import com.services.domain.User;

@Controller
```

```
@SpringBootApplication (scanBasePackages={"com.services"})
public class DemoApplication {

    @Autowired
    private UserService userService;

    @RequestMapping("/")
    @ResponseBody
    String home() {
        User user = null;
        return "Hello " + userService.getUsername(user) + ". How are
you?";
    }

    public static void main(String[] args) {
        SpringApplication.run(DemoApplication.class, args);
    }
}
```

Introduction to Spring Web MVC

In this section, we will learn the key elements of the **Spring Web model-view-controller (Spring Web MVC)** framework, and how to quickly get started with a Spring web application using the Spring Web MVC components. The following will be covered in detail in this section:

- Key building blocks of a Spring Web MVC application
- Introduction to the Dispatcher servlet

Key building blocks of a Spring Web MVC application

In this section, we will learn about the key building blocks of a Spring web MVC application. The following diagram represents the key building blocks:

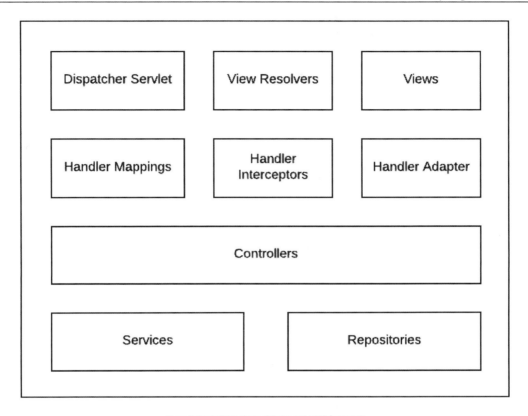

Figure 2: Key building blocks of Spring web MVC framework

The following are the details in relation to the preceding diagram:

- **Dispatcher servlet**: Dispatcher servlet, also termed the **front controller**, is at the core of the Spring Web MVC framework. Simply speaking, the Dispatcher servlet determines which `controller` class and method needs to be called when a page request or an API request arrives. In addition, it sends the response using the appropriate JSP page or JSON/XML objects. It dispatches the incoming requests to the appropriate handlers (custom controllers) with different handler mappings. This is integrated with the Spring IOC container, which allows it to use all the features that the Spring framework provides.

- **Handler Mappings**: Handler mappings are used to map the request URL with the appropriate handlers such as controllers. The Dispatcher servlet uses the handler mappings to determine the controllers which will process the incoming requests. The handler mappings are specified in the XML file, or as annotations such as @RequestMapping, @GetMapping, or @PostMapping, and so on. The following diagram represents the @RequestMapping annotation that is used for URL mapping.
- **Handler Interceptors**: Handler interceptors are used to invoke preprocessing and post-processing logic before and after the invocation of the actual handler method respectively.
- **Controllers**: These are custom controllers created by the developers and used for processing the incoming requests. The controllers are tagged with annotations such as @Controller or @RestController. Controllers are used to access the application behavior through one or more service interfaces. Controllers are used to interpret the user input, pass them to the services for implementation of business logic, and transform the service output into a model which is presented to the user as a view. The following diagram shows the @Controller annotation which represents the DemoApplication class to play the role of a controller:

```
                              Controller

@Controller
@SpringBootApplication (scanBasePackages={"com.services"})
public class DemoApplication {

    @Autowired
    private UserService userService;

    @RequestMapping("/")          Handler Mappings
    @ResponseBody
    String home() {
        User user = null;
        return "Hello " + userService.getUsername(user) + ". How are you?";
    }

    public static void main(String[] args) {
        SpringApplication.run(DemoApplication.class, args);
    }
}
```

Figure 3: Representing handler mappings (URL mapping) and Controller annotation

- **Services**: These are the components coded by the developers. These components contain the business logic. One or more methods of services are invoked from within the `Controller` methods. Spring provides annotations such as `@Service` for identifying services. The following code represents the service class `UserService`, which consists of a method, `getUsername`. Pay attention to the `@Service` annotation. Note how the instance of `UserService` is defined in `@Controller`, as shown in the preceding code, and the method `getUsername` is invoked on the instance of `UserService`.

```
import org.springframework.beans.factory.annotation.Autowired;
import org.springframework.stereotype.Service;

import com.services.dao.UserDAO;
import com.services.domain.User;

@Service ("userService")
public class UserService {

    @Autowired
    private UserDAO userDAO;

    public String getUsername(User user) {
        return userDAO.getUsername(user);
    }
}
```

- **Data Access Objects (DAO)**: The classes which represent DOA, are used to do data processing with the underlying data sources. These classes are annotated with annotations such as `@Repository`. The preceding code of `UserService` consists, a DAO, namely, `UserDAO`. Note the `@Repository` annotation used by the class, `UserDAO`, in the following code:

```
import org.springframework.stereotype.Repository;

import com.services.domain.User;

@Repository ("userDAO")
public class UserDAO {

    public String getUsername(User user) {
        return "Albert Einstein";
    }
}
```

- **View Resolvers**: View resolvers are components which map view names to views. They help in rendering models in the browser based on different view technologies such as JSP, FreeMarker, JasperResports, Tiles, Velocity, XML, and so on. Spring comes with different view resolvers such as `InternalResourceViewResolver`, `ResourceBundleViewResolver`, `XMLViewResolver`, and others. View resolvers are used by the Dispatcher servlet to invoke the appropriate view components.
- **Views**: Views are used to render the response data on the UI. They can be represented using different technologies such as JSP, Velocity, Tiles, and so on.

Introduction to the Dispatcher servlet

In this section, we will learn about the core component of a Spring web MVC application, the Dispatcher servlet.

As introduced in the previous section, Dispatcher servlet is the front controller which processes the user requests by invoking the appropriate components such as handler mappings, interceptors, adapters, custom controllers, services, DOA, view resolver, and finally, the views. The following diagram represents the web request/response workflow of the Dispatcher servlet:

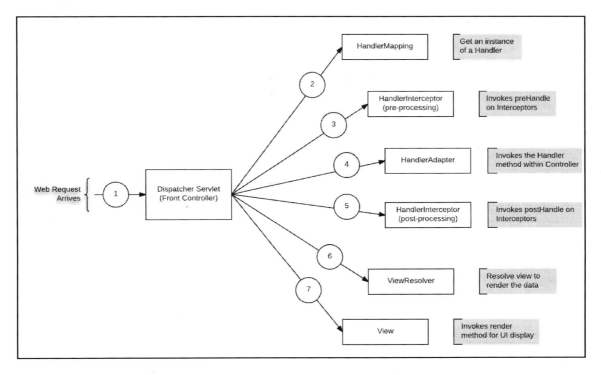

Figure 4: Web request/response flow across the Dispatcher servlet

As per the preceding diagram, the journey of a request/response through a Spring web MVC application looks like the following:

1. The user requests arrive at the server, and are intercepted by the Dispatcher servlet.
2. The Dispatcher servlet gets a handler object (primarily, an instance of `HandlerExecutionChain`) from the `HandlerMapping` object based on the URL mapping. URL mappings can be defined with the `web.xml` file or as annotations on the Controllers' methods.

3. One or more instances of the `HandlerInterceptor` objects are retrieved from the handler object, and preprocessing logic is processed on the request object.

4. The instance of `HandlerAdapter` is retrieved from the handler object, and the `handle` method is invoked. This results in execution of logic within the `controller` class. In the preceding diagram (*Figure 3*), the request with `RequestMapping` as "/" leads to the execution of code within the `home` method as part of this step.

5. The post-processing logic on the `HandlerInterceptor` instances is executed. This is the final step before the `rendering` method is invoked.

6. The `ViewResolver` instance is used to retrieve the appropriate view component.

7. The `render` method is invoked on the instance of view.

Building Hello World web application with Spring Boot

In this section, we will learn how to quickly build a web application using Spring Boot. The following will be covered in this section:

- The **Spring Tool Suite** (**STS**) setup in Eclipse IDE
- Introduction to Spring Boot
- Building the Hello World web app using Spring Boot

The Spring STS Setup in Eclipse IDE

Spring Tool Suite (**STS**) provides the development environment for Spring-powered enterprise applications. This can be easily downloaded from the Eclipse marketplace in the following manner:

1. Within the Eclipse IDE, click on **Help | Eclipse Marketplace...** and search for Spring STS by submitting Spring STS in the `Find` text field. The search result would show up different versions of STS for different Eclipse versions.

2. Choose the appropriate version and install. The most current version is `3.9.0.RELEASE`.

3. Restart Eclipse, and you are all set to create your first Spring Boot web application.

Introduction to Spring Boot

Spring Boot is a quick and easy way to get up and running with production-grade standalone applications in no time. If you hated all the XML configurations required to be set for creating a Spring web application, Spring Boot helps us to get away with all those troubles, and lets us focus on developing the application from the word go. The following are some of the key attributes of a Spring Boot application:

- Requires no XML configuration or code generation.
- Automatically configures Spring wherever appropriate and possible.
- Supports embedded web servers such as Tomcat, Jett, and so on. One of the key disadvantages while working with the Spring web framework prior to Spring Boot was deploying these apps explicitly on the web server either manually, or using some tools/scripts. This is no more required with Spring Boot, as it comes with support for embedded web servers.
- Helps to quickly and easily get started with microservices development. Spring Boot has seen great adoption in recent times thanks to the advent of micro-services architecture style apps. Spring Boot supports creation of micro-services in the form of a JAR file, which could easily be deployed within a server container.
- Supports features such as health checks, metrics, and so on.
- Provides useful annotations such as `@ConfigurationProperties` to accomplish tasks such as loading properties' details from the `application.properties` file.

Building Hello World web app using Spring Boot

In this section, we will go through the steps required to build a Hello World Web App using Spring Boot. The following given steps assume that you have set up Spring STS within your Eclipse IDE by following the steps given earlier. Now, with the steps given next, one can set up the Hello World web app in an easy manner:

1. Press *Ctrl + N* to open up the **Project creation Wizard** dialog box.
2. Write `spring` in the **Wizards** text field. This will show various project options related to Spring projects. Select the option **Spring Starter Project**, and click on **Next**.

3. Name the project `HelloWorld`, or leave the default name `demo`, and click on **Next**:

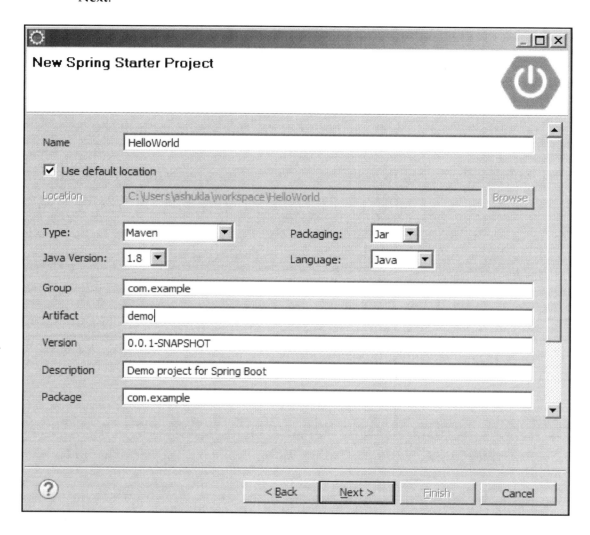

4. Select **Web** in the list of dependencies as shown in the following screenshot, and click on **Finish**:

5. Clicking on **Finish** will create a `HelloWorld` project whose file structure will look as seen in the following screenshot. Pay attention to the annotation `@SpringBootApplication` in the `HelloWorldApplication` class shown in the screenshot. Spring applications are commonly found to be annotated with annotations such as `@Configuration`, `@EnableAutoConfiguration`, and `@ComponentScan`. Spring Boot came up with `@SpringBootApplication` as an alternative to using three annotations together:

6. Right-click on the project, and start **Spring Boot App,** as shown in the following screenshot. It will start the app on the embedded Tomcat server. Access the URL `http://localhost:8080` on your browser. It will show up a page with the heading as **Whitelabel Error Page** followed by some content.

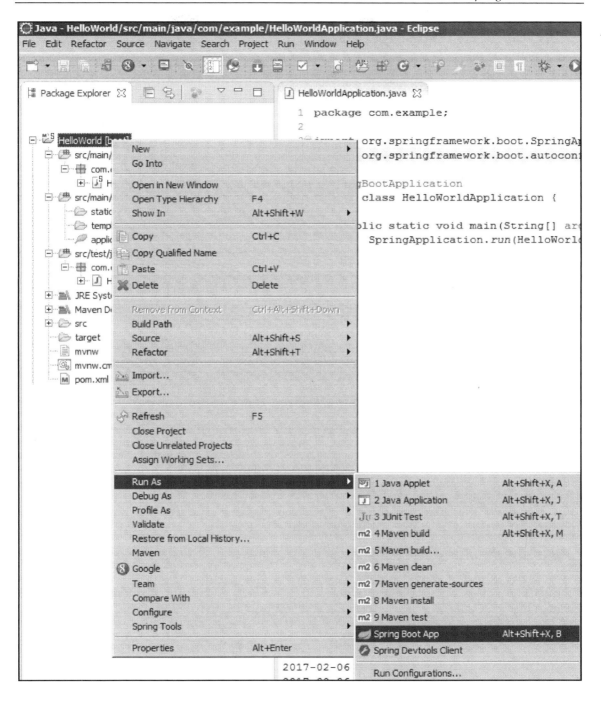

7. At times, the project may not run successfully due to one or more errors encountered during setting up the project. One can open the Problems View, and find out if there are any issues. As creating and running a Maven project requires the dependencies to be downloaded from the internet, it is to be ensured that the internet connection is active while setting up and running the project.

8. It is time to write some custom code in the `HelloWorldApplication` Java file, and run the app. Place the following code (in bold) as shown and run the app. Access the URL `http://localhost:8080`, and you will find the following getting printed: `Hello World. How are you?`. Pay attention to the usage of the `@Controller` annotation, which is required to annotate a class as a controller. In case one wants the class to serve REST APIs, one can use either `@Controller` and `@ResponseBody` together appropriately at the class and method level, or use `@RestController` at the class level:

```
@Controller
@SpringBootApplication
public class HelloWorldApplication {

    @RequestMapping("/")
    String home() {
        return "Hello world. How are you?";
    }

    public static void main(String[] args) {
        SpringApplication.run(HelloWorldApplication.class, args);
    }
}
```

9. When wanting to use the JSP files for displaying views, the following steps needed to be taken:

- Include the following code in the `pom.xml` file. This is done to enable JSP support:

```
<dependency>
    <groupId>org.apache.tomcat.embed</groupId>
    <artifactId>tomcat-embed-jasper</artifactId>
</dependency>
<dependency>
    <groupId>javax.servlet</groupId>
    <artifactId>jstl</artifactId>
</dependency>
```

- The following needs to be put in
  src/main/resources/application.properties in order to define the
  template prefix and suffix for the JSP files:

  ```
  spring.mvc.view.prefix=/WEB-INF/jsp/
  spring.mvc.view.suffix=.jsp
  ```

- Create the JSP files in the folder src/main/resources/META-
  INF/resources/WEB-INF/jsp/. For the sake of this current example, let's call
  the file as index.jsp.

- The code for @Controller would look like the following to render
  the index.jsp file. Note the absence of the @ResponseBody annotation on the
  home() method. This is why the JSP file, index.jsp, is rendered. Otherwise, a
  string object would have been returned as a response leading to errors while
  rendering.

```
@Controller
@SpringBootApplication
public class HelloWorldApplication {

    @RequestMapping("/")
    String home() {
        return "index";
    }

    public static void main(String[] args) {
        SpringApplication.run(HelloWorldApplication.class,
args);
    }
}
```

Implementing Controllers

Before we go into the details of understanding the different aspects of implementing the
controllers, let's quickly go over how controllers take part in the MVC workflow.

The following is the workflow representing the processing of a web request and the
response by a controller:

1. The requests are first intercepted by the Dispatcher servlet.

2. The Dispatcher servlet does the initial stage of request processing by resolving locale/themes, performing activities such as taking snapshots of the request attributes, and making framework objects available to handlers and view objects.

3. Once the initial processing is done as mentioned in the preceding step, an appropriate handler is determined and invoked for further processing the request. It is the `handleRequest` method that is invoked on the handler instance, which, in turn, invokes the appropriate method on the appropriate controller determined using `HandlerMappings`.

4. The controller then processes the request, and returns an instance of `ModelAndView` appropriately.

5. The instance of `ModelAndView` is further processed by the Dispatcher servlet to send out the response to the user.

Let us start building the sample healthcare app for doctors and patients. This app will be used to illustrate the controllers' implementations with multiple examples. In this section, we will see how to implement the controllers for handling users' requests for accessing the home page, signup form, login form, and so on. In the previous section, we have seen how to build a Hello World web app using Spring Boot. We will start implementing controllers using the Spring Boot app.

The following are the different controllers which are used to process requests for accessing the home page, signup form, and login page:

- `UserAccountController`
- `RxController`
- `DoctorSearchController`

We will see the implementation of the preceding controllers in code examples listed as follows. In the most trivial form, controller classes can be implemented in the following manner:

- The `controller` class can be annotated with `@Controller` or `@RestController` annotations at the class level. The code samples given below represent the usage of both types of annotations. `@RestController` is used as a convenience annotation to represent the annotations such as `@Controller` and `@ResponseBody`. When used at the class level, the controller can serve REST API requests.

- When using the `@Controller` or `@RestController` annotation, request mappings can be provided using one of the following techniques:

    - **Using RequestMapping Annotation at Method Level**: The following code represents the `RequestMapping` annotation at the method level, `home()`. Spring framework 4.3 introduced annotations such as `@GetMapping`, `@PostMapping`, `@PutMapping`, and so on to simplify mappings for common HTTP method types such as `GET`, `POST`, `PUT`, and so on respectively. These new annotations enhance code readability. In the following code, the aforementioned annotations have been used interchangeably for providing greater clarity and ease of understanding. When the application is started, accessing `http://localhost:8080/` would lead to a display of the view, `index.jsp` file. Note the `controller` class `HealthApplication`.

```
@Controller
@SpringBootApplication
public class HealthApplication {

    @RequestMapping("/")
    String home() {
        return "index";
    }

    public static void main(String[] args) {
        SpringApplication.run(HelloWorldApplication.class,
args);

    }
}
```

    - In the code given next, the `@GetMapping` annotation is used in place of `@RequestMapping`, as shown in the preceding code sample. `GetMapping` is a composed annotation which acts as a shortcut for `@RequestMapping (method = RequestMethod.GET)`. When the application is started, accessing `http://localhost:8080/` will print `Hello world. This is a health application!`.

```
@RestController
@SpringBootApplication
public class HealthApplication {
```

```
@GetMapping("/")
String home() {
    return "Hello world. This is a health application!";
}

public static void main(String[] args) {
    SpringApplication.run(HelloWorldApplication.class,
args);
}
}
```

- **Using RequestMapping Annotation at both, Method & Class Level:** The following code represents RequestMapping at both the class and the method level. When the URL such as `http://localhost:8080/account/` is accessed, one will be taken to the login page. Note that a URL such as `http://localhost:8080/account` (without trailing "/") would result in an error. The point to note is that the login method does not have URL mapping with the RequestMapping annotation. This, primarily, acts as a catch--all method to handle all the requests with different paths represented by using "/*" (defined at the class level) except /account/. When a URL such as `http://localhost:8080/account/signup` is accessed, the signup page is displayed. Similar is the case with the URL `http://localhost:8080/account/forgotpassword` which would open up the forgot password page.

```
@Controller
@RequestMapping("/account/*")
public class UserAccountController {

  @RequestMapping
  public String login() {
   return "login";
  }

  @GetMapping("/signup")
  public String signup() {
   return "signup";
  }

  @GetMapping("/forgotpassword")
  public String forgotpassword() {
   return "forgotpassword";
  }
}
```

- **Using RequestMapping Annotations with Http Requests Type**: In the following example, the HTTP request type Get is mapped to the method login:

```
@Controller
@RequestMapping("/account/login")
public class LoginController {
 //
 // @GetMapping can as well be used
 //
 @RequestMapping(method = RequestMethod.GET)
 public String login() {
  return "login";
 }
}
```

In the next section, we will learn the concepts and examples of handling request parameters in relation to handling forms such as signup, login, and so on as discussed in this section.

Handling request parameters

There are different ways in which user request parameters can be handled. We shall be taking the example of the signup form to understand the following concepts related to the most common ways of handling request parameters:

- Using the RequestParam annotation: This is used to bind the method parameters to web request parameters
- Using the RequestBody annotation: This is used to bind the method parameter to the body of the web request
- Using the PathVariable annotation: This is used to bind the method parameter to the URI template variable

The RequestParam annotation

In this section, we will learn how to use the `RequestParam` annotation for reading web request parameters in the `controller` class. The following image shows what the signup form looks like with three input fields such as **Nick Name**, **Email address**, and **Password**:

New User Signup

Nick Name

nickname

Email address

Email

Password

Password

Submit

Figure: New User Signup form

On submission of the preceding form, the user request parameters will be handled using the `@RequestParam` annotation. The `RequestParam` annotation is used to bind a method parameter to a web request parameter. The following code displays the binding of method parameters such as `nickname`, `emailAddress`, and `password` with web request parameters such as `nickname`, `emailaddress`, and `password` respectively. In simple words, the frontend has to send parameters with keys as nickname, email address, and password for the code given next to work.

```
@Controller
@RequestMapping("/account/*")
public class UserAccountController {

    @GetMapping("/signup")
    public String signup() {
        return "signup";
```

```
        }

    @PostMapping("/signup/process")
    public String processSignup(ModelMap model,
    @RequestParam("nickname") String nickname,
    @RequestParam("emailaddress") String emailAddress,
    @RequestParam("password") String password) {
        model.addAttribute("login", true);
        model.addAttribute("nickname", nickname);
        return "index";
    }
}
```

The RequestBody annotation

In this section, we will learn when and how to use the RequestBody annotation (@RequestBody) for handling web requests.

The RequestBody annotation is used to bind the method parameter with the body of the incoming request. In the process of binding, HttpMessageConverters converts the body of the request appropriately (most commonly into the parameter object) based on the content type of the request.

The RequestBody annotation is most commonly used in scenarios dealing with REST APIs.

The following example demonstrates the usage of the @RequestBody annotation using a domain object, User, which is made a parameter to the controller method:

```
@RestController
public class RestDemoController {

    @PostMapping("/hello")
    public HelloMessage getHelloMessage(@RequestBody User user) {
        HelloMessage helloMessage = new HelloMessage();
        String name = user.getName();
        helloMessage.setMessage( "Hello " + name + "! How are you
doing?");
        helloMessage.setName(name);
        return helloMessage;
    }
}
```

In the preceding example, note some of the following:

- The @PostMapping annotation maps the REST API endpoint, /hello, with the handler method, getHelloMessage. Recall that @PostMapping is a composed annotation which acts as a shortcut for @RequestMapping (method = RequestMethod.POST).
- The @RequestBody annotation is used with the User object. This binds (or maps) the method parameter, user of type User, with the body of the web request. The body of the request arrives in the following JSON format:

  ```
  {"name": "Calvin Hobbes"}
  ```

The HttpMessageConverter method converts the preceding into the User object, whose code looks like the following:

```
public class User {
  private String name;

  public String getName() {
    return name;
  }

  public void setName(String name) {
    this.name = name;
  }
}
```

- The @RestController annotation, a convenient annotation, which is itself annotated with @Controller and @ResponseBody annotations, and is used for programming REST API integration endpoints.
- The HelloMessage class is returned as a response. The following is the code for HelloMessage:

```
public class HelloMessage {
  private String message;
  private String name;
  public String getMessage() {
    return message;
  }
  public void setMessage(String message) {
    this.message = message;
  }
  public String getName() {
    return name;
  }
```

```
    public void setName(String name) {
      this.name = name;
    }
}
```

The `HttpMessageConverter` method converts the preceding response object into the following response message:

```
{"message": "message text goes here...", "name": "name goes here..."}
```

The PathVariable annotation

In this section, we will learn how to use the `PathVariable` annotation for handling request parameters.

The `PathVariable` annotation is used to bind a method parameter to a URI template variable. A URI template is a URI-like string containing one or more variables. For example, in the following code, `/{nickname}` is a URI template consisting of `nickname` as a variable. A method can have multiple `@Pathvariable` annotations to bind multiple variables present in the URI template. `PathVariable` is seen to be mainly used in the REST web service. Later, while going through Angular chapters, you will see that `PathVariable` is very similar to handling routing parameters using the `ActivatedRoute` concept:

```
@Controller
@SpringBootApplication
public class HealthAppApplication {

  @RequestMapping("/")
  public String home() {
    return "index";
  }

  @GetMapping("/{nickname}")
  public String home(ModelMap model, @PathVariable String nickname) {
    model.addAttribute("name", nickname);
    return "index";
  }

  public static void main(String[] args) {
    SpringApplication.run(HealthAppApplication.class, args);
  }
}
```

Both RequestParam and PathVariable can be used to read the request parameters. @RequestParam is used to retrieve the query parameters from the request URL. On the other hand, @PathVariable is used to retrieve one or more placeholders from the URI. URLs without query parameters, for example, paths, tend to be cached. The following code demonstrates the usage of both RequestParam and PathVariable. Different URLs will be handled using different methods represented in the code as follows:

- URL (http://localhost:8080, localhost:8080/?name=calvin): This URL consists of a parameter such as *name*. The value of this parameter is obtained using RequestParam. Note that as required = false is declared with the @RequestParam definition in the code example given next, thus, a request URL such as http://localhost:8080/ would also get mapped to the usingRequestParam method.
- URI (http://localhost:8080/calvin): This URL consists of a name which can be handled using a placeholder variable whose value can be obtained using the PathVariable method.

The following code displays the usage of both RequestParam and PathVariable:

```
@Controller
@SpringBootApplication
public class HealthAppApplication {
 //
 // RequestParam is used to retrieve value of parameter, name.
 //
 @RequestMapping("/")
 public String usingRequestParam(Model model,
               @RequestParam(value="name", required=false) String
nickname) {
    model.addAttribute("nickname", nickname);
    return "index";
 }

 @RequestMapping("/{nickname}")
  public String usingPathVariable(Model model, @PathVariable String
nickname)
  {
    model.addAttribute("nickname", nickname);
    return "index";
  }
}
```

In the next section, you will learn how to use interceptors to handle web requests-response, before and after the requests are handled by the controller respectively.

Handling Interceptors

In this section, we will learn about some of the following:

- Why use interceptors?
- How to implement interceptor methods such as pre-handle and post-handle to process the web requests before and after the requests get processed by the controllers respectively.

Interceptors' implementation provides methods for intercepting incoming requests before it gets processed by the controller classes or, intercepting the outgoing response after being processed by the controller and before being fed to the client. Interceptor methods help to get away with boilerplate code which is required to be invoked on each request and response. For example, let's take the authentication scenario where every request need to be checked for an authenticated session before being processed by the code in the controller. If the session is not found to be authenticated, the request is forwarded to the login page, else the request is forwarded to the controller for further processing. Given that the controller logic could span across multiple controller classes, and the aforementioned authentication logic needs to be processed before one or more controllers processes the incoming requests, it is suitable to put the authentication processing in the interceptor method. Another example of using interceptor methods includes measuring the time spent in the method execution.

For implementing interceptors for processing web requests-response, custom interceptor classes need to be implemented. Custom interceptor classes need to implement one or all of the methods provided in the HandlerInterceptor interface which are as follows:

- preHandle: The code within the preHandle method gets executed before the controller method is invoked
- postHandle: The code within the postHandle method is executed after the controller method is invoked
- afterCompletion: The code within afterCompletion is executed after the view gets rendered

In the following example, we will use an interceptor to process web requests arriving from the signup form. The following steps are required to be taken:

- **Create an Interceptor class**: Create an `Interceptor` class extending the `HandlerInterceptorAdapter` class. In the following example, only the `preHandle` method is implemented. Other methods such as `postHandle` and `afterCompletion` are not provided with the implementation:

```java
public class SignupInterceptor extends HandlerInterceptorAdapter {

@Override
public boolean preHandle(HttpServletRequest request,
        HttpServletResponse response, Object handler) throws
Exception {

    String emailAddress = request.getParameter("emailaddress");
    String password = request.getParameter("password");

    if(StringUtils.isEmpty(emailAddress) ||
    StringUtils.containsWhitespace(emailAddress) ||
    StringUtils.isEmpty(password) ||
    StringUtils.containsWhitespace(password)) {
      throw new Exception("Invalid Email Address or Password.
                         Please try again.");
    }

    return true;
}

@Override
public void afterCompletion(HttpServletRequest request,
                            HttpServletResponse response,
                            Object handler, Exception exception)
throws Exception {
  ...
}

@Override
public void postHandle(HttpServletRequest request,
            HttpServletResponse response,
            Object handler, ModelAndView modelAndView)
throws Exception {
  ...
}
}
```

- **Implement the Configuration class**: Implement a custom @Configuration class by extending WebMvcConfigurerAdapter, thereby adding the interceptor with appropriate path patterns within the addInterceptors method. If the path pattern is not specified, the interceptor is executed for all the requests.

  - **@Configuration**
    ```
    public class AppConfig extends WebMvcConfigurerAdapter {

    @Override
    public void addInterceptors(InterceptorRegistry registry) {
    registry.addInterceptor(new
    SignupInterceptor()).addPathPatterns("/account/signup/process");
    }
    }
    ```

- Make sure that the controller with the appropriate URI pattern is implemented as specified within the addInterceptors method in the aforementioned @Configuration class.

  - **@Controller**
    @RequestMapping("/account/*")
    ```
    public class UserAccountController {

    @RequestMapping("/signup")
    public String signup() {
    return "signup";
    }

    @RequestMapping("/signup/process")
    public String processSignup(ModelMap model,
    @RequestParam("nickname") String nickname,
     @RequestParam("emailaddress") String emailAddress,
    @RequestParam("password") String password) {
      model.addAttribute("login", true);
      model.addAttribute("nickname", nickname);
      return "index";
    }

    }
    ```

In the next section, you will learn about the different types of responses from controllers.

Handling Response

The following are some of the common types of responses returned from controllers:

- An instance of `ModelAndView`
- Using `@ResponseBody`

Response as an instance of ModelAndView

`ModelAndView` is a container object to hold both Model and View. With `ModelAndView` as a return object, the controller returns the both model and view as a single return value. The model is a map object which makes it possible to store key-value pairs. The following code sample represents the usage of `ModelAndView` in a Controller:

```
@Controller
@RequestMapping("/account/*")
public class UserAccountController {

    @PostMapping("/signup/process")
    public ModelAndView processSignup(ModelMap model,
@RequestParam("nickname")          String  nickname,
@RequestParam("emailaddress")
    String emailAddress, @RequestParam("password") String password) {
        model.addAttribute("login", true);
        model.addAttribute("nickname", nickname);
        model.addAttribute("message", "Have a great day ahead.");
        return new ModelAndView("index", model);
    }
}
```

The following code samples represent the different ways in which an instance of `ModelAndView` is returned with different sets of information:

```
// Will result in display of index.jsp page
return new ModelAndView("index");

// Will result in display of index.jsp page.
//The JSP page could consist of code such as "Hello ${name}"
//which will get displayed as "Hello Calvin Hobbes"

return new ModelAndView("index", "name", "Calvin Hobbes");
```

```
// Will result in display of index.jsp page.
// The JSP page could consist of code such as
//"Hello ${model.firstName} ${model.lastName}"
//which will get displayed as "Hello Calvin Hobbes"

UserInfo userInfo = new UserInfo();
userInfo.setFirstName("Calvin");
userInfo.setLastName("Hobbes");
return new ModelAndView("index", "model", userInfo);

// Will result in display of index.jsp page.
// The JSP page could consist of code such as "Hello ${name}"
// which will get displayed as "Hello Calvin Hobbes"

Map<String, Object> map = new HashMap<String, Object>();
map.put("name", "Calvin Hobbes");
return new ModelAndView("index", map);
```

Using @ResponseBody annotation

This section represents the concepts related to the usage of the @ResponseBody annotation for returning a response to the client request.

The @ResponseBody annotation can be applied both at the class level and the method level. When @ResponseBody is applied at the class level along with the @Controller annotation, another annotation such as @RestController can be used instead.

The @ResonseBody annotation represents the fact that the value returned by the method will form the body of the response. When the value returned is an object, the object is converted into an appropriate JSON or XML format by HttpMessageConverters. The format is decided based on the value of the produce attribute of the @RequestMapping annotation, and also the type of content that the client accepts. Take a look at the following example:

```
@Controller
public class RestDemoController {

    @RequestMapping(value="/hello", method=RequestMethod.POST,
produces="application/json")
    @ResponseBody
    public HelloMessage getHelloMessage(@RequestBody User user) {
      HelloMessage helloMessage = new HelloMessage();
      String name = user.getName();
      helloMessage.setMessage( "Hello " + name + "! How are you doing?");
      helloMessage.setName(name);
```

```
        return helloMessage;
    }
}
```

Creating a RESTful web service

In this section, you will learn how to create a RESTful web service. The concepts explained earlier in this chapter will be used.

The following are some of the key aspects of creating a RESTful web service. Let's take the example of retrieving the doctors' list based on the specialties, location, and so on.

- **Create a controller representing the RESTful endpoint**: In the following code, note the usage of the @RestController annotation, which is used to represent the annotation @Controller and @ResponseBody. The controller has a method, searchDoctor, for handling the request represented using the URL such as /doctors?location=xxx&speciality=yyy. Note the @RequestMapping annotation and its attributes, especially, "produces", which signifies the fact that the output sent to the user will be in the JSON format.

```
@RestController
public class DoctorSearchController {

    @Autowired
    DoctorService docService;

    @RequestMapping(value="/doctors", method=RequestMethod.GET,
                    produces="application/json")
    public DoctorList searchDoctor(
            @RequestParam(value="location", required=false) String
location,
            @RequestParam(value="speciality", required=false) String
speciality)
    {
        DoctorList docList = docService.find(location, speciality);
      return docList;
    }
}
```

The following is how the `DoctorService` implementation may look like:

```
@Service
public class DoctorServiceImpl implements DoctorService {

    @Autowired
    private DoctorDAO doctorDAO;

    @Override
    public List<Doctor> findByLocationAndSpeciality(String location,
String
    speciality) {
        return doctorDAO.findByLocationAndSpeciality(location,
specialityCode);
    }
}
```

The following is how the `DoctorDAO` implementation may look like:

```
@Repository
@Transactional
public class DoctorDAOImpl implements DoctorDAO {

    private SessionFactory sessionFactory;

    @Autowired
    public DoctorDAOImpl(SessionFactory sessionFactory) {
        this.sessionFactory = sessionFactory;
    }

    @Override
    public List<Doctor> findByLocationAndSpeciality(String location,
String speciality) {
        Session session = this.sessionFactory.getCurrentSession();
        TypedQuery<Doctor> query =
session.getNamedQuery("findByLocationAndSpeciality");
        query.setParameter("location", location);
        query.setParameter("speciality", speciality);
        List<Doctor> doctors = query.getResultList();
        return doctors;
    }
}
```

- **Create a RESTful API**: For retrieving the list of doctors based on location and speciality, the URL could look like
  `http://localhost:8080/doctors?location=xxx&speciality=yyy`.

- **Identify the method of processing incoming requests data**: @RequestParam will be used to process the incoming requests data as mentioned in the preceding URL. In the previous code, note how @RequestParam is used for processing the value of both the location and the specialty parameter. The following code represents the same:

```
public DoctorList searchDoctor(
@RequestParam(value="location", required=false)
String location,
@RequestParam(value="specialty", required=false)
String speciality) {
    // Code goes here
}
```

- **Create a class representing ResponseBody**: The return value is the DoctorList object, which consists of a list of Doctors. The following code represents the DoctorList object which is a list of the Doctor object:

```
// The class representing the list of Doctor; Returned as a response
public class DoctorList {
  private List<Doctor> doctors;

  public DoctorInfo(List<Doctor> doctors) {
    this.setDoctors(doctors);
  }
  public List<Doctor> getDoctors() {
    return doctors;
  }
  public void setDoctors(List<Doctor> doctors) {
    this.doctors = doctors;
  }
}
```

The following represents the Doctor class which is returned as part of the response object:

```
public class Doctor {

  private String id;
  private String firstName;
  private String lastName;
  private String specialityCode;

  public String getId() {
    return id;
  }
  public void setId(String id) {
    this.id = id;
```

```
  }
  public String getFirstName() {
    return firstName;
  }
  public void setFirstName(String firstName) {
    this.firstName = firstName;
  }
  public String getLastName() {
    return lastName;
  }
  public void setLastName(String lastName) {
    this.lastName = lastName;
  }
  public String getSpecialityCode() {
    return specialityCode;
  }
  public void setSpecialityCode(String specialityCode) {
    this.specialityCode = specialityCode;
  }
}
```

- **Client response**: The client receives the response body in the JSON format. The following is a sample response which is returned by the execution of the preceding code:

```
[{
 "id": "doc1",
 "firstName": "Calvin",
 "lastName": "Hobbes",
 "specialityCode": "pediatrics"
},
{
  "id": "doc2",
  "firstName": "Susan",
  "lastName": "Storm",
  "specialityCode": "cardiology"
}]
```

Dockerizing a Spring Boot application

In this section, you will learn how to Dockerize a Spring Boot application. The detailed introduction to Docker and the related aspects such as Docker images, containers, Dockerfile, and so on is provided in `Chapter 2`, *Preparing Spring Web Development Environment*. In case, you are new to Docker, it may be a good idea to get an understanding of Docker before going ahead with this section.

The following are some of the reasons why it may be a good idea to Dockerize a Spring Boot application:

- **Containerized Springboot App-- a Microservice**: It aligns well with the cloud-native architecture style, which recommends containerizing a microservice (using Docker or other runtimes such as rkt), and managing these containers using container orchestration tools such as Kubernetes, Docker Swarm, and so on. It should be noted that Spring Boot can be used to create a microservice. Thus, one may need to Dockerize a Spring Boot microservice when creating a cloud-native app.
- **Quick Dev/QA environments**: A containerized/Dockerized Spring Boot app is easy to commission or decommission.
- **Continuous delivery made easy**: It is easy to achieve a continuous delivery of containerized/Dockerized Spring Boot app in different environments such as QA, UAT, production.

It should be noted that Docker can be used while working with both Maven and Gradle, details of which will be presented in the next chapter while understanding the aspects of build. The following are some of the key aspects of Dockerizing a Spring Boot app. The same instructions can be used to wrap Spring boot micro-services within Docker containers.

- **Dockerfile**: The first step is to create the Dockerfile which will be used to build the Docker image. The following is the content of the Dockerfile. Save the Dockerfile as Dockerfile in the root folder.

```
FROM frolvlad/alpine-oraclejdk8:slim
VOLUME /tmp
ADD target/demo-0.0.1-SNAPSHOT.jar app.jar
RUN sh -c 'touch /app.jar'
ENV JAVA_OPTS=""
ENTRYPOINT [ "sh", "-c", "java $JAVA_OPTS -
          Djava.security.egd=file:/dev/./urandom -jar /app.jar" ]
```

- Build and test the Spring Boot app:

1. Go to the Spring Boot app root folder. Make sure that you saved Dockerfile in the root folder. Execute the following command to build the Docker image:

```
docker built -t springboot-app:latest .

// In case you are executing the above command from another folder
docker built -t springboot-app:latest -f path_to_dockerfile.
```

- Execute the following command to start and access the container:

```
// Start the container; Name of the container is sbapp
docker run -tid -p 8080:8080 --name sbapp springboot-app:latest

// Access the container
docker exec -ti sbapp bash

// Access the logs
docker logs sbapp
```

Once started, open the REST client, and test the preceding RESTful API with URL as `http://localhost:8080/doctors?location=xxx&speciality=yyy`.

Summary

In this chapter, you learnt the fundamentals of the Spring web framework with a focus on understanding the key concepts such as IOC container, Dispatcher servlet, implementing controllers, web requests and response handling, using custom interceptors, and so on. You also learnt how to create a web application using Spring Boot, how to create a RESTful web service, and finally, how to Dockerize a Spring Boot application.

In the next chapter, you will learn how to prepare a Spring web development environment.

2
Preparing the Spring Web Development Environment

In this chapter, we will go into the details of setting up the development environment for working with Spring web applications. The following are the key areas that we will look into:

- Installing the Java SDK
- Installing/configuring Maven
- Installing the Eclipse IDE
- Installing/configuring the Apache Tomcat server
- Installing/configuring the MySQL database
- Introducing Docker containers
- Setting up the development environment using Docker Compose

Installing the Java SDK

First and foremost, we will install Java SDK. We will work with Java 8 throughout this book. Go ahead and access this page (`http://www.oracle.com/technetwork/java/javase/downloads/jdk8-downloads-2133151.html`). Download the appropriate JDK kit. For Windows/Linux, there are two different versions--one for x86 and another for x64. One should select the appropriate version, and download the appropriate installable file. Once downloaded, double-click on the executable file for Windows, or unTAR and install appropriately for Linux. The instructions for installing Java on Linux can be found on this page (`https://docs.oracle.com/javase/8/docs/technotes/guides/install/linux_jdk.html`).

The following instructions help one install Java on Windows OS. Double-clicking on the EXE file would start the installer. Once installed, the following needs to be done:

1. Set `JAVA_HOME` as the path where JDK is installed.
2. Include the path in `%JAVA_HOME%/bin` in the environment variable. One can do that by adding the `%JAVA_HOME%/bin` directory to his/her user `PATH` environment variable--open up the system properties (Windows key + *Pause*), select the **Advanced** tab, and the **Environment Variables** button, then add or select the `PATH` variable in the user variables with the value.

Once done with the preceding steps, open a shell and type the command `java -version`. It should print the version of Java you installed just now.

 Next, let us try and understand how to install and configure Maven, a tool for building and managing Java projects. Later, in the coming chapters, we will deal with Spring Boot, which uses Maven to create boilerplate web applications.

Installing/configuring Maven

Maven is a tool which can be used for building and managing Java-based projects. The following are some of the key benefits of using Maven as a build tool:

- It provides a simple project setup that follows best practices--it gets a new project or module started in seconds.
- It allows a project to build using its **Project Object Model (POM)** and a set of plugins that are shared by all projects, providing a uniform build system. POM is defined in an XML file, namely, `pom.xml`, which defines the project configuration and dependencies along with their versions. One can manage the dependencies version from `pom.xml`.
- Based on the project templates (also called **archtype***)*, Maven supports scaffolding, based on which the standard folder structure is created along with the base controller files, unit tests, and so on.

- It allows usage of the large and growing repository of libraries and metadata to use out of the box. The project dependencies are installed in the local repository specified by path, such as `${user.home}/.m2/repository`. Once installed, all the logged-in users can build from this common local repository. The settings related to the local repository can be found in the `settings.xml` file, which can be found in one of the folders such as `${maven.home}/conf` or `${user.home}/.m2`. More details related to `settings.xml` can be found on this page: `https://maven.apache.org/settings.html`
- Based on model-based builds, it provides the ability to work with multiple projects at the same time. Any number of projects can be built into predefined output types such as a **Java archive (JAR)**, **Web archive (WAR)**, **Enterprise archive (WAR)**, or distribution based on metadata about the project, without the need to do any scripting in most cases.

One can download Maven from `https://maven.apache.org/download.cgi`. Before installing Maven, make sure that Java is installed and configured (`JAVA_HOME`) appropriately, as mentioned in the previous section. On Windows, you could check the same by typing the command `echo %JAVA_HOME%`:

1. Extract the distribution archive in any directory. If it works on Windows, install an unzip tool such as WinRAR. Right-click on the ZIP file, and unzip it. A directory (with the name `apache-maven-3.3.9`, the version of Maven at the time of writing) holding files such as `bin`, `conf`, and so on will be created.
2. Add the bin directory of the created directory, `apache-maven-3.3.9`, to the PATH environment variable. To do that, add the bin directory to the user PATH environment variable by opening up the system properties (Windows Key + *Pause*), select the **Advanced** tab and the **Environment Variables** button, and then add or select the `PATH` variable in the user variables with the value.
3. Open a new shell, and type `mvn -v`. The result should print the Maven version along with details including the Java version, Java home, OS name, and so on.

Now, let's look at how can we create a Java project using Maven from the command prompt before we get on to creating a Maven project in the Eclipse IDE. Use the following `mvn` command to create a Java project:

```
mvn archetype:generate -DgroupId=com.healthapp
                       -DartifactId=HealthApp
                       -DarchetypeArtifactId=maven-archetype-quickstart
                       -DinteractiveMode=false
```

Pay attention to some of the following in the preceding command:

- `archetype:generate`: This is used to create a new project from an archetype. Archetype is a Maven project templating toolkit. Executing a command the `mvn archetype:generate` asks the developers a set of questions for setting up the project. In order to avoid these questions, Maven provides a flag, `interactiveMode`, which needs to be set to `false`.
- `groupId`: This represents the name of the package.
- `artifactId`: This represents the name of the project.
- `archetypeArtifactId`: This represents the name of the template from which the project is scaffolded.
- `interactiveMode`: This,when set to `false`, avoids the interactivity of the Maven Archetype plugin.

With the `archetype:generate` and `-DarchetypeArtifactId=maven-archetype-quickstart` templates, the following project directory structure is created:

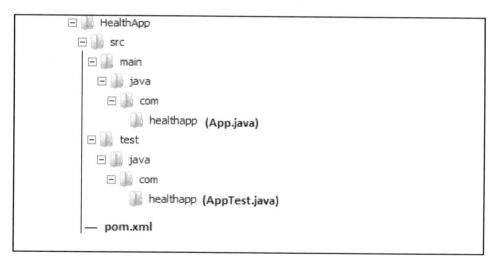

Figure 1.1: Maven project folder structure

In the preceding diagram, the `healthapp` folders within the `src/main` and `src/test` folders consist of a `Hello World` program named as `App.java`, and a corresponding test program such as `AppTest.java`. Also, a `pom.xml` file is created in the top-most folder.

In the next section, we will install the Eclipse IDE, and create a maven project using the functionality provided by the IDE.

Installing the Eclipse IDE

In this section, we will set up the Eclipse IDE, a tool used by Java developers to create Java EE and web applications. Go to the Eclipse website at `http://www.eclipse.org`, and download the latest version of Eclipse and install it. As we shall be working with web applications, select the option **Eclipse IDE for Java EE Developers** while downloading the IDE.

As you launch the IDE, it will ask you to select a folder for the workspace. Select the appropriate path, and start the IDE.

The following are some of the different types of projects that developers could work on using IDE:

- A new Java EE web project.
- A new JavaScript project. This option will be very useful when you work with a standalone JavaScript project, and plan to integrate with the server components using APIs.
- Check out the existing Eclipse projects from Git, and work on them.
- Import one or more existing Eclipse projects from the filesystem or archive.

Import the existing Maven project in Eclipse

In the previous section, we created a Maven project, namely, HealthApp. We will now see how we to import this project into the Eclipse IDE:

1. Click on **File | import**.
2. Type `Maven` in the search box under **Select an import source**.
3. Select **Existing Maven Projects**.
4. Click on **Next**.
5. Click on **Browse**, and select the **HealthApp** folder which is the root of the Maven project. Note that it contains the **pom.xml** file.
6. Click on **Finish**.

The project will be imported in Eclipse. Make sure this is what it looks like:

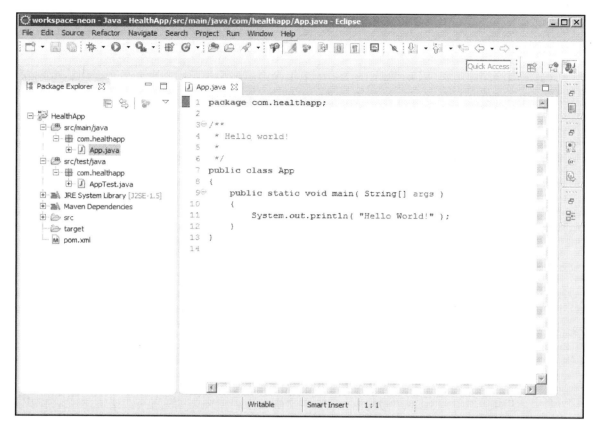

Figure 1.2: Maven project imported into Eclipse

Let's also see how one can create a new Maven project with the Eclipse IDE.

Creating a new Maven project in Eclipse

Follow the instructions given to create a new Java Maven project with the Eclipse IDE:

1. Click on **File | New | Project**.
2. Type Maven in the search box under Wizards.
3. Select **Maven project**.
4. A dialog box with the title **New Maven Project**, having the option **Use default Workspace location** as checked, appears.

5. Make sure that **Group Id** is selected as **org.apache.maven.archetypes** with **Artifact Id** selected as `maven-archetype-quickstart`.

6. Give a name to **Group Id**, say, `com.orgname`. Give a name to **Artifact Id**, say, `healthapp2`.

7. Click on **Finish**.

As a result of the preceding steps, a new Maven project will be created in Eclipse. Make sure this is what it looks like:

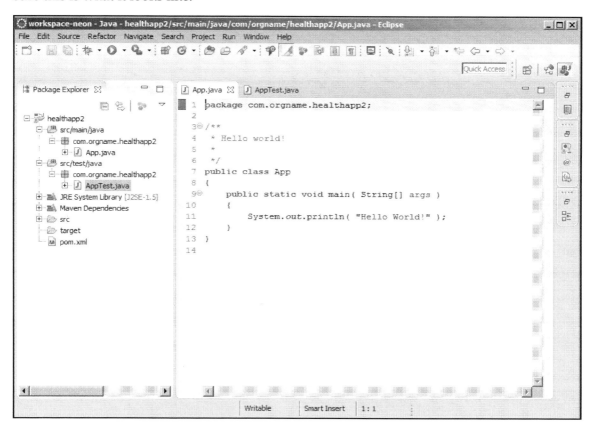

Figure 1.3: Maven project created within Eclipse

In the next section, we will see how to install and configure the Tomcat server.

Installing/configuring the Apache Tomcat server

One can skip this section when working with a Spring Boot project. This is because starting a Spring boot application, using `public static void main` as an entry point, launches an embedded web server and, thus, one would not require starting a server such as Tomcat.

In this section, we will learn about some of the following:

- How to install and configure the Apache Tomcat server
- Common deployment approaches with the Tomcat server
- How to add the Tomcat server in Eclipse

The Apache Tomcat software is an open-source implementation of the Java servlet, **JavaServer Pages (JSPs)**, Java Expression Language, and Java WebSocket technologies. We will work with Apache Tomcat 8.x version in this book. We will look at both, the Windows and Unix version of Java. One can go to `http://tomcat.apache.org/` and download the appropriate version from this page. At the time of installation, it requires you to choose the path to one of the JREs installed on your computer. Once the installation is complete, the Apache Tomcat server is started as a Windows service. With the default installation options, one can then access the Tomcat server by accessing the URL `http://127.0.0.1:8080/`.

A page such as the following will be displayed:

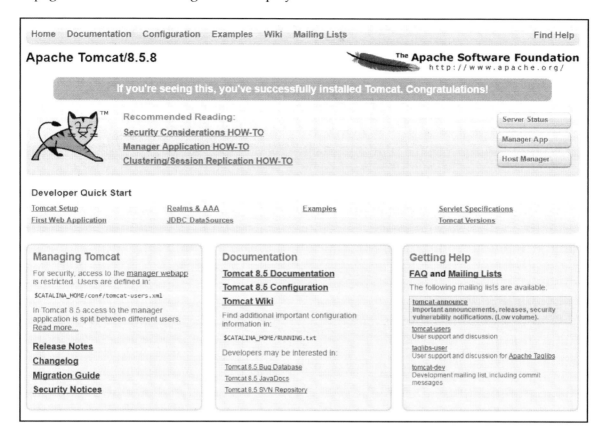

Figure 1.4: Apache Tomcat Server Homepage

The following is what the Tomcat's folder structure looks like:

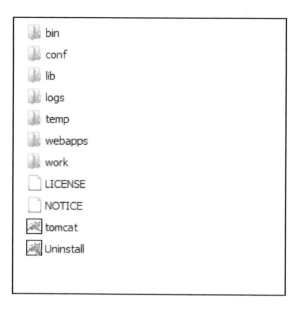

Figure 1.5: Apache Tomcat folder Structure

In the preceding image, note the `webapps` folder which will contain our web apps. The following description uses variable names such as the following:

- `$CATALINA_HOME`: The directory into which Tomcat is installed.
- `$CATALINA_BASE`: The base directory against which most relative paths are resolved. If you have not configured Tomcat for multiple instances by setting a `CATALINA_BASE` directory, then `$CATALINA_BASE` will be set to the value of `$CATALINA_HOME`.

The following are the most commonly used approaches to deploy web apps in Tomcat:

1. Copy the unpacked directory hierarchy into a subdirectory in the directory `$CATALINA_BASE/webapps/`. Tomcat will assign a context path to your application based on the subdirectory name you choose.

2. Copy the **web application archive (WAR)** file into the directory `$CATALINA_BASE/webapps/`. When Tomcat is started, it will automatically expand the web application archive file into its unpacked form, and execute the application that way. Simply speaking, be it an HTML page/folder or WAR package, copying it inside the `webapps` and starting the Tomcat server will extract the war to a folder. Thus, it is important that after copying the war file to the `webapps` folder, you restart the Tomcat server.

Let us learn how to configure Apache Tomcat from within Eclipse. This would be very useful, as you could start and stop Tomcat from Eclipse while working with your web applications.

Adding/configuring Apache Tomcat in Eclipse

In this section, we will learn how to add and configure Apache Tomcat in Eclipse. This will help to start and stop the server from within the Eclipse IDE.

The following steps need to be taken to achieve this objective:

1. Make sure you are in Java EE perspective.
2. Click on the **Servers** tab in the lower panel. You will find a link saying **No servers are available. Click this link to create a new server...**. Click on this link.
3. Type `Tomcat` under **Select the server type**. It would show a list of Tomcat servers with different versions. Select **Tomcat v8.5 Server**, and click on **Next**.
4. Select the Tomcat installation directory. Click on the **Installed JREs...** button, and make sure that the appropriate JRE is checked. Click on **Next**.
5. Click on **Finish**. This would create an entry for the Tomcat server in the **Servers** tab.
6. Double-click on Tomcat server. This would open up a configuration window where multiple options such as **Server Locations**, **Server Options**, **Ports** can be configured.
7. Under Server Locations, click on the **Browse Path** button to select the path to the `webapps` folder within your local Tomcat installation folder. Once done, save it using *Ctrl + S*.
8. Right-click on the **Tomcat Server** link listed under the **Servers** panel, and click on **Start**.
9. This should start the server. You should be able to access the Tomcat page on the URL `http://localhost:8080/`.

Installing/configuring the MySQL database

In this section, you will learn how to install the MySQL database. Go to the MySQL Downloads site (`https://www.mysql.com/downloads/`), and click on **Community (GPL) Downloads** under the MySQL community edition. On the next page, you will see a listing of several MySQL software packages. Download the following:

- MySQL Community Server
- MySQL Connector for Java development (Connector/J)

Installing/configuring the MySQL server

In this section, we will explain how to download, install, and configure the MySQL database and a related utility, MySQL Workbench. Note that MySQL Workbench is a unified visual tool which can be used by database architects, developers, and DBA for activities such as data modeling, SQL development, comprehensive administration tools for server configuration, user administration, and so on.

Follow the instructions given for installation and configuration of the MySQL server and workbench:

1. Click on the **Download** link under **MySQL Community Server (GPL)** found as the first entry on the **MySQL Community Downloads** page. We shall be working with the Windows version of MySQL in the following instructions. However, one should be able to download and install MySQL on Linux using the installers provided on the page `https://dev.mysql.com/doc/refman/5.7/en/linux-installation.html`.

2. Click on the **Download** button against the entry **Windows (x86, 32-bit), MySQL Installer MSI**. This would download an `.exe` file such as `mysql-installer-community-5.7.16.0.exe`.

3. Double-click on the installer to start the installation.

4. As you progress ahead after accepting the license terms and condition, you would find the interactive UI such as the one shown in the following screenshot. Choose the appropriate version of the MySQL server and also of MySQL Workbench, and click on **Next**.

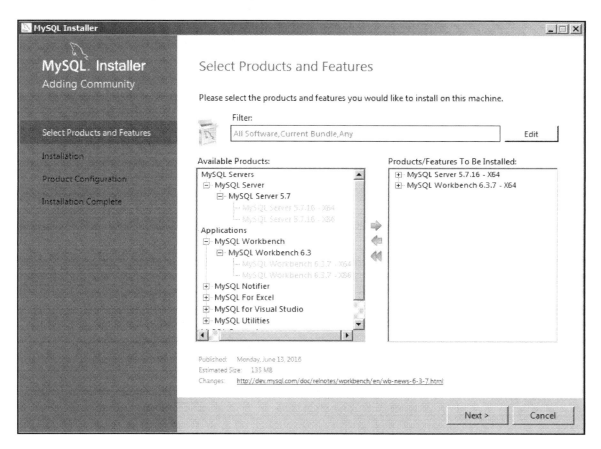

Figure 1.6: Selecting and installing MySQL Server and MySQL Workbench

5. Clicking on **Execute** would install the MySQL server and MySQL Workbench as shown in the following screenshot:

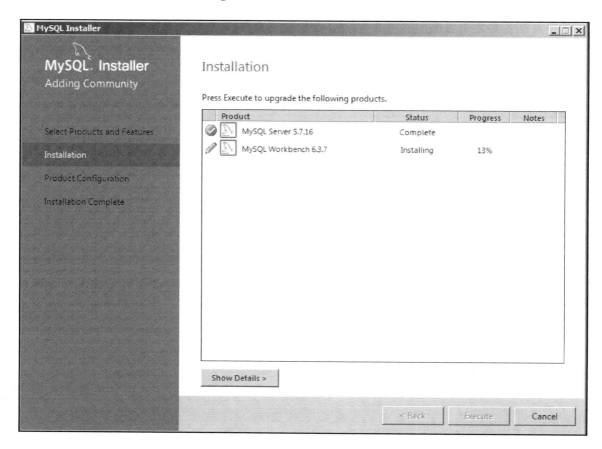

Figure 1.7: MySQL Server and Workbench installation in progress

6. Once the installation is complete, the next few steps would require you to configure the MySQL database including setting the root password, adding one or more users, opting to start the MySQL server as a Windows service, and so on. The quickest way is to use the default instructions as much as possible, and finish the installation. Once all is done, you would see a UI such as the following:

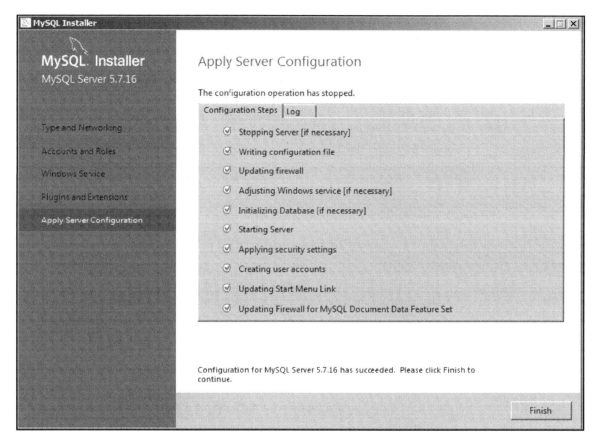

Figure 1.8: Completion of MySQL Server and Workbench installation

7. Clicking on the **Finish** button will take you on to the next window, where you could choose to start MySQL Workbench. The following screenshot shows what the MySQL Workbench would look like after you click on the MySQL server instance on the Workbench homepage, enter the root password, and execute the **Show databases** command:

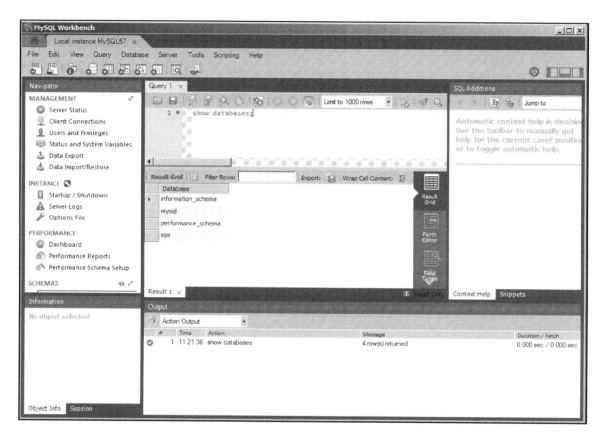

Figure 1.9: MySQL Workbench

Using the MySQL connector

Before testing the MySQL database connection from a Java program, one would need to add the MySQL JDBC connector library to the classpath. In this section, you will learn how to configure/add the MySQL JDBC connector library to the classpath while working with the Eclipse IDE or command console.

The MySQL connector (`Connector/J`) comes in a ZIP file, (`*.tar.gz`). The MySQL connector is a concrete implementation of the JDBC API. Once extracted, one can see a JAR file with a name such as `mysql-connector-java-xxx.jar`. The following are the different ways in which this JAR file is dealt with while working with or without IDEs such as Eclipse:

- While working with the Eclipse IDE, one can add the JAR file to the class path by adding it as a library to the `Build Path` in the project's properties.
- While working with the command console, one needs to specify the path to the JAR file in the `-cp` or `-classpath` argument when executing the Java application. The following is the sample command representing the preceding:

```
java -cp .;/path/to/mysql-connector-java-xxx.jar
com.healthapp.JavaClassName
```

Note the "`.`" in the classpath (`-cp`) option. This is there to add the current directory to the classpath as well such that `com.healthapp.JavaClassName` can be located.

Connecting to the MySQL database from a Java class

In this section, you will learn how to test the MySQL database connection from a Java program. Note that this section is intended only to help you test the database connection from the Java class. In reality, we will use `Springboot DataSourceBuilder` to create a datasource bean, which will be used for connecting with the database.

Before executing the code shown as follows in your Eclipse IDE, make sure to do the following:

1. Add the MySQL connector JAR file by right-clicking on the top-level project folder, clicking on **Properties**, clicking on **Java Build Path**, and then, adding the `mysql-connector-java-xxx.jar` file by clicking on **Add External JARs...**:

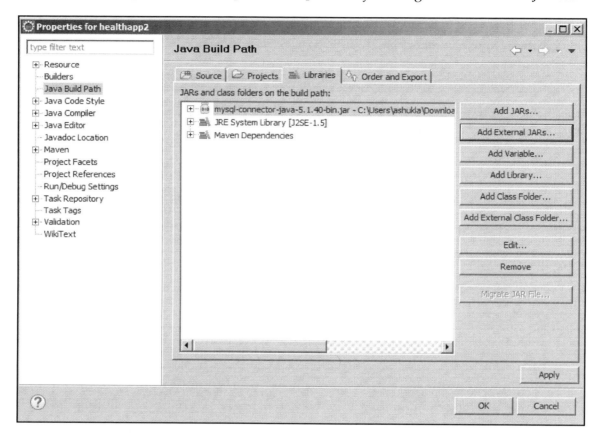

Figure 1.10: Adding MySQL Java Connector to Java Build Path in Eclipse IDE

2. Create a MySQL database, namely, `healthapp`. You can do that by accessing MySQL Workbench, and executing the MySQL command **create database healthapp**. The following screenshot represents the same:

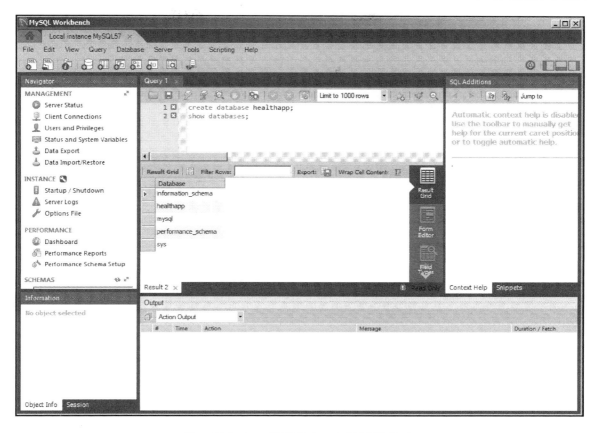

Figure 1.11: Creating new MySQL Database using MySQL Workbench

3. Once done with the preceding steps, use the following code to test the connection to the MySQL database from your Java class. On successful connection, you should be able to see Database connected! be printed:

```
import java.sql.Connection;
import java.sql.DriverManager;
import java.sql.SQLException;

/**
 * Sample program to test MySQL database connection
 */
public class App
{
    public static void main( String[] args )
    {
        String url =
```

```
        "jdbc:mysql://localhost:3306/healthapp";
        String username = "root";
        String password = "r00t"; //Root password set
        during MySQL installation procedure as
        described above.

        System.out.println("Connecting database...");

        try {
            Connection connection =
            DriverManager.getConnection(url, username,
            password);
            System.out.println("Database connected!");
        }
        catch (SQLException e) {
            throw new IllegalStateException("Cannot
            connect the database!", e);
        }
    }
}
```

Introduction to Docker

In this section, we will learn about Dockers and related concepts. The primary reason why Docker was introduced is that Docker is a virtualization technology which helps IT organizations, including developers, QA, and IT staff, achieve some of the following:

- Helps to create cloud-native applications by containerizing apps/microservices using Docker. Note that Spring Boot is used for building microservices. These Spring Boot apps/microservices can be containerized using Docker, and deployed and managed on any Cloud platform using container-orchestration tools such as Kubernetes, Mesos, Docker Swarm, and so on. Thus, it is important to get an understanding of Docker.
- Enhances application portability by enabling Dev/QA team develop and test applications in a quick and easy manner in any environment.
- Helps to break the barriers between the Dev/QA and Operations teams during the **software development life cycle (SDLC)** processes.
- Optimizes infrastructure usage in the most appropriate manner.

In this section, we will emphasize the first point in the preceding list, which would help us set up Spring web application development in a quick and easy manner.

So far, we have seen the traditional ways in which we could set up the Java web application development environment by installing different tools in independently, and later, configuring them appropriately. In a traditional setup, one would be required to set up and configure Java, Maven, Tomcat, MySQL server, and so on, one tool at a time, by following manual steps. On the same lines, you could see that all of the steps described in the preceding sections have to be performed one-by-one manually. The following are some of the disadvantages of setting up development/test environments in this manner:

- **Conflicting runtimes**: If a need arises to use software packages (say, different versions of Java and Tomcat) of different versions to run and test the same web application, it can become very cumbersome to manually set up the environment having different versions of the software.
- **Environments getting corrupted**: If more than one developers are working in a particular development environment, there are chances that the environment could get corrupted due to the changes made by one developer which the others are not aware of. That, generally leads to developers/teams productivity loss due to the time spent in fixing the configuration issue or re-installing the development environment from scratch.
- **"Works for me" syndrome**: Have you come across another member of your team saying that the application works in their environment although the application seems to have broken?
- **New Developers/Testers on-boarding**: If there is a need to quickly on-board the new developers, manually setting up the development environment takes some significant amount of time depending upon the applications' complexity.

All of the preceding disadvantages can be taken care of by making use of the Dockers technology. In this section, we will learn briefly about some of the following:

- What are Docker containers?
- What are the key building blocks of Docker containers?
- Installing Dockers
- Useful commands to work with Docker containers

What are Docker containers?

In this section, we will try and understand what are Docker containers while comparing them with real-world containers. Simply speaking, Docker is an open platform for developing, shipping, and running applications. It provides the ability to package and run an application in a loosely isolated environment called a container.

Before going into the details of Docker containers, let us try and understand the problems that are solved by real-world containers.

What are real-world containers good for?

The following picture represents real-world containers which are used to package anything and everything, and then, transport the goods from one place to another in an easy and safe manner:

Figure 1.12: Real-world containers

The following diagram represents the different forms of goods, which need to be transported from one place to another using different forms of transport mechanisms:

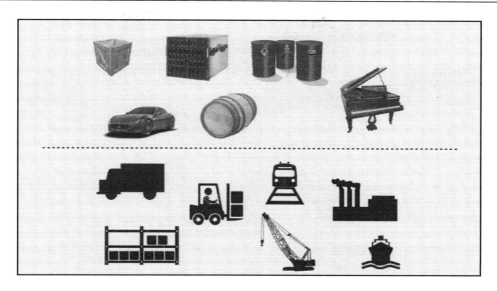

Figure 1.13: Different forms of goods vis-a-vis different form of transport mechanisms

The following diagram displays the matrix representing the need to transport each of the goods via different transport mechanisms. The challenge is to make sure that these goods get transported in an easy and safe manner:

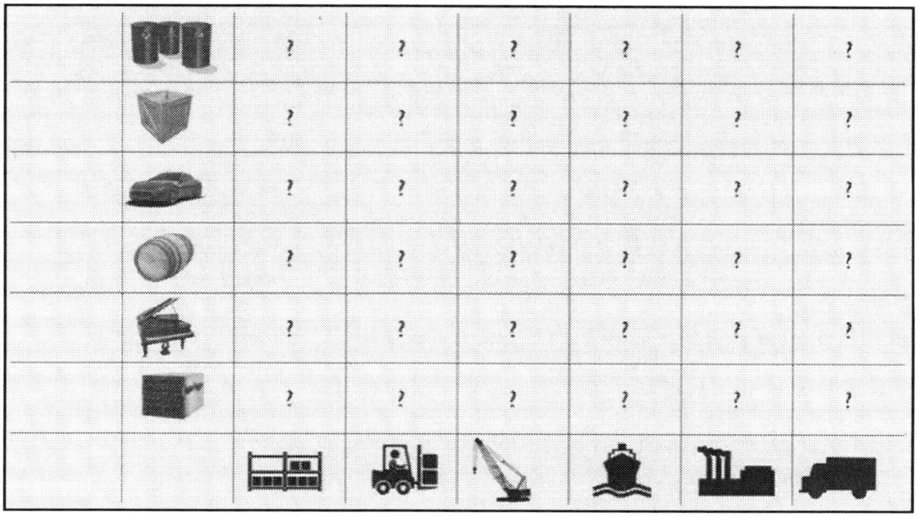

Figure 1.14: Complexity associated with transporting goods of different types using different transport mechanisms

In order to solve the preceding problem of transporting the goods in a safe and easy manner, irrespective of the transport medium, containers are used. Look at the following diagram:

Figure 1.15: Goods can be packed within containers, and containers can be transported.

How do Docker containers relate to real-world containers?

Now imagine the act of moving a software application from one environment to another environment starting from development right up to production. The following diagram represents the complexity associated with making different application components work in different environments:

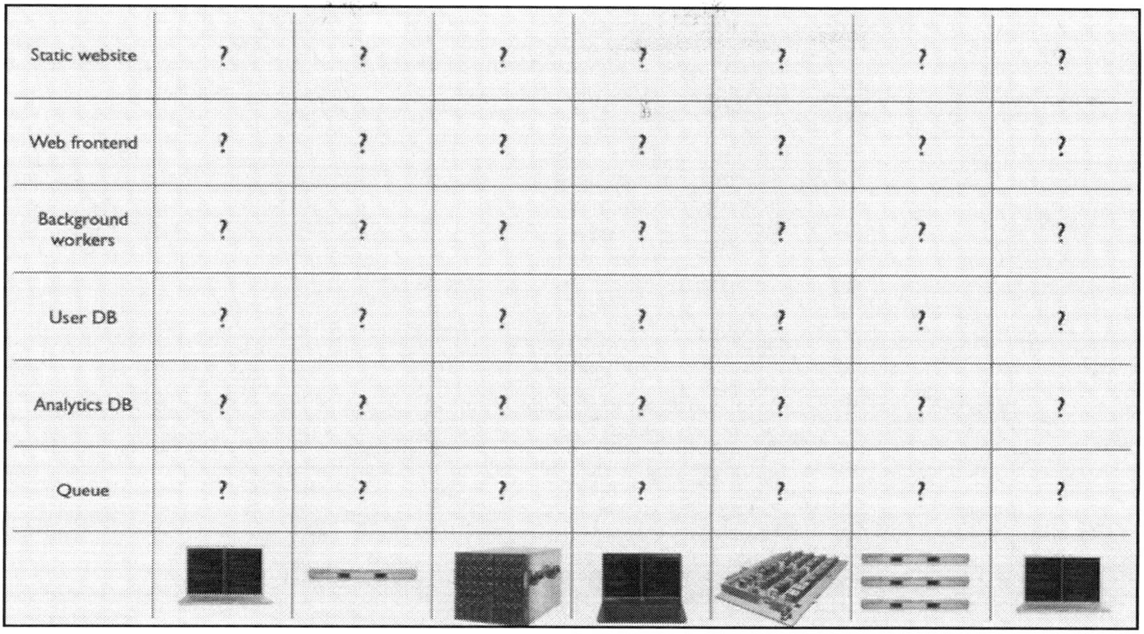

Static website	?	?	?	?	?	?	?
Web frontend	?	?	?	?	?	?	?
Background workers	?	?	?	?	?	?	?
User DB	?	?	?	?	?	?	?
Analytics DB	?	?	?	?	?	?	?
Queue	?	?	?	?	?	?	?

Figure 1.16: Complexity associated with making different application components work in different environments

As per the preceding diagram, to make different application components work in different environments (different hardware platforms), one would need to make sure that the environment-compatible software versions and their related configurations are set appropriately. Doing this using manual steps can be a really cumbersome and error-prone task.

This is where Docker containers fit in. The following diagram represents containerizing different application components using Docker containers. As like real-world containers, it would become very easy to move the containerized application components from one environment to another with fewer or no issues:

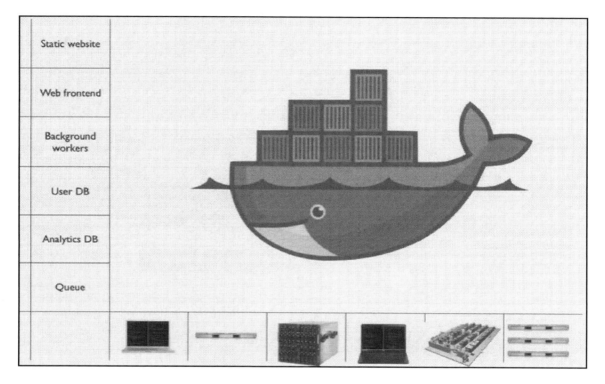

Figure 1.17: Docker containers to move application components across different environments

Docker containers

In simple terms, Docker containers provide an isolated and secure environment for the application components to run. The isolation and security allows one or many containers to run simultaneously on a given host. Often, for simplicity's sake, Docker containers are loosely termed as lightweight-VMs (Virtual Machine). However, they are very different from traditional VMs. Docker containers do not need hypervisors to run like virtual machines, and thus, multiple containers can be run on a given hardware combination.

Virtual machines include the application, the necessary binaries and libraries, and an entire guest operating system, all of which can amount to tens of GBs. On the other hand, Docker containers include the application and all of its dependencies, but share the kernel with other containers, running as isolated processes in the user space on the host operating system. *Docker containers are not tied to any specific infrastructure: they run on any computer, on any infrastructure, and in any cloud.* This very aspect makes them look like a real-world container. The following diagram sums it all up:

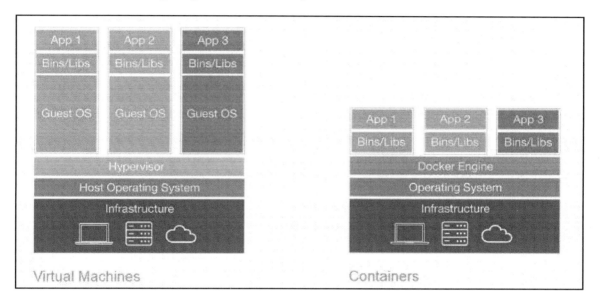

Figure 1.18: Difference between traditional VMs and Docker containers

Listed next are some of the key building blocks of the Docker technology:

- **Docker Container**: An isolated and secured environment for applications to run.
- **Docker engine**: A client-server application having the following components:
  - Daemon process used to create and manage Docker *objects*, such as images, containers, networks, and data volumes.
  - A REST API interface
  - A **command-line interface (CLI)** client
- **Docker client**: A client program that invokes the Docker engine using APIs.
- **Docker host**: The underlying operating system sharing kernel space with the Docker containers. Until recently, the Windows OS needed Linux virtualization to host Docker containers.

- **Docker hub**: The public repository used to manage Docker images posted by various users. Images made public are available for all to download in order to create containers using those images.

What are the key building blocks of Dockers containers?

For setting up our development environment, we will rely on Docker containers, and assemble them together using the tool called **Docker compose**, which we shall learn about a little later.

Let us understand some of the following, which can also be termed as the key building blocks of Docker containers:

- **Docker image**: In simple terms, a Docker image can be thought of as a class in Java. Docker containers can be thought of as running instances of the image as like having one or more instances of a Java class. Technically speaking, Docker images consist of a list of layers that are stacked on top of each other to form a base for the containers' root file system. The following diagram represents a command which can be used to create a Docker container using an image named `hello-world`:

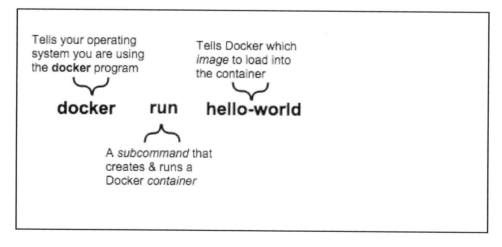

Figure 1.19: Docker command representing creation of Docker container using a Docker image.

In order to set up our development environment, we will require the images of the following to create the respective Docker containers: Tomcat and MySQL

- **Dockerfile**: A `Dockerfile` is a text document that contains all the commands which could be called on the command line to assemble or build an image. The `docker build` command is used to build an image from a `Dockerfile` and a context. In order to create custom images for Tomcat and MySQL, it may be required to create a `Dockerfile`, and then build the image. The following is a sample command for building an image using a `Dockerfile`:

```
docker build -f tomcat.df -t tomcat_debug .
```

The preceding command would look for the Dockerfile `tomcat.df` in the current directory specified by ".", and build the image with the tag `tomcat_debug`.

Installing Docker

Now that you have got an understanding of Docker, let's install Docker. We shall look into the steps that are required to install Dockers on the Windows OS. However, one can download the appropriate installer for Docker toolbox based on the OS requirements. Perform the following steps to install Docker:

1. Download the Windows version of the Docker Toolbox from the webpage https://www.docker.com/products/docker-toolbox.
2. The Docker toolbox comes as an installer which can be double-clicked for a quick setup and launch of the docker environment. The following come with the Docker toolbox installation:
    - Docker Machine for running docker-machine commands
    - Docker Engine for running the docker commands
    - Docker Compose for running the docker-compose commands--this is what we are looking for
    - Kitematic, the Docker GUI
    - A shell preconfigured for a Docker command-line environment
    - Oracle VirtualBox

Setting up the development environment using Docker compose

In this section, we will learn how to set up an on-demand, self-service development environment using Docker compose. The following are some of the points covered in this section:

- What is Docker compose
- The Docker compose script for setting up the development environment

What is Docker compose?

Docker compose is a tool for defining and running multi-container Docker applications. One will require to create a Compose file to configure the application's services. The following steps are required to be taken in order to work with Docker compose:

- Define the application's environment with a Dockerfile so it can be reproduced anywhere.
- Define the services that make up the application in `docker-compose.yml` so they can be run together in an isolated environment.
- Lastly, run `docker-compose`, and Compose will start and run the entire application.

As we are going to set up a multi-container application using Tomcat and MySQL as different containers, we will use Docker compose to configure both of them, and then, assemble the application.

Docker Compose Script for setting up the Dev Environment

In order to come up with a Docker compose script which can set up our Spring Web App development environment with one script execution, we will first set up images for the following by creating independent Dockerfiles:

- Tomcat 8.x with Java and Maven installed as one container
- MySQL as another container

Setting up the Tomcat 8.x as a container service

The following steps can be used to set up Tomcat 8.x along with Java 8 and Maven 3.x as one container:

1. Create a folder, and put the following files within the folder. The source code for the files will be given as follows:
   - tomcat.df
   - create_tomcat_admin_user.sh
   - run.sh

2. Copy the following source code for tomcat.df:

```
FROM phusion/baseimage:0.9.17

RUN echo "deb http://archive.ubuntu.com/ubuntu trusty main
universe" > /etc/apt/sources.list

RUN apt-get -y update

RUN DEBIAN_FRONTEND=noninteractive apt-get install -y -q python-
software-properties software-properties-common

ENV JAVA_VER 8
ENV JAVA_HOME /usr/lib/jvm/java-8-oracle

RUN echo 'deb http://ppa.launchpad.net/webupd8team/java/ubuntu
trusty main' >> /etc/apt/sources.list && \
    echo 'deb-src http://ppa.launchpad.net/webupd8team/java/ubuntu
trusty main' >> /etc/apt/sources.list && \
    apt-key adv --keyserver keyserver.ubuntu.com --recv-keys
C2518248EEA14886 && \
    apt-get update && \
    echo oracle-java${JAVA_VER}-installer shared/accepted-oracle-
license-v1-1 select true | sudo /usr/bin/debconf-set-selections && \
    apt-get install -y --force-yes --no-install-recommends oracle-
java${JAVA_VER}-installer oracle-java${JAVA_VER}-set-default && \
    apt-get clean && \
    rm -rf /var/cache/oracle-jdk${JAVA_VER}-installer

RUN update-java-alternatives -s java-8-oracle

RUN echo "export JAVA_HOME=/usr/lib/jvm/java-8-oracle" >> ~/.bashrc

RUN apt-get clean && rm -rf /var/lib/apt/lists/* /tmp/* /var/tmp/*
ENV MAVEN_VERSION 3.3.9
```

```
        RUN mkdir -p /usr/share/maven \
  && curl -fsSL
http://apache.osuosl.org/maven/maven-3/$MAVEN_VERSION/binaries/apache-maven
-$MAVEN_VERSION-bin.tar.gz \
  | tar -xzC /usr/share/maven --strip-components=1 \
  && ln -s /usr/share/maven/bin/mvn /usr/bin/mvn

        ENV MAVEN_HOME /usr/share/maven

        VOLUME /root/.m2

        RUN apt-get update && \
          apt-get install -yq --no-install-recommends wget pwgen ca-
certificates && \
          apt-get clean && \
          rm -rf /var/lib/apt/lists/*
        ENV TOMCAT_MAJOR_VERSION 8
        ENV TOMCAT_MINOR_VERSION 8.5.8
        ENV CATALINA_HOME /tomcat

        RUN wget -q
https://archive.apache.org/dist/tomcat/tomcat-${TOMCAT_MAJOR_VERSION}/v${TO
MCAT_MINOR_VERSION}/bin/apache-tomcat-${TOMCAT_MINOR_VERSION}.tar.gz && \
  wget -qO-
https://archive.apache.org/dist/tomcat/tomcat-${TOMCAT_MAJOR_VERSION}/v
${TOMCAT_MINOR_VERSION}/bin/apache-tomcat-
${TOMCAT_MINOR_VERSION}.tar.gz.md5 | md5sum
-c - && \
          tar zxf apache-tomcat-*.tar.gz && \
          rm apache-tomcat-*.tar.gz && \
          mv apache-tomcat* tomcat
        ADD create_tomcat_admin_user.sh /create_tomcat_admin_user.sh
        RUN mkdir /etc/service/tomcat
        ADD run.sh /etc/service/tomcat/run
        RUN chmod +x /*.sh
        RUN chmod +x /etc/service/tomcat/run

        EXPOSE 8080

        CMD ["/sbin/my_init"]
```

3. Copy the following code in a file named `create_tomcat_admin_user.sh`. This file should be created in the same folder as the preceding file, `tomcat.df`. While copying into notepad and later using with the Docker terminal, you may find *Ctrl + M* inserted at the end of the line. Make sure that those lines are appropriately handled and removed:

```bash
#!/bin/bash

if [ -f /.tomcat_admin_created ]; then
 echo "Tomcat 'admin' user already created"
 exit 0
fi

PASS=${TOMCAT_PASS:-$(pwgen -s 12 1)}
_word=$( [ ${TOMCAT_PASS} ] && echo "preset" || echo "random" )

echo "=> Creating an admin user with a ${_word} password in Tomcat"
sed -i -r 's/<\/tomcat-users>//' ${CATALINA_HOME}/conf/tomcat-users.xml
    echo '<role rolename="manager-gui"/>' >>
${CATALINA_HOME}/conf/tomcat-users.xml
    echo '<role rolename="manager-script"/>' >>
${CATALINA_HOME}/conf/tomcat-users.xml
    echo '<role rolename="manager-jmx"/>' >>
${CATALINA_HOME}/conf/tomcat-users.xml
    echo '<role rolename="admin-gui"/>' >>
${CATALINA_HOME}/conf/tomcat-users.xml
    echo '<role rolename="admin-script"/>' >>
${CATALINA_HOME}/conf/tomcat-users.xml
    echo "<user username="admin" password="${PASS}" roles="manager-
gui,manager-script,manager-jmx,admin-gui, admin-script"/>" >>
${CATALINA_HOME}/conf/tomcat-users.xml
    echo '</tomcat-users>' >> ${CATALINA_HOME}/conf/tomcat-users.xml
    echo "=> Done!"
    touch /.tomcat_admin_created

    echo
"======================================================================"
echo "You can now configure to this Tomcat server using:"
echo ""
echo " admin:${PASS}"
echo ""
echo
"======================================================================"
```

4. Copy the following code in a file named as run.sh in the same folder as the preceding two files:

```
#!/bin/bash

if [ ! -f /.tomcat_admin_created ]; then
 /create_tomcat_admin_user.sh
fi

exec ${CATALINA_HOME}/bin/catalina.sh run
```

5. Open up a Docker terminal, and go to the folder where these files are located.
6. Execute the following command to create the Tomcat image. In a few minutes, the Tomcat image will be created:

```
docker build -f tomcat.df -t demo/tomcat:8 .
```

7. Execute this command, and make sure that an image with the name demo/tomcat is found:

```
docker images
```

8. Next, run a container with the name tomcatdev using the following command:

```
docker run -ti -d -p 8080:8080 --name tomcatdev -v "$PWD":/mnt/
demo/tomcat:8
```

9. Open a browser, and type the URL as http://192.168.99.100:8080/. You should be able to see the following page be loaded. Note the URL and the Tomcat version, 8.5.8. This is the same version that we installed earlier (check *Figure 1.4*):

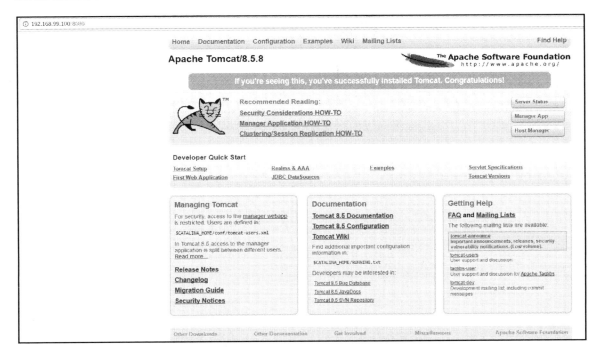

Figure 1.20: Tomcat 8.5.8 installed as a Docker container

10. You can access the container through the terminal with the following command. Make sure to check the Tomcat installation inside the folder /tomcat. Also, execute the commands java -version and mvn -v to check the version of Java and Maven respectively:

```
docker exec -ti tomcatdev /bin/bash
```

In this section, you learnt to set up Tomcat 8.5.8 along with Java 8 and Maven 3.x as one container.

Setting up MySQL as a container service

In this section, you will learn how to set up MySQL as a container service. In the Docker terminal, execute the following command:

```
docker run -ti -d -p 3326:3306 --name mysqldev -e MYSQL_ROOT_PASSWORD=r00t
-v "$PWD":/mnt/ mysql:5.7
```

The preceding command sets up MySQL 5.7 version within the container, and starts the `mysqld` service. Open MySQL Workbench, and create a new connection by entering the details such as those shown in the following screenshot; click on **Test Connection**. You should be able to establish the connection successfully:

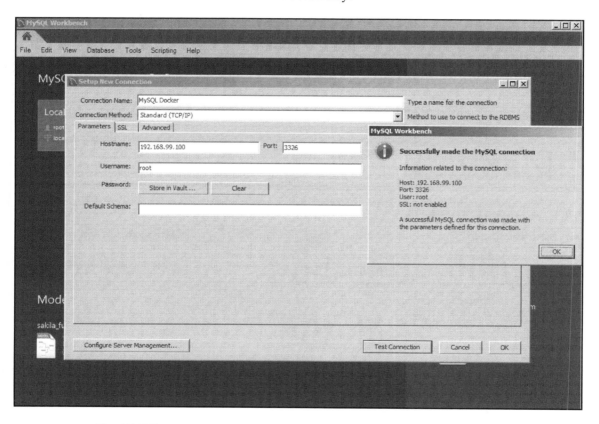

Figure 1.21: MySQL server running in the container and accessible from host machine at 3326 port using MySQL Workbench

Docker compose script to set up the development environment

Now that we have set up both Tomcat and MySQL as individual containers, let's create a Docker compose script using which both the containers can be started simultaneously, thereby, starting the Dev environment.

1. Save the following source code as `docker-compose.yml` in the same folder as the aforementioned files:

```
version: '2'
services:
    web:
      build:
        context: .
        dockerfile: tomcat.df
      ports:
        - "8080:8080"
      volumes:
        - .:/mnt/
      links:
        - db
    db:
      image: mysql:5.7
      ports:
        - "3326:3306"
      environment:
        - MYSQL_ROOT_PASSWORD=r00t
```

2. Execute the following command to start and stop the services:

```
// For starting the services in the foreground
docker-compose up

// For starting the services in the background (detached mode)
docker-compose up -d

// For stopping the services
docker-compose stop
```

3. Test whether both the default Tomcat web app and MySQL server can be accessed. Access the URL 192.168.99.100:8080, and make sure that the web page as shown in Figure 1.20 is displayed. Also, open MySQL Workbench and access the MySQL server at IP 192.168.99.100 and port 3326 (as specified in the preceding docker-compose.yml file).

Summary

In this chapter, you learnt about preparing development environment for building Spring web app. Details on how to setup tomcat server, MySQL database, eclipse IDE were presented. IN next chapter, we will learn about aspects of data processing using Spring and Hibernate.

3

Data Access Layer with Spring and Hibernate

Given that Java applications need to persist data in the database, there are different approaches to achieve this objective, including using JDBC APIs or an **Object/Relational Mapping (ORM)** framework. An ORM framework greatly simplifies the process of storing and retrieving the data from the database by means of mapping the Java objects with the data stored in the database. Some of the popular ORM frameworks are Hibernate and MyBatis. In this chapter, you will learn about Hibernate and its concepts in relation with how Hibernate can be used with Spring apps to interact with the databases. We will cover the following topics in this chapter:

- An introduction to Hibernate
- Setting up Hibernate with Spring
- Designing domain objects and database tables
- An introduction to NamedQuery and Criteria
- Common Hibernate operations
- Transaction management

An introduction to Hibernate

First and foremost, let's try to understand what Hibernate is and why it is worth using. Hibernate is most popularly known as an Object/Relational Mapping framework. It was devised back in the year 2001 by Gavin King, while working with Cirrus technologies, as an alternative to the **Enterprise JavaBeans** (**EJB**) style of persistence to provide better persistence capabilities to Java applications. The project details can be accessed on its homepage, `http://www.hibernate.org`. Initially started as an ORM framework, Hibernate has spun off into many projects, such as Hibernate Search, Hibernate Validator, Hibernate OGM (for NoSQL databases), and so on. In this chapter, you will learn about the Hibernate ORM framework (`http://hibernate.org/orm/`).

Before getting into the details of Hibernate, let's understand why it is good to use an ORM framework such as Hibernate. The following are some of the key reasons:

- The most important reason is that an ORM framework, such as Hibernate, allows you to work with a rich, object-oriented business domain model, and is still able to store and write effective queries quickly against relational and NoSQL databases.
- It helps make data access more portable and abstract. As a result of the abstraction brought into the data access layer, it provides the flexibility to move to different database software in an easier manner.
- It allows in speeding up the development by not only avoiding writing repetitive code such as mapping query fields to object member fields and vice versa, but also generate boilerplate code for basic CRUD operations.

Here are some of the salient features of the Hibernate framework:

- **Object/Relational Mapping**: The ORM feature tends to solve the problem of the mismatch of the Java domain object model with regards to the relational database table format based on which the domain data gets stored in the database. Hibernate, as an ORM framework, allows the mapping of the Java domain object with database tables and vice versa. As a result, business logic is able to access and manipulate database entities via Java objects. It helps speed up the overall development process by taking care of aspects such as transaction management, automatic primary key generation, managing database connections and related implementations, and so on. This is considered to be the most important feature of Hibernate ORM.
- **JPA provider**: Hibernate does support the **Java Persistence API** (**JPA**) specification. JPA is a set of specifications for accessing, persisting, and managing data between Java objects and relational database entities.

- **Idiomatic persistence**: Any class that follows object-oriented principles such as inheritance, polymorphism, and so on, can be used as a persistent class.
- **High performance and scalability**: Hibernate supports techniques such as different fetching strategies, lazy initialization, optimistic locking, and so on, to achieve high performance, and it scales well in any environment.
- **Easy to maintain**: Hibernate is easier to maintain as it requires no special database tables or fields. It generates SQL at system initialization time. It is much quicker and easier to maintain compared to JDBC.

The following diagram represents the application architecture of a Java application, making use of Hibernate as an ORM framework and connecting with a database:

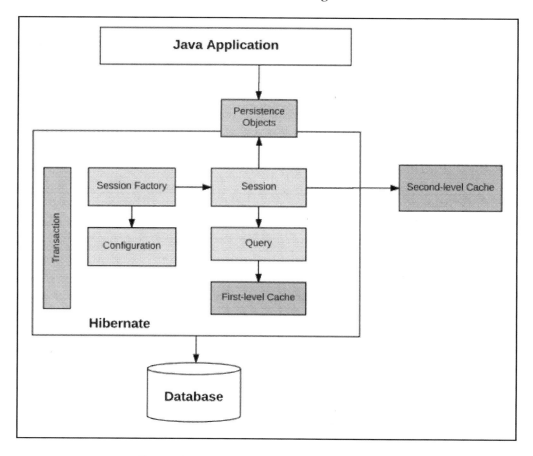

Figure 1: Application architecture representing key building blocks of Hibernate

The following represents some details of the key building blocks of Hibernate, which are shown in the preceding diagram:

- **Configuration**: This represents the **Configuration** used by **Session Factory** to work with **Java Application** and the **Database**. It represents an entire set of mappings of an application Java Types to an SQL database. Instance of `org.hibernate.cfg.Configuration` is used to build an immutable `org.hibernate.SessionFactory`. It is represented by files, such as `hibernate.properties` or `hibernate.cfg.xml`. Alternatively, configuration can also be represented using `@Configuration` annotation. The following code represents a class annotated with the `@Configuration` annotation:

```
/@Configuration
public class AppConfig
{
 @Bean(name = "dataSource")
 public DataSource getDataSource() {
 ...
 }

 @Bean(name = "sessionFactory")
 ...
 }

 @Bean(name = "transactionManager")
 public HibernateTransactionManager getTransactionManager(
 SessionFactory sessionFactory) {
 ...
 }
}
```

- **Session Factory**: Java application requests Hibernate Session Factory for a session object. Session Factory uses configuration files, such as `hibernate.properties` or `hibernate.cfg.xml` to configure Hibernate for the application and instantiates the session object appropriately. Alternatively, the `SessionFactory` bean could also be created in the class annotated with `@Configuration`. This is represented by the `org.hibernate.SessionFactory` class. The following code sample represents the instantiation of the `SessionFactory` bean in a class annotated with `@Configuration` as shown in the preceding example.

```
@Bean(name = "sessionFactory")
public SessionFactory getSessionFactory(DataSource dataSource)
{
 LocalSessionFactoryBuilder sessionBuilder = new
   LocalSessionFactoryBuilder(dataSource);
```

```
sessionBuilder.scanPackages("com.book.healthapp.domain");
return sessionBuilder.buildSessionFactory();
}
```

- **Session**: This object represents the interaction between the application and the database. This is represented by the `org.hibernate.Session` class. The instance of a session can be retrieved from the `SessionFactory` bean. The following code represents the instantiation of a session instance using `SessionFactory`:

```
@Repository
@Transactional
public class UserDAOImpl implements UserDAO {

  @Autowired private SessionFactory sessionFactory;

  @Override
  public List<User> findByEmail(String email) {
    Session session = this.sessionFactory.getCurrentSession();
    ...
  }
}
```

- **Query**: This interface allows one to query the database for one or more objects. Hibernate provides different techniques to query database, including **NamedQuery** and **Criteria API**, which are discussed in one of the later sections.
- **First-level cache**: This represents the default cache used by Hibernate `Session` object while interacting with the database. It is also called as **session cache** and caches objects within the current session. All requests from the `Session` object to the database must pass through the first-level cache or session cache. One must note that the first-level cache is available with the session object until the `Session` object is live. Each `Session` object, that way, would have its session cache or first-level cache and, is not accessible to any other `Session` object.
- **Transaction**: This object enables you to achieve data consistency. This is represented by the class, `org.hibernate.Transaction`. Instances of transaction which are single-threaded, short-lived objects are created using `TransactionFactory` (`org.hibernate.TransactionFactory`).

In addition to the preceding points, the application architecture diagram also represents some of the following:

- **Persistent objects**: Simply speaking, persistent objects are plain old Java objects (POJOs), which get persisted as one of the rows in the related table in the database. These objects get represented using configuration files, such as `hibernate.cfg.xml` or `hibernate.properties`. Alternatively, persistent objects are also represented using the `@Entity` annotation. While in the session scope, Hibernate synchronizes the state of persistent objects with a corresponding table in database. The following represents the persistent `User` object with `@Entity` annotation:

```
@Entity
@Table(name="user")
public class User {
    @Id
    @GeneratedValue(strategy=GenerationType.IDENTITY)
    private int id;
    ...
}
```

- **Second-level cache**: This cache is used to store objects across sessions. Note that this is unlike session or first-level cache, which caches objects within the current session. Second-level cache needs to be explicitly enabled and one would be required to provide the cache provider for a second-level cache. One of the common second-level cache providers is **EhCache**.

The Spring framework supports integration with Hibernate for managing different aspects of ORM, achieving clear application layering and loose coupling of application objects. In the next section, you will learn about how to setup Hibernate with Spring.

Setting up Hibernate with Spring

There are different approaches to integrating Hibernate with Spring. One of them represents defining Hibernate-related configuration in the XML application context file, and, the other one is based on the usage of appropriate annotations. In this section, you will learn to setup Hibernate with Spring using the annotation method.

In order to setup Hibernate with Spring, one would need to do following:

- Setting up data source information in the `application.properties` file, which can be found in the `src/main/resources` folder when working with a Spring Boot application.
- Use annotations to wire `LocalSessionFactoryBean` into the `SessionFactory` object within DAO.

Setting up data source information in the application.properties file

Place the following configuration-related code in the `application.properties` file. The following code represents the database server address as `127.0.0.1:3306` and the database as `healthapp`:

```
spring.datasource.driverClassName=com.mysql.jdbc.Driver
spring.datasource.url=jdbc:mysql://127.0.0.1:3306/healthapp
spring.datasource.username=root
spring.datasource.password=root
```

Using annotations to wire a SessionFactory bean

The following are some of the key steps which are required to be taken in order to wire `LocalSessionFactoryBean` with the `SessionFactory` instance in the DAO objects:

- Configure bean definitions
- Autowire `SessionFactory` instance in DAOs

Configure bean definitions

First and foremost, one will be required to configure bean definitions in order to inject a `SessionFactory` instance as a member variable in DAOs. In order to configure bean definitions, it is recommended to have a class annotated with `@Configuration` annotation. The following is the code that represents class for configurating bean definitions:

```
@Configuration
@EntityScan("com.book.healthapp.domain")
@EnableTransactionManagement
@PropertySource("classpath:application.properties")
```

```
public class AppConfig {
    ...
}
```

Pay attention to some of the following in the earlier given code:

- `@Configuration` annotation: This is used to indicate that the class can have one or more `@Bean` annotated methods. These `@Bean` annotated methods are used by the Spring IOC container to generate bean definitions which are used to serve the requests at runtime. It should be noted that the `@Configuration` annotation is meta-annotated with `@Component`, and thus, are candidates of component scanning.

- `@EntityScan` annotation: This is used to configure the base packages, which are used to scan the packages for JPA entity classes.

- `@EnableTransactionManagement` annotation: This is used to register one or more Spring components, which are used to power annotation-driven transaction management capabilities. It is similar to having `<tx:annotation-driven>` in an XML namespace.

- `@PropertySource` annotation: These are used in conjunction with a `@Configuration` annotation. It provides a declarative mechanism for associating the application property file (consisting of key-value pairs) with the environment.

The next steps are to configure some of the following bean definitions in the pre-mentioned class:

- **DataSource**: The following code represents the bean definition (`dataSource`) for the data source to be used with Hibernate Session Factory:

```
@Value("${spring.datasource.driverClassName}") String
  driverClassName;
@Value("${spring.datasource.url}") String url;
@Value("${spring.datasource.username}") String username;
@Value("${spring.datasource.password}") String password;

@Bean(name = "dataSource")
public DataSource getDataSource() {
  DataSource dataSource = DataSourceBuilder
    .create()
    .username(username)
    .password(password)
    .url(url)
    .driverClassName(driverClassName)
    .build();
```

```
        return dataSource;
    }
```

- **SessionFactory**: The following code configures a session factory bean (sessionFactory), which can be injected in DAOImpl classes. Note the use of LocalSessionFactoryBuilder for creation of sessionFactory. The scanPackages method invoked on sessionBuilder instance instructs the annotated classes to be used for mapping definitions:

```
@Bean(name = "sessionFactory")
public SessionFactory getSessionFactory(DataSource dataSource)
{
    LocalSessionFactoryBuilder sessionBuilder = new
LocalSessionFactoryBuilder(dataSource);
    sessionBuilder.scanPackages("com.book.healthapp.domain");
    return sessionBuilder.buildSessionFactory();
}
```

- **HibernateTransactionManager**: The following code configures a HibernateTransactionManager (TransactionManager) for SessionFactory. Configuring a TransactionManager for SessionFactory would avoid code in DAO classes to explicitly take care of transaction management concerns:

```
@Bean(name = "transactionManager")
public HibernateTransactionManager getTransactionManager(
    SessionFactory sessionFactory) {
    HibernateTransactionManager transactionManager = new
        HibernateTransactionManager(sessionFactory);
    return transactionManager;
}
```

Summing it up, all the following code can be used for configuring bean definitions:

```
@Configuration
@EntityScan("com.book.healthapp.domain")
@EnableTransactionManagement
@PropertySource("classpath:application.properties")
public class AppConfig {

    @Value("${spring.datasource.driverClassName}") String
driverClassName;
    @Value("${spring.datasource.url}") String url;
    @Value("${spring.datasource.username}") String username;
    @Value("${spring.datasource.password}") String password;
```

```
@Bean(name = "dataSource")
public DataSource getDataSource() {
   DataSource dataSource = DataSourceBuilder
     .create()
     .username(username)
     .password(password)
     .url(url)
     .driverClassName(driverClassName)
     .build();
     return dataSource;
}

@Bean(name = "sessionFactory")
  public SessionFactory getSessionFactory(DataSource dataSource) {
     LocalSessionFactoryBuilder sessionBuilder = new
       LocalSessionFactoryBuilder(dataSource);
     sessionBuilder.scanPackages("com.book.healthapp.domain");
     return sessionBuilder.buildSessionFactory();
}

@Bean(name = "transactionManager")
public HibernateTransactionManager getTransactionManager(
  SessionFactory sessionFactory) {
     HibernateTransactionManager transactionManager = new
       HibernateTransactionManager(sessionFactory);
     return transactionManager;
  }
}
```

Autowire SessionFactory in DAOs

Once the bean definitions get configured, the next step is to autowire SessionFactory in
DAO classes. The following code represents how to autowire SessionFactory in DAO
classes:

```
@Repository
@Transactional
public class UserDAOImpl implements UserDAO {

  @Autowired private SessionFactory sessionFactory;

  @Override
  public List<User> findByEmail(String email) {
    return this.sessionFactory.getCurrentSession()
    .createQuery("from User u where u.email = :email")
    .setString("email", email)
```

```
        .list();
    }
}
```

Note some of the following terms in the preceding code:

- @Repository: This annotation is used to represent the fact that the class can be used to CRUD operations with the domain objects from encapsulating storage, including methods for retrieval, search, and persistence of the objects.
- @Autowired: This annotation is used to autowire an instance of SessionFactory.
- @Transactional: This annotation is used to automatically handle the transaction-related concerns, such as transaction propagation and so on. For classes or methods with @Transactional, Spring creates a proxy for the objects and injects the behaviors before, after, or around the method calls appropriately.

Design domain objects and database tables

Before moving ahead, let's design the Java POJOs and the related tables in the database. Let's recall that we are trying to create a Healthcare-based web application comprising of domain objects, such as doctors, patients, hospitals, and so on. The following are some the domain objects for the preceding mentioned application:

- User
- Doctor: For a doctor, one would want to record health centers where he/she makes a visit and, also, his/her qualification
- Rx (representing prescription)
- Medicine
- Health centres (representing clinic, hospital, and so on)

The following are different tables, which can be created for capturing data related with preceding domain objects:

- user
- doctor
- doctor_location
- doctor_qualification

- health_centre
- medicine
- rx
- rx_medicine

Let's take a look at the Java code for one of the domain object and the related MySQL table code. Other domain objects and tables would follow a similar pattern of code.

User

The following code represents the Java code for User. Pay attention to some of the following annotations in the following code given:

- @Entity: This, simply speaking, is used to represent a class that can be mapped to a table
- @Table: This is optionally used in conjunction with the @Entity annotation to map the table name with the entity class
- @Id: This is used to represent the primary identifier of the entity or table
- @Column: This is used to map the field in the entity class with the column in the related table

```
@Entity
@Table(name="user")
public class User {
  // Define the variables; Provide the mapping with
  //the table column name appropriately
  @Id
  @GeneratedValue(strategy=GenerationType.IDENTITY)
  private int id;
  private String email;
  private String password;
  @Column(name = "first_name") private String firstname;
  @Column(name = "last_name") private String lastname;
  ...

  // Getter and Setter methods

  public int getId() {
    return id;
  }
  public void setId(int id) {
    this.id = id;
```

```
      }
      public String getEmail() {
        return email;
      }
      public void setEmail(String email) {
        this.email = email;
      }
      ...
    }
```

The following code represents the corresponding user table in MySQL:

```
CREATE TABLE `user` (
 `id` bigint(20) NOT NULL AUTO_INCREMENT,
 `email` varchar(50) NOT NULL,
 `password` varchar(20) NOT NULL,
 `first_name` varchar(20) NOT NULL,
 `last_name` varchar(20) DEFAULT NULL,
 `age` int(11) DEFAULT NULL,
 `gender` int(11) DEFAULT NULL,
 `contact_number` varchar(15) DEFAULT NULL,
 `alternate_contact_number` varchar(15) DEFAULT NULL,
 `address` varchar(100) DEFAULT NULL,
 `city_code` varchar(20) DEFAULT NULL,
 `state_code` varchar(20) DEFAULT NULL,
 `country_code` varchar(20) DEFAULT NULL,
 `create_time` timestamp NOT NULL DEFAULT CURRENT_TIMESTAMP,
 `last_updated` timestamp NOT NULL DEFAULT CURRENT_TIMESTAMP,
 PRIMARY KEY (`id`),
 UNIQUE KEY `email` (`email`)
) ENGINE=InnoDB AUTO_INCREMENT=7 DEFAULT CHARSET=latin
```

In a similar fashion, one will be required to create other domain objects such as doctor, rx, medicine, health centre, and corresponding tables for them.

Introduction to NamedQuery and Criteria

Before we go on to understand some of the common hibernate operations, let's look into what NamedQuery and Criteria API are. This concept will be referred in the next section for performing data retrieval operations.

What is NamedQuery?

NamedQuery in Hibernate is a way to provide alias names to one or more queries, which are static in nature. The primary coding problem that gets solved with NamedQuery is the queries lying all around, and thus, gets difficult to manage. NamedQuery allows queries to be segregated at one place and accessed later via alias names. They are parsed/prepared once, and are thus considered as more optimal than other query mechanisms such as Criteria. NamedQuery can be defined using annotation or mapping files. In this section, we shall take a look at examples using NamedQuery and related annotations.

The following are some of the key annotations in relation with NamedQuery:

- `@NamedQuery`: This is used to define a **Java Persistence Query Language (JPQL)** query and later access it using a name
- `@NamedQueries`: This is used to group multiple instances of `@NamedQuery`

The following is an example of both of the earlier mentioned annotations. In the example here, two different NamedQuery has been used to illustrate the concept of `@NamedQuery`. Each `@NamedQuery` has two attributes, such as name and query. Attribute `name` is used to associate an alias name (such as `findByEmail` or `findByEmailAndPassword`) to the query and, attribute `query` is used to associate the actual query.

```
@NamedQueries({
    @NamedQuery(
        name = "findByEmail",
        query = "from User u where u.email = :email"
    ),
    @NamedQuery(
        name = "findByEmailAndPassword",
        query = "from User u where u.email = :email and u.password =
:password"
})
```

In the preceding section, we saw the User domain object. The code related to `NamedQuery` annotations will go in `User.java`. Thus, `User.java` would look like the following:

```
package com.book.healthapp.domain;

import java.sql.Timestamp;

import javax.persistence.Column;
import javax.persistence.Entity;
import javax.persistence.GeneratedValue;
import javax.persistence.GenerationType;
import javax.persistence.Id;
```

```java
import javax.persistence.NamedQueries;
import javax.persistence.NamedQuery;
import javax.persistence.Table;

@Entity
@Table(name="user")
@NamedQueries({
  @NamedQuery(
    name = "findByEmail",
    query = "from User u where u.email = :email"
  ),
  @NamedQuery(
    name = "findByEmailAndPassword",
    query = "from User u where u.email= :email and u.password =
:password"
  ),
})
public class User {

  @Id
  @GeneratedValue(strategy=GenerationType.IDENTITY)
  private int id;
  private String email;
  private String password;
  @Column(name = "first_name") private String firstname;
  @Column(name = "last_name") private String lastname;
  private int age;
  private int gender;
  @Column(name = "contact_number")
  private String contactNumber;
  @Column(name = "alternate_contact_number")
  private String alternateContactNumber;
  private String address;
  @Column(name = "city_code") private String cityCode;
  @Column(name = "state_code") private String stateCode;
  @Column(name = "country_code") private String countryCode;
  @Column(name = "create_time") private Timestamp createTime;
  @Column(name = "last_updated") private Timestamp lastUpdated;

  public int getId() {
    return id;
  }
  public void setId(int id) {
    this.id = id;
  }
  public String getEmail() {
    return email;
  }
```

```
      public void setEmail(String email) {
        this.email = email;
      }
      public String getPassword() {
        return password;
      }
      public void setPassword(String password) {
        this.password = password;
      }
      ...
    }
```

With NamedQuery `findByEmail`, this is how `UserDAOImpl` would look like. Compare the following code with the code given under the section, *Use Annotations to Autowire a SessionFactory Bean*:

```
    @Repository
    @Transactional
    public class UserDAOImpl implements UserDAO {

      @Autowired private SessionFactory sessionFactory;

      @Override
      public List<User> findByEmail(String email) {
        Session session = this.sessionFactory.getCurrentSession();
        Query query = session.getNamedQuery("findByEmail");
        query.setString("email", email);
        return query.list();
      }
    }
```

What is Criteria?

The Criteria API can be used to dynamically create queries at runtime, also termed as dynamic queries. They are considered to be a preferred choice for some of the following reasons:

- There are multiple variables and search criteria which need to be applied, based on one or more filter conditions at runtime.
- Criteria queries are typesafe, and thus provide compile time type checking.

The following represents an example displaying the use of the Criteria API,
createCriteria:

```
public List<User> findByEmailAndPassword(String email, String password) {
    Session session = this.sessionFactory.getCurrentSession();
    return session.createCriteria(User.class)
      .add(Restrictions.eq("email", email))
      .add(Restrictions.eq("password", password))
      .list();
}
```

Common Hibernate operations

In this section, you will learn some of the common Hibernate operations which are used to
process data from the database.

The following are some of the key operations:

- Data retrieval
- Save/persist
- Update/merge
- Save or update

Data retrieval

Data retrieval can be done using NamedQuery, Criteria, or a simple Hibernate query
mechanism as illustrated in the previous sections. Here are the best practices:

- Criteria can be used to dynamically create queries at runtime. The usage of
  Criteria for static queries should be avoided due to the disadvantages, such
  as cost, associated with translating a JPQL query to SQL every time it is accessed.
- NamedQuery allows queries to be accessed using alias names while making it
  easy to manage queries. NamedQuery is the preferred choice for static queries.

Save/persist operation

Transient instances of persistent classes can be saved in the database using Session APIs such as save or persist. Transient instances are the one which do not have any representation in the database, including an identifier value. These transient instances need to be attached with a Hibernate session for them to be saved in the database. It may be recalled that classes are annotated as persistent entities using annotations such as @Entity at class level.

The following are some of the APIs that are used to save the persistent object in the database:

```
Serializable save(Object object) throws HibernateException
Serializable save(String entityName, Object object) throws
HibernateException

void persist(Object object) throws HibernateException
void persist(String entityName, Object object) throws
HibernateException
```

Both save and persist methods result in SQL INSERT. It is recommended that both these methods should be executed within transaction boundaries. Refer to the following section to understand key aspects of transaction boundaries. The primary difference between persist and save APIs is the fact that the persist API does not necessarily ensure or guarantee that the identifier is assigned to the persistent object immediately. However, the save method is executed immediately, irrespective of the state of the transaction and the identifier is returned thereafter.

In addition, care needs to be taken when using save or persist API in case of detached instances. Such instances are the persistent instances which have entries in the database but which are not attached to any open Hibernate session object. Invoking save API on detached instances would result in the creation of a new record in the database silently. On the other hand, the persist API would result in the exception being thrown complaining of the detached entity being passed to the persist method.

The following code sample represents the use of the save method to persist the user object. Note the invocation of the flush() method to make sure that user object is persisted:

```
Session session = this.sessionFactory.openSession();
Serializable userId = session.save(user);
session.flush();
```

The following code sample represents the use of the save method when done within a transaction boundary. Note that the transaction management is handled programmatically. In the later section, the same code is represented using declarative transaction management:

```
Session session = this.sessionFactory.openSession();
session.beginTransaction();
Serializable userId = session.save(user);
session.getTransaction().commit();
session.close();
```

The following code sample represents the use of the persist method:

```
Session session = this.sessionFactory.openSession();
session.beginTransaction();
session.persist(user);
session.getTransaction().commit();
session.close();
```

Update/merge operation

Update or merge operation are Session APIs, which results in an SQL Update. The update() method results in the update of a persistent instance with the ID of the given detached instance, while the merge() method results in the state of the detached instance getting copied onto the persistent object with the same ID. The following are the related APIs:

```
void update(Object object) throws HibernateException
void update(String entityName, Object object) throws HibernateException

Object merge(Object object) throws HibernateException
Object merge(String entityName, Object object) throws
HibernateException
```

The following happens as a result of invocation of the update method:

- The detached instance passed to the update method is persisted and the state is transitioned from detached to persistent.

The following code sample represents the use of the update method:

```
@Override
 public void update(User user) {
    Session session = this.sessionFactory.openSession();
    User persistentUser = (User) session.load(User.class, new
                          Integer(user.getId()));
```

```
Transaction tx = session.beginTransaction();
persistentUser.setFirstName(user.getFirstname());
persistentUser.setLastname(user.getLastname());
session.update(persistentUser);
tx.commit();
}
```

The following happens as a result of invocation of merge() method:

- A persistent entity having ID matching with the ID of detached instance is obtained
- Values from passed detached instance is copied to the persistent instance
- The updated persistent object is returned

The following code sample represents the usage of the merge method:

```
@Override
public void update(User user) {
  Session session = this.sessionFactory.openSession();
  Transaction tx1 = session.beginTransaction();
  User persistentUser = (User) session.load(User.class, new
   Integer(user.getId()));
  tx1.commit();
  Transaction tx2 = session.beginTransaction();
  user.setEmail(persistentUser.getEmail());
  user.setPassword(persistentUser.getPassword());
  session.merge(user);
  tx2.commit();
}
```

The saveOrUpdate operation

The saveOrUpdate operation is used for persisting (save or update) both transient and detached instances based on whether data already exists in the database. It results in SQL INSERT or SQL UPDATE. It is recommended to use the saveOrUpdate method within transaction boundaries. The following represents the saveOrUpdate API:

```
void saveOrUpdate(Object object) throws HibernateException
```

The code sample represents the use of the saveOrUpdate API for saving data as a result of a new user signup with the HealthApp, or, updating the user profile data for the logged in user:

```
Session session = this.sessionFactory.openSession();
session.beginTransaction();
```

```
session.saveOrUpdate(user);
session.getTransaction().commit();
session.close();
```

Transaction management

In this section, you will learn about some of the important aspects of transaction management with a focus on declarative transaction management. Before going into the details of declarative transaction management, let's try and understand how Spring deals with transaction management.

Transaction management is primarily about defining a transaction boundary in relation to the following to ensure data consistency:

- When a transaction gets started
- Data being persisted
- When the transaction gets rolled back
- When the transaction is closed

Here are some of the key aspects of a Spring transaction boundary:

- **Isolation**: It represents the transaction boundary by determining the extent to which a transaction is isolated from other transactions.
- **Propagation**: It represents the scope of the transaction, for example, whether a code needs to be executed within a new transaction or continue executing within the existing transaction. In a later section, different transaction propagation is dealt with.
- **Timeout**: It is used to define how long the transaction would run before timing out and rolling back automatically.
- **Read-only status**: It is used to represent whether a code can just read the data without being able to write or update it.

Spring supports following two types of transaction management:

- **Programmatic transaction management**: Developers have to write programs/code to carry out transaction management. However, it is not recommended as it is error prone.

- **Declarative transaction management**: It is supported by Spring using the Spring AOP framework. Simply speaking, an annotation such as `@Transactional` is used to achieve declarative transaction management. In the following section, we will go over the related details.

Regardless of whether one adopts programmatic or declarative transaction management, it is of utmost importance to define the appropriate implementation of `PlatformTrasactionManager`. The following are some of the most commonly used implementations:

- **DataSourceTransactionManager**: When working with JDBC, it is recommended to use Spring's `DataSourceTransactionManager`. The following code represents defining the data source alternatively in either an XML file or `@Configuration` class:

```
// When defined in XML file
//
<bean id="dataSource"
class="org.apache.commons.dbcp.BasicDataSource" destroy-
method="close">
    <property name="driverClassName"
value="${jdbc.driverClassName}" />
    <property name="url" value="${jdbc.url}" />
    <property name="username" value="${jdbc.username}" />
    <property name="password" value="${jdbc.password}" />
</bean>

// When defined in @Configuration class
//
@Bean(name = "dataSource")
public DataSource getDataSource() {
  DataSource dataSource = DataSourceBuilder
    .create()
    .username(username)
    .password(password)
    .url(url)
    .driverClassName(driverClassName)
    .build();
  return dataSource;
}
```

The following represents a code sample for defining PlatformTransactionManager implementation in both an XML file or @Configuration class, which makes use of dataSource created as shown in preceding code sample:

```
// When defined in XML file
//
<bean id="transactionManager"
class="org.springframework.jdbc.datasource.DataSourceTransactionManager">
    <property name="dataSource" ref="dataSource"/>
</bean>

// To be Defined within @Configuration class
//
@Bean(name = "transactionManager")
public DataSourceTransactionManager getTransactionManager(DataSource
dataSource) {
    return transactionManager = new
DataSourceTransactionManager(dataSource);
}
```

- **JtaTransactionManager**: In case **Java Transaction API (JTA)** is used, then, the container DataSource instance is obtained through **Java Naming and Directory Interface (JNDI)** in conjunction with JtaTransactionManager. The following code samples demonstrates the creation of DataSource and JtaTransactionManager bean:

```
@Configuration
@EnableTransactionManagement
public class AppConfigJPA {

  @Bean(name = "dataSource")
  public DataSource dataSource() {
    JndiObjectFactoryBean dataSource = new
JndiObjectFactoryBean();
    dataSource.setJndiName("jdbc:healthapp");
    return dataSource;
  }

  @Bean(name = "transactionManager")
  public JtaTransactionManager transactionManager() {
    return new JtaTransactionManager();
  }
}
```

- **HibernateTransactionManager**: In this chapter, as our focus is Hibernate, let's look into the aspect of how Hibernate can be used for doing database transactions. One would require to create a `SessionFactory` bean, which can be used to retrieve a Hibernate `Session` instance.

  `HibernateTransactionManager` needs a reference of `SessionFactory`. The following code sample demonstrates the creation of `DataSource`, `SessionFactory`, and `HibernateTransactionManager` bean:

```
@Configuration
@EnableTransactionManagement
@PropertySource("classpath:application.properties")
public class AppConfig {

  @Value("${spring.datasource.driverClassName}") String
    driverClassName;
  @Value("${spring.datasource.url}") String url;
  @Value("${spring.datasource.username}") String username;
  @Value("${spring.datasource.password}") String password;
  //
  // Create a DataSource bean
  //
  @Bean(name = "dataSource")
  public DataSource getDataSource() {
    DataSource dataSource = DataSourceBuilder
      .create()
      .username(username)
      .password(password)
      .url(url)
      .driverClassName(driverClassName)
      .build();
    return dataSource;
  }
  //
  // Create a SessionFactory bean
  //
  @Bean(name = "sessionFactory")
    public SessionFactory getSessionFactory(DataSource
      dataSource) {
    LocalSessionFactoryBuilder sessionBuilder = new
      LocalSessionFactoryBuilder(dataSource);
    sessionBuilder.scanPackages("com.book.healthapp.domain");
    return sessionBuilder.buildSessionFactory();
  }
  //
  // Create a HibernateTransactionManager bean
  //
  @Bean(name = "transactionManager")
```

```
public HibernateTransactionManager getTransactionManager(
  SessionFactory sessionFactory) {
  HibernateTransactionManager transactionManager = new
    HibernateTransactionManager(sessionFactory);
  return transactionManager;
  }
}
```

Declarative transaction management

Out of two types of transaction management that Spring supports, the declarative transaction management is the recommended way to manage the transactions. The following are some of the fundamental concepts in relation to declarative transaction management:

- An annotation such as @EnableTransactionManagement should be added to the Configuration class in order to support transaction annotations such as @Transactional. The following represents the sample code:

  ```
  @Configuration
  @EnableTransactionManagement
  public class AppConfig
  {
    ...
  }
  ```

- The @Transactional annotation can be used to represent a single database transaction within the scope of a persistent context. It can be used at both class level or the public methods of the class. The reason for having @Transactional at method level is to allow methods to handle aspects of transaction management differently from the class level. The following are some of the key attributes of @Transactional annotation, which further describes subtle aspects of transaction management:
  - **Propagation**: It's parameters are used to define how transactions relate to each other. It supports options such as REQUIRED, REQUIRES_NEW, MANDATORY, NEVER, and so on. The REQUIRED option ensures that the code always run within a transaction boundary by running the code in the current transaction or by creating a new transaction if none exists.
    The REQUIRES_NEW option creates a new transaction for the code to run.

- Let's understand these parameters and how they represent a transaction boundary using the code example given here. As part of signing up, users' data (such as doctors and patients with HealthApp) needs to be persisted in the database and a confirmation email needs to be sent asking the user to verify their identity. This can be achieved using two custom services, UserService and EmailService, where UserService saves the user data in the database and calls EmailService to send a confirmation. The following code represents the same:

```
@Service
@Transactional(propagation=Propagation.REQUIRED)
public class UserServiceImpl implements UserService {

    private UserDAO userDAO;
    private EmailService emailService;

    @Autowired
    public UserServiceImpl(UserDAO userDAO, EmailService
    emailService) {
        this.userDAO = userDAO;
        this.emailService = emailService;
    }

    @Override
    public User save(User user) {
        User user = userDAO.save(user);
        this.emailService.sendConfirmationEmail(user);
        return user;
    }
}
```

Note that UserService mandates that user signup code needs to execute in either an existing transaction or in a new transaction. This is achieved using the Propagation.REQUIRED parameter:

```
@Service
@Transactional(propagation=Propagation.REQUIRES_NEW)
public class EmailServiceImpl implements EmailService {
    @Override
    public void sendConfirmationEmail(User user) {
        try {
            // Code for sending email
        } catch(EmailException ex) {
        }
    }
}
```

In the preceding code, notice that `EmailService` sends an email in a new transaction (`REQUIRES_NEW`). This ensures that if there is an error in sending an email, the entire user signup process is not rolled back, including removing the new user data from the database.

Similarly, the following code demonstrates the use of `Propagation.Mandatory`. It is mandated that the call made to save the user in the database was made as part of an existing or live transaction. In a sense, this also ensures the database operation security.

```
@Repository
@Transactional(propagation=Propagation.MANDATORY)
public class UserDAOImpl implements UserDAO {

   private SessionFactory sessionFactory;
   @Autowired
   public UserDAOImpl(SessionFactory sessionFactory) {
     this.sessionFactory = sessionFactory;
   }

   @Override
   public User save(User user) {
     Session session =
this.sessionFactory.openSession();
     session.save(user);
     session.close();
     return user;
   }
}
```

- **Isolation**: it is used to represent the transaction isolation level. Its parameters are used to define the data contract between different transactions. It supports options such as `READ_UNCOMMITTED`, `READ_COMMITTED`, `REPEATABLE_READ`, and so on. Option such as `READ_COMMITTED` ensure that no dirty data reads are allowed.

The following code represents the transaction management achieved in a **declarative** manner where a new transaction is created for saving the user using both save and persist methods:

```
@Transactional(propagation=Propagation.REQUIRES_NEW)
   public User save(User user) {
     Session session = this.sessionFactory.openSession();
     session.save(user);
```

```
    session.close();
    return user;
  }

@Transactional(propagation=Propagation.REQUIRES_NEW)
public void save(User user) {
  Session session = this.sessionFactory.openSession();
  session.persist(user);
  session.close();
}
```

This is unlike the following code, where transaction management is handled in a *programmatic* manner:

```
public User save(User user) {
  Session session = this.sessionFactory.openSession();
  session.beginTransaction();
  Serializable userId = session.save(user);
  session.getTransaction().commit();
  session.close();
}
```

It can be noted from the preceding example that the code becomes clean and easy to read by making use of the @Transactional annotation, or, in other words, declarative transaction management.

Summary

In this chapter, you learnt about how to use Spring and Hibernate to perform CRUD operations on data with an underlying database such as MySQL. In the next chapter, you will learn different aspects of testing and running a Spring-based web application. We will look into aspects of unit testing, debugging, and running the Spring web app within Docker.

4

Testing and Running Spring Web App

One of the most important aspect of writing a highly maintainable & robust code is to complement code with its unit tests. This increases the code testability which, in turn, enhances the maintainability of the code. In this chapter, you will primarily learn about unit testing and running the Spring web app. The following are some of the topics which will be covered:

- How to run the Spring Boot app
- Introduction to unit testing fundamentals
- Introduction to JUnit 5
- Mocking dependencies using Mockito
- Unit testing controllers, services, and DAOs

How to run the Spring Boot app

In this section, you will learn about three different techniques using to run the Spring Boot app.

- **Using Eclipse IDE**: This is pretty straightforward. One can run from within the Eclipse IDE using the following two different methods:
  - Right-click on the project and click on `Run as > Spring Boot App`. This will run the Spring Boot app.
  - Click on the green-color button in the toolbar. This will open a a few options. Click on `Run as > Spring Boot App` to run the app.

- **Using Command Prompt**: One could do the following to run the Spring Boot app from Command Prompt:
  - Build the app using the following command. This will create a jar or war file within the target directory:

```
mvn clean package
```

  - Execute the following command to run the app assuming that the jar file is created within the target directory. Note that `healthapp` is the artifact ID, which is assigned during the creation of the app. The value artifact ID can also be found in the `pom.xml` file:

```
java -jar target/healthapp-0.0.1-SNAPSHOT.jar
```

- **Using Docker**: As described in one of the previous chapters, Docker containers help deploy apps in local or remote environments in a quick and easy manner. This essentially means that, using Docker, one should be able to quickly run the app locally or through remote environments including Development, QA, and UAT servers, without much ado. The following represents the steps one needs to take in order to achieve the aforementioned objective of running the Spring Boot app anytime, anywhere, with one script execution:

1. **First and foremost, containerize or dockerize the Spring Boot app** using a Dockerfile. It is a two-step process to containerize the app. Firstly, one needs to create a Dockerfile, and secondly, one is required to build an image using that Dockerfile. Once an image is built, one or more containers using that image can be started. The following represents the sample Dockerfile for our Spring Boot app, the HealthApp. Name the file as "Dockerfile" and save it in the project root folder:

```
FROM frolvlad/alpine-oraclejdk8:slim
VOLUME /tmp
ADD target/healthapp-0.0.1-SNAPSHOT.jar app.jar
RUN sh -c 'touch /app.jar'
ENV JAVA_OPTS=""
ENTRYPOINT [ "sh", "-c", "java $JAVA_OPTS -
Djava.security.egd=file:/dev/./urandom -jar /app.jar" ]
```

Once the Dockerfile is created, execute the following command from the project root folder, where the Dockerfile is saved, to build the image. Note "." represents the current folder where the Docker runtime would look for Dockerfile:

```
# Build the docker image within project root folder
docker build -t ImageName:tag .
```

1. **Upload the Docker image in the image repository**: Push the container image in a container registry such as the Docker Hub (http://www.dockerhub.com). The following code can be used to push the image to Docker Hub. Note that one would be required to create a Docker Hub user account and a repository prior to trying the following commands for pushing the images:

```
# Login into Docker Hub
docker login -u="dockerhubLogin" -p="dockerhubPassword"

# Tag the docker image
docker tag dockerhubUser/repositoryName:tag imageName:tag

# Push docker image into Docker Hub
docker push dockerhubUser/repositoryName:tag
```

2. **Run the Spring Boot app anytime, anywhere**: When required to run the app anytime and anywhere, pull the image and run the container using the following commands:

```
docker pull dockerhubUser/repositoryName:tag

docker run -tid -p 8080:8080 --name springbootapp -v
/c/Users:/mnt dockerhubUser/repositoryName:tag
```

Once started, the app can be accessed at port 8080 using URLs such as http://127.0.0.1:8080. The advantage of containerizing is the flexibility that it brings in relation with running the app on-demand anywhere, be it the local environment, dev/test environment, or cloud platforms. The following is the code for the Dockerfile, which can be used to containerize the app.

For our Spring Boot app, in order to truly containerize the Spring Boot app, we will also need to pass the database parameters as environment variables and execute the following command:

```
docker run -tid -p 8080:8080 --name springbootapp -v /c/Users:/mnt -e
DB_HOST=172.17.0.2 -e DB_PORT=3306 -e DB_NAME=healthapp -e DB_USERNAME=root
-e D
B_PASSWORD=root --link mysql dockerhubUser/repositoryName:tag
```

To achieve this, one may be required to parameterize the database details in the `application.properties` file in following manner:

```
spring.datasource.url=jdbc:mysql://${DB_HOST}:${DB_PORT}/${DB_NAME}
spring.datasource.username=${DB_USERNAME}
spring.datasource.password=${DB_PASSWORD}
```

Introduction to unit testing fundamentals

Before getting on to understanding key aspects of JUnit 5, let's try and understand some of the basic concepts around unit testing. In this section, the following will be dealt with:

- What is unit testing?
- Why write unit tests?
- Unit testing naming conventions

What is unit testing?

Simply speaking, unit testing is about **testing a block of code in isolation**. This essentially means that any dependency within the code will be mocked, and it is just the block of code which will be tested. In case the dependencies are not mocked, the block of code tested along with dependencies forms part of what can be called **integration testing**. On similar lines, Martin Fowler states that unit tests can be of two different types. They are solitary tests (a block of code tested in isolation) and sociable tests (a block of code tested without mocking dependencies, or simply speaking, integration testing). Read the details at https:/ /martinfowler.com/bliki/UnitTest.html.

The following diagram depicts the concept of unit and integration testing:

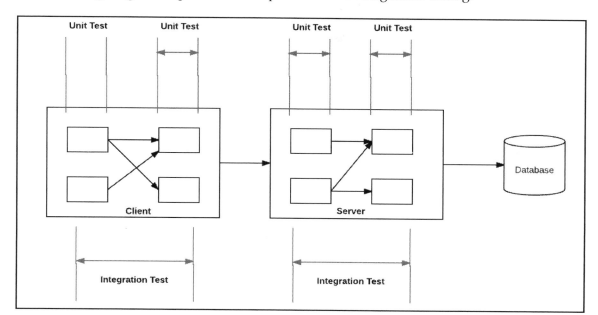

Figure 1: Unit tests and integration tests

The following are some of the key building blocks of unit tests:

- **Spies**: When there is a need to examine some of the following in relation to a function, spies are used. Note that spies, however, do not prevent a function from getting called.
    - Arguments passed to the function
    - Return value
    - Exceptions thrown

- **Mocks**: These can be termed as *test replacements* or *test doubles*. They can be used in place of actual function calls. Mocks help isolated the block of code from dependencies. One can pre-program the function behavior and expectations using Mock and later verify them using Mock APIs. Other types of test doubles are stubs, fake objects, and so on.

- **Stubs**: These are a kind of test double, which provide predefined or canned answers to the method calls. The primary difference between mocks and stubs is that one can assert against the mock object, whereas one cannot assert against a stub.

- **Fakes**: These are a kind of test double, which are actually a working implementation but take shortcuts and are not suited for production. These are classes created primarily for testing purposes.

There are different mocking frameworks, which can be used for mocking the dependencies. In this chapter, you will, however, learn about different aspects of mocking with a very popular framework named Mockito (http://site.mockito.org/).

Why write unit tests?

The following are some of the reasons why it is of utmost importance to write unit tests:

- **Help reduce bugs**: A code having good unit test coverage will result in lesser bugs appearing during different SDLC stages such as QA, UAT, and production. As a result, this will help creating a robust product whose changes can be deployed in production in a quicker manner.
- **Highly maintainable code base**: A code which is easy to change is the code which is easy to maintain, and hence, can be termed as highly maintainable code. A code being supported by unit tests becomes *easy to change/refactor*, and hence, highly maintainable code as one or more unexpected changes would lead to failure of the unit test cases. In that manner, *code testability* can be termed as one of the key pillars of code maintainability apart from modularity and reusability.
- **Deliver Business at Speed**: Given that business wants to *continuously deliver* enhanced products with new features/functionality, this is only possible if and only if engineering teams adopt the state of *continuous testing*. And, in order to achieve the state of continuous testing, unit and integration tests are the key. These unit and integration tests can be run as part of automated **continuous integration** (**CI**) builds, and, failure of these tests could result in build failure notifying the stakeholders.

Unit testing naming conventions

One of the common concerns found in relation to writing unit tests is related to naming conventions which need to be used for giving proper names to unit tests. Unit tests should be written in such a manner that they should rather act as an alternate piece of documentation for actual code. Keeping this aspect in mind, some of the strategies which can be used for choosing an appropriate naming convention for unit tests are listed here:

- **Unit tests starting with the keyword, "test"**: This is the most simple and the traditional approach, which is used by many developers, most specifically, beginners. In older versions of JUnit, this is how unit tests used to be recognized by the unit testing framework while executing unit tests. Unit test methods are found with their name starting with the keyword, `test`. Thus, in order to write unit test for the method, `doesUserExist`, one would write the corresponding test as `testDoesUserExist`. It works, but is not the recommended way for naming unit tests. The primary reason is that in order to test different flows of the method, `doesUserExist`, it is commonly seen that developers end up writing tests, such as `testDoesUserExist1`, `testDoesUserExist2`, and so on, which impacts the readability/usability of unit tests. Given that there are tags, such as `@Test`, one can use alternate techniques, such as some of the following, to name unit tests.

- **Unit tests starting with actual method names**: Quite often, it is found that developers tend to associate method names with corresponding unit tests. Thus, for the method `doesUserExist`, unit test methods can be written as `doesUserExist_invalidUser_throwsException`. It may not be the most appropriate way as the actual method names may get changed, which may result in ambiguity while reading the unit tests.

- **Unit tests starting with the keyword, "Should"**: This technique looks to be a better technique for naming unit tests as it enhances the readability/usability of unit tests and helps make unit tests alternate documentation of the actual code. For a method such as `doesUserExist`, the unit tests could be named `should_throwException_forUsersNotFoundInDatabase`. Alternatively, one could also name the corresponding unit test `shouldThrowExceptionForUsersNotFoundInDatabase`. Given that JUnit 5 supports the `@DisplayName` tag, the detail could also be written with this tag in the following manner: `@DisplayName` (this should throw an exception if the user is not found in the database). The usage of `@DisplayName` will be illustrated in one of the later sections of this chapter.

Introduction to JUnit 5

In this section, you will learn about JUnit 5 fundamentals, including some of the following:

- Architectural building blocks of JUnit 5
- How to get set up with JUnit 5 and run unit tests

Architectural building blocks of JUnit 5

JUnit 5 is a rewrite of JUnit. The following are three key building blocks of JUnit 5 along with support for the custom testing framework, which along with their components, are represented in the following diagram:

- JUnit Platform
- JUnit Jupiter
- JUnit Vintage

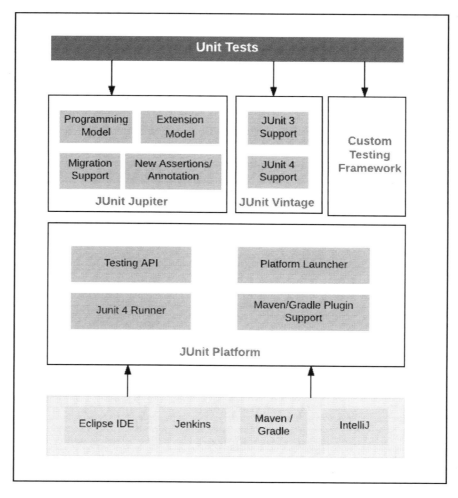

Figure 2: JUnit 5 technology/application architecture

Unlike earlier versions of JUnit, JUnit 5 has been split into following three sub-projects in addition to the great flexibility of plugging in one's own custom testing engine/framework:

- **JUnit Platform**: JUnit platform is the foundation building block of JUnit 5. The most important feature of JUnit 5 platform, which makes it standout, is the ability to allow the custom testing framework/engine to be plugged in, through the Testing API. This very capability (the Testing API) of the platform allows support for running JUnit tests using the JUnit 5 testing engine (Jupiter), earlier JUnit versions (the JUnit 3.x, JUnit 4.x) testing engine (Vintage), or any other custom testing engine. The following are some of the key platform components:
    - Testing API for plugging in custom developed test engine
    - Console Launcher for discovering and executing tests from the console
    - Gradle and Maven plugin support for discovering and executing tests
    - Runner to allow execution of Junit tests in the JUnit 4 environment
- **JUnit Jupiter**: This provides a test engine for running unit tests written with JUnit 5. The following are some of the key aspects of JUnit Jupiter:
    - Programming and extension model for writing unit tests and extensions.
    - Support for migrating unit tests written with JUnit 4 to JUnit Jupiter.
    - New assertion methods, which work with Java 8 Lambdas.
    - Support for annotations such as `@DisplayName`, which allow custom display names consisting of spaces, emojis, special character, and so on. Here is the sample code:

        - ```
          @Test
          @DisplayName("Throws exception if user with given
          email does not exist")
          void Should_throwException_When_UserDoesNotExist() {
              ...
          }
          ```

        The preceding unit test is written for the following method in the `UserServiceImpl` class:

        - ```
          @Override
          public User doesUserExist(String email) throws
          UserNotFoundException {
          ```

```
                    List<User> users = (List<User>)
                userDAO.findByEmail(email);
                  if(users.size() == 0) {
                    throw new UserNotFoundException("User does not
                exist in the database.");
                  }
                  return users.get(0);
                }
```

- **JUnit Vintage**: Provides a test engine for running unit tests written with earlier JUnit versions such as JUnit 3 and JUnit 4.

Setting up and running JUnit tests

The following code when put in pom.xml helps one get set up with JUnit 5:

```xml
<properties>
    <junit.jupiter.version>5.0.0-M4</junit.jupiter.version>
    <junit.vintage.version>${junit.version}.0-M4</junit.vintage.version>
 <junit.platform.version>1.0.0-M4</junit.platform.version>
</properties>

<dependencies>
    <dependency>
      <groupId>org.junit.platform</groupId>
      <artifactId>junit-platform-surefire-provider</artifactId>
      <version>${junit.platform.version}</version>
    </dependency>
    <dependency>
      <groupId>org.junit.jupiter</groupId>
      <artifactId>junit-jupiter-api</artifactId>
      <version>${junit.jupiter.version}</version>
      <scope>test</scope>
    </dependency>
    <dependency>
      <groupId>org.junit.jupiter</groupId>
      <artifactId>junit-jupiter-engine</artifactId>
      <version>${junit.jupiter.version}</version>
    </dependency>
    <dependency>
      <groupId>org.junit.vintage</groupId>
      <artifactId>junit-vintage-engine</artifactId>
      <version>${junit.vintage.version}</version>
    </dependency>
</dependencies>
```

```xml
<build>
  <plugins>
    <plugin>
      <artifactId>maven-compiler-plugin</artifactId>
      <version>3.1</version>
      <configuration>
        <source>${java.version}</source>
        <target>${java.version}</target>
      </configuration>
    </plugin>
    <plugin>
      <artifactId>maven-surefire-plugin</artifactId>
      <version>2.19.1</version>
      <configuration>
        <includes>
         <include>**/Test*.java</include>
         <include>**/*Test.java</include>
         <include>**/*Tests.java</include>
         <include>**/*TestCase.java</include>
        </includes>
      </configuration>
      <dependencies>
        <dependency>
          <groupId>org.junit.platform</groupId>
          <artifactId>junit-platform-surefire-provider</artifactId>
          <version>${junit.platform.version}</version>
        </dependency>
        <dependency>
          <groupId>org.junit.jupiter</groupId>
          <artifactId>junit-jupiter-engine</artifactId>
          <version>${junit.jupiter.version}</version>
        </dependency>
        <dependency>
          <groupId>org.junit.vintage</groupId>
          <artifactId>junit-vintage-engine</artifactId>
          <version>${junit.vintage.version}</version>
        </dependency>
      </dependencies>
    </plugin>
  </plugins>
</build>
```

At the time of writing, JUnit 5 is supported in Eclipse Oxygen (4.7) and IntelliJ version 2016.2. We shall, however, take a look at how to run JUnit 5 manually using the Maven plugin.

In addition to the preceding code, for running JUnit 5 with Spring 5, one would require to update the `pom.xml` in the following manner. It would allow the usage of the `SpringExtension` class, which integrates the Spring 5 `TestContext` framework into the JUnit 5 Jupiter programming model:

```
<parent>
  <groupId>org.springframework.boot</groupId>
  <artifactId>spring-boot-starter-parent</artifactId>
  <version>2.0.0.BUILD-SNAPSHOT</version>
</parent>

<repositories>
  <repository>
    <id>spring-snapshots</id>
    <name>Spring Snapshots</name>
    <url>https://repo.spring.io/libs-snapshot</url>
    <snapshots>
      <enabled>true</enabled>
    </snapshots>
  </repository>
</repositories>
```

Once done with the preceding code, create the following sample class for `UserService` and name it as `UserServiceTests.java`. Place the file within a package, say, `com.book.healthapp`, under the folder `src/test/java`. Note the usage of the `@ExtendWith` annotation. Note that the code given here is intended to give an idea of how a unit test skeleton class may look like. Executing the code given here would result in test failures. Refer to one of the later sections wherein the code for `UserService` and related unit tests are described:

```
package com.book.healthapp;

import static org.junit.Assert.*;

import org.junit.jupiter.api.AfterEach;
import org.junit.jupiter.api.BeforeEach;
import org.junit.jupiter.api.DisplayName;
import org.junit.jupiter.api.Test;

@ExtendWith(SpringExtension.class)
public class UserServiceTests {
```

```
@BeforeEach
public void setUp() throws Exception {
}

@AfterEach
public void tearDown() throws Exception {
}

@Test
@DisplayName("Throws exception if user with given email does not
  exist")
void Should_throwException_When_UserDoesNotExist() {
fail("Not yet implemented");
}

@Test
@DisplayName("Throws exception if user with given email & password is
  not found in the database")
void Should_throwException_When_UnmatchingUserCredentialsFound() {
fail("Not yet implemented");
}
}
```

Go to Command Prompt and run the following command. This will run the build and perform the tests.

```
mvn -DDB_HOST=127.0.0.1 -DDB_PORT=3306 -DDB_NAME=healthapp -
DDB_USERNAME=<username> -DDB_PASSWORD=<password> clean package
```

If, you just want to run the tests, the following command can be used:

```
mvn -DDB_HOST=127.0.0.1 -DDB_PORT=3306 -DDB_NAME=healthapp -
DDB_USERNAME=root -DDB_PASSWORD=root clean test
```

The following output in relation to the execution of test cases will be displayed on the console:

```
Running com.book.healthapp.UserServiceTests
Tests run: 2, Failures: 2, Errors: 0, Skipped: 0, Time elapsed: 0.037 sec
<<< FAILURE! - in com.book.healthapp.UserServiceTests
Should_throwException_When_UserDoesNotExist() Time elapsed: 0.02 sec <<<
FAILURE!
java.lang.AssertionError: Not yet implemented
 at
com.book.healthapp.UserServiceTests.Should_throwException_When_UserDoesNotE
xist(UserServiceTests.java:23)

Should_throwException_When_UnmatchingUserCredentialsFound() Time elapsed:
```

```
0.001 sec <<< FAILURE!
java.lang.AssertionError: Not yet implemented
 at
com.book.healthapp.UserServiceTests.Should_throwException_When_UnmatchingUs
erCredentialsFound(UserServiceTests.java:29)

...

Results :

Failed tests:
 UserServiceTests.Should_throwException_When_UnmatchingUserCredentialsF
ound:29 Not yet implemented
 UserServiceTests.Should_throwException_When_UserDoesNotExist:23 Not
 yet implemented

Tests run: 2, Failures: 2, Errors: 0, Skipped: 0
```

In the next section, we will take a look at Mockito concepts before understanding and writing real unit tests.

Mocking dependencies using Mockito

In this section, we will learn about the basic fundamentals in relation to mocking dependencies (or, using test doubles) within a class/function. As explained in one of the preceding sections, some of the key building blocks of unit tests are spies, mocks, stubs, fakes, and so on. There are different Java mocking frameworks which provide these features. In this section, we will look into Mockito and related concepts.

The following are key considerations when using mocking:

- Identify objects in the block of code (class/methods under test) which need to be mocked or spied. These could be data access objects (DAOs), services, and so on.
- Create mock objects.
- Pre-program the behavior of mock objects.
- Execute the code or invoke the function/method under test.
- Verify the behavior or examine the function/method arguments/return objects based on whether a mock or spy was used, respectively.

Getting set up with Mockito

In order to get set up with Mockito, one would require to put the following code within `pom.xml`:

```
<properties>
    <mockito.version>1.10.19</mockito.version>
</properties>

<dependency>
    <groupId>org.mockito</groupId>
    <artifactId>mockito-core</artifactId>
    <version>${mockito.version}</version>
</dependency>
```

One may want to note that when using Spring, one can include the following code in `pom.xml` that would mean inclusion of JUnit and a mocking framework such as Mockito:

```
<dependency>
    <groupId>org.springframework.boot</groupId>
    <artifactId>spring-boot-starter-test</artifactId>
    <scope>test</scope>
</dependency>
```

The preceding code leads imports JUnit, the Spring Boot test, and related libraries such as AssertJ (assertion library), and so on.

Introduction to mocking techniques

In this section, you will learn about different mocking techniques which will be used for mocking the dependencies of a class. In the example given here, mocking techniques are described using the `UserServiceTests` class, which comprises of unit tests for the `UserServiceImpl` class. This class has a dependency, namely, `UserDAO`, which is a data access object used to interact with the underlying database, and, whose methods such as `findByEmail` is invoked to find whether a user exists in the database. The given the principles of unit tests, where we need to create test replacements or test doubles for the dependencies, we will create a test double for the dependency, `UserDAO`. There are three different techniques, as discussed here, to creates test doubles. They are as follows:

- Using `@Mock` annotation
- Using `Mockito.mock` API
- Using `@Mockbean` annotation provided by Spring Boot

While using the preceding techniques, it can be noted that the method invocation on UserDAO such as findByEmail is pre-programmed using Mockito APIs.

The following is the code sample of UserServiceImpl for which mocking techniques are described in this section:

```
@Service
public class UserServiceImpl implements UserService {
  //
  // Dependent class which needs to be mocked
  //
  private UserDAO userDAO;

  @Autowired
  public UserServiceImpl(UserDAO userDAO) {
    this.userDAO = userDAO;
  }
  @Override
  public User doesUserExist(String email) throws UserNotFoundException    {
    //
    // findByEmail method which needs to be pre-programmed
    //
    List<User> users = (List<User>) userDAO.findByEmail(email);
    if(users.size() == 0) {
      throw new UserNotFoundException("User does not exist in the
      database.");
    }
    return users.get(0);
  }
}
```

The following are some of the different ways in which Mockito can be used to mock the dependencies:

- @Mock annotation, part of Mockito framework, can be used to mock and inject the test doubles in place of actual dependencies. Note some of the following aspects of mocking in the following code:
  - Identify the dependent objects; userDAO is the dependent object.
  - Mock the dependent object; the UserDAO object is mocked using the @Mock annotation.
  - Create the service with the Mock instance of UserDAO

- Preprogram the behavior of the mocked instance; take a look at the following code where the findByEmail method when invoked on the UserDAO object, userDAO, would return an instance of ArrayList:

```
Mockito.when(this.userDAO.findByEmail(email)).thenReturn(new
ArrayList<User>());
```

- Verify the behavior of the method invocation. The following code represents the same. Note the usage of the **Java 8 Lambda expression** in the assertion method, assertThatThrownBy:

```
assertThatThrownBy(()->this.userService.doesUserExist(email)).isInstanceOf(
UserNotFoundException.class)
 .hasMessage("User does not exist in the database.");
```

- The @Disabled tag is used to disable one or more unit tests. This is a new feature in JUnit 5.
- Methods such as setUp() and tearDown() decorated with the @BeforeEach and @AfterEach annotations are executed before and after execution of each of the unit tests, respectively.
- The following code represents usage of the @Mock annotation to mock the UserDAO instance:

```
@ExtendWith(SpringExtension.class)
public class UserServiceTests {

  @Mock
  private UserDAO userDAO;
  private UserService userService;

  @BeforeEach
  public void setUp() throws Exception {
   this.userService = new UserServiceImpl(this.userDAO);
  }

  @AfterEach
  public void tearDown() throws Exception {
  }

  @Test
  @DisplayName("Throws exception if user with given email does not exist")
  public void     Should_throwException_When_UserDoesNotExist() {
    String email = "foo@bar.com";
    Mockito.when(this.userDAO.findByEmail(email)). thenReturn(new
```

```
ArrayList<User>());
    assertThatThrownBy(() ->
this.userService.doesUserExist(email)).isInstanceOf(UserNotFoundException.c
lass)
    .hasMessage("User does not exist in the database.");
}

@Disabled
@Test
@DisplayName("Throws exception if user with given email & password is not
found in the database")
  void  Should_throwException_When_UnmatchingUserCredentialsFound() {
    fail("Not yet implemented");
  }
}
```

- The `mock()` method is an API of Mockito which can be used as an alternate technique to get the mock instance for the actual dependencies. The following code represents the usage of the `Mockito.mock()` method:

```
@ExtendWith(SpringExtension.class)
public class UserServiceTests {

  private UserDAO userDAO;
  private UserService userService;

  @BeforeEach
  public void setUp() throws Exception {
    this.userDAO = Mockito.mock(UserDAO.class);
    this.userService = new UserServiceImpl(this.userDAO);
  }

  //...Same as the code given above

}
```

- The `@Mockbean` annotation, provided by **Spring Boot**, can be used to mock one or more components which are part of `ApplicationContext`. The following code represents the usage of the `@Mockbean` annotation:

```
@ExtendWith(SpringExtension.class)
public class UserServiceTests {

  @MockBean
  private UserDAO userDAO;
  private UserService userService;
```

```
@BeforeEach
public void setUp() throws Exception {
  this.userService = new UserServiceImpl(this.userDAO);
}

//...Same as the code given above

}
```

Unit testing controllers, services, and DAOs

In this section, we will take a look at how to perform unit testing with components such as controllers, services, and DAOs. We shall also look at some of the features of JUnit 5.

Unit tests for controllers

Let's understand some of the following concepts before we get to look at the source codes for controllers and the corresponding unit tests written using JUnit 5:

- MockMvc: This is a Spring MVC component primarily used for writing unit tests with controllers components. Simply speaking, MockMvc is used to mock the Spring MVC container. The following is what the code looks like when using MockMvc:

  ```
  private MockMvc mockMvc;

  @MockBean
  private UserService userService;

  @BeforeEach
  public void setUp() throws Exception {
    this.mockMvc = MockMvcBuilders.standaloneSetup(new
  UserAccountController(this.userService)).build();
  }
  ```

In the preceding code, UserService, a dependency within the controller, is mocked using the @MockBean annotation. Within the setUp() function, the standaloneSetup method is invoked on MockMvcBuilders in order to test the UserAccountController in isolation.

- @MockBean: Inspite of the fact that MockMvc is used to mock the MVC container, there are objects which are part of ApplicationContext, which need to be mocked. This is where the @MockBean annotation is used to mock one or more dependencies within a controller. In the preceding code, it is used to mock the UserService instance.

The following code represents UserAccountController:

```
@RestController
@RequestMapping("/account/*")
public class UserAccountController {

  final static Logger logger =
    LoggerFactory.getLogger(UserAccountController.class);

  private UserService userService;

  @Autowired
  public UserAccountController(UserService userService) {
    this.userService = userService;
  }

  @PostMapping(value="/login/process", produces="application/json")
  public @ResponseBody ExecutionStatus processLogin(ModelMap model,
    @RequestBody User reqUser) {

    User user = null;
    try {
      user = userService.isValidUser(reqUser.getEmail(),
        reqUser.getPassword());
    } catch (UnmatchingUserCredentialsException ex) {
      logger.debug(ex.getMessage(), ex);
    }
    if(user == null) {
      return new ExecutionStatus("USER_LOGIN_UNSUCCESSFUL", "Username or
        password is incorrect. Please try again!");
    }
    return new ExecutionStatus("USER_LOGIN_SUCCESSFUL", "Login
      Successful!");
  }

}
```

The following code represents the JUnit 5 unit test code for the preceding controller. Note the usage of some of the following annotations from JUnit 5 and the relevant annotations from Spring 5:

- @BeforeEach: This represents the code which is run before each unit test.
- @Test: This represents the unit test.
- @DisplayName:: This is the JUnit 5 annotation used for giving descriptive text for unit tests.
- @Tag: This annotation is used to tag the classes and methods. This can later be used for test discovery and execution.
- @ExtendWith (SpringExtension.class): This integrates the Spring 5 Test Context framework with JUnit 5:

```
@ExtendWith(SpringExtension.class)
@Tag("Controller")
public class UserAccountControllerTest {

  private MockMvc mockMvc;
  @MockBean
  private UserService userService;

  @BeforeEach
  public void setUp(TestInfo testInfo) throws Exception {
  this.mockMvc = MockMvcBuilders.standaloneSetup(new
    UserAccountController(this.userService)).build();
  }

  @Test
  @DisplayName("Should return error message for when user not existing
    in the database tries to login.")
  public void Should_ReturnErrorMessage_ForUnmatchingUser() throws
  Exception {

  User user = new User();
  user.setEmail("foo@bar.com");
  user.setPassword("foobar");
  //
  // Create JSON Representation for User object;
  // Gson is a Java serialization/deserialization library to
  // convert Java Objects into JSON and back
  //
  Gson gson = new Gson();
  String jsonUser = gson.toJson(user);
  //
  // Pre-program the behavior of Mock; When isValidUser method
```

```
    // is invoked, return null object
    //
    Mockito.when(this.userService.isValidUser("foo@bar.com",
    "foobar")).thenReturn(null);
    //
    // Invoking the controller method
    //
    MvcResult result = this.mockMvc.perform(
    post("/account/login/process")
    .contentType(MediaType.APPLICATION_JSON)
    .content(jsonUser))
    .andExpect(status().isOk())
    .andReturn();
    //
    // Verify the program behavior; Assert the response object
    //
    MockHttpServletResponse response = result.getResponse();
    ObjectMapper mapper = new ObjectMapper();
    ExecutionStatus responseObj =
    mapper.readValue(response.getContentAsString(),
    ExecutionStatus.class);
    assertTrue(responseObj.getCode().equals("USER_LOGIN_UNSUCCESSFUL"));
    assertTrue(responseObj.getMessage().equals("Username or password is
    incorrect. Please try again!"));
    }
}
```

Unit tests for Services

The following represents the implementation for UserService. Note some of the CRUD methods used to update the User object:

```
@Service
public class UserServiceImpl implements UserService {

  private UserDAO userDAO;

  @Autowired
  public UserServiceImpl(UserDAO userDAO) {
    this.userDAO = userDAO;
  }

  @Override
  public User save(User user) {
    return userDAO.save(user);
  }
```

```
@Override
public void update(User user) {
  userDAO.update(user);
}

@Override
public User doesUserExist(String email) throws UserNotFoundException   {
  List<User> users = (List<User>) userDAO.findByEmail(email);
  if(users.size() == 0) {
    throw new UserNotFoundException("User does not exist in the
      database.");
  }
  return users.get(0);
}
}
```

The following represents unit tests code for the `UserService` implementation, as shown earlier. Note that `@MockBean` is used to mock the DAO component referenced within `UserServiceImpl`, as shown in the following code. Pay attention to some of the following:

- Usage of Java 8 Lambdas in the assertion method.
- TestInfo passed as an argument to the `setUp` method. The TestInfo instance is used to retrieve the information about the current test, such as display name, test class, test method, and so on.
- The `@Tag` annotation is used to tag the unit test which can later be used for test discovery.
- The `@RepeatedTest` annotation is used to repeat the tests for n number of times where n is the number passed to the annotation, as shown in the following example:

```
@ExtendWith(SpringExtension.class)
@Tag("Service")
public class UserServiceTests {

  @MockBean
  private UserDAO userDAO;
  private UserService userService;

  @BeforeEach
  public void setUp(TestInfo testInfo) throws Exception {
    this.userService = new UserServiceImpl(this.userDAO);
    String displayName = testInfo.getDisplayName();
    assertTrue(displayName.equals("Should return error message for when
      user not existing in the database tries to login."));
```

```
}

@AfterEach
public void tearDown() throws Exception {
}

@Test
@RepeatedTest(5)
@DisplayName("Throws exception if user with given email does not
  exist")
public void Should_throwException_When_UserDoesNotExist() {
String email = "foo@bar.com";
Mockito.when(this.userDAO.findByEmail(email)).thenReturn(new
  ArrayList<User>());
//
// Usage of Java 8 Lambda expression in assertion method
//
assertThatThrownBy(() ->
this.userService.doesUserExist(email)).isInstanceOf(UserNotFoundException.c
lass)
  .hasMessage("User does not exist in the database.");
  }
}
```

Unit tests for DAO components

The following code represents the implementation for the UserDAO interface. In the code, note some of the following which will be required to be mocked for testing DAO objects in isolation:

- SessionFactory instance
- Session

```
@Repository
@Transactional
public class UserDAOImpl implements UserDAO {

  private SessionFactory sessionFactory;

  @Autowired
  public UserDAOImpl(SessionFactory sessionFactory) {
      this.sessionFactory = sessionFactory;
  }

  @Override
```

```
public List<User> findByEmail(String email) {
    Session session = this.sessionFactory.getCurrentSession();
    TypedQuery<User> query = session.getNamedQuery("findByEmail");
    query.setParameter("email", email);
    return query.getResultList();
    }
}
```

The following code represents the unit tests for the UserDAOImpl code as shown previously. Note the usage of the @MockBean annotation to mock SessionFactory and session instances:

```
@ExtendWith(SpringExtension.class)
@Tag("DAO")
public class UserDAOTest {

    @MockBean
    private SessionFactory sessionFactory;
    @MockBean
    private Session session;

    private UserDAO userDAO;

    @BeforeEach
    public void setUp() throws Exception {
        //
        // Pre-program the mocking behavior resulting into
        // returning a mock instance of Session when getCurrentSession
        // method is invoked on sessionFactory instance
        //
        Mockito.when(this.sessionFactory.getCurrentSession()).
          thenReturn(this.session);
        this.userDAO = new UserDAOImpl(this.sessionFactory);
    }

    @Test
    public void should_returnEmptyList_forUnmatchingUser() {
        Query query = Mockito.mock(Query.class);
        Mockito.when(this.session.getNamedQuery("findByEmail")).
          thenReturn(query);
        Mockito.when(query.getResultList()).thenReturn(new ArrayList());

        List list = userDAO.findByEmail("foo@bar.com");
        assertAll("Users",
            () -> assertNotEquals(list, null),
            () -> assertEquals(list.size(), 0));
    }
}
```

In the preceding unit test, note some of the following:

- **Grouped assertions**, `assertAll`: This results in the execution of all the assertions and all the failures are reported together.

Summary

In this chapter, you have primarily learned about different aspects of doing unit tests with Spring Boot web apps using JUnit 5. We looked into aspects such as JUnit 5 architecture building blocks, setting up JUnit 5, running JUnit tests, mocking with Mockito, and writing unit tests for controllers, services, and DAOs components. In the next chapter, you will learn about the different aspects of Spring Security.

5

Securing Web App with Spring Security

In this chapter, you will learn about concepts related to Spring Security, such as authentication, authorization, CSRF protection and so on. The concepts related with OAuth2 based authentication and authorization has been dealt in later part of the chapter. You will learn about how to use OAuth2 based authentication and authorization for Angular and Spring web app. Following are some of the topics covered in this chapter:

- Introduction to Spring Security
- Handling the login authentication
- CSRF protection for API requests
- Handling the logout request
- OAuth2 based authentication/authorization

Introduction to Spring Security

Spring Security is a framework which provides comprehensive security functionality in relation to the two most important application security concerns--authentication and authorization:

- Authentication is related to ensuring that a principal is who it claims to be. A principal is an entity which can perform one or more actions in the application. Thus, the principal can be a user, a device, or an external system/client which interacts with the system.
- Once a principal is authenticated, it needs to be determined whether the principal can perform the desired action or not. This process is called authorization.

Spring Security supports different authentication models, including some of the most common ones such as Http basic authentication, simple form-based authentication, OpenID authentication, OAuth2 based authentication/authorization and so on.

In this section, you will learn about the following:

- Spring Security high-level architecture
- Setting up Spring Security

Spring Security high level architecture

In this section, you will learn about the architecture building blocks of the Spring Security framework:

- Core building blocks
- Authentication
- Authorization (accesscontrol)

Spring Security architecture - core building blocks

Some of the following are the most important components of the Spring Security:

- `SecurityContextHolder`: One of the key objects, `SecurityContextHolder` is used to hold the security context information of the principal (users, external system, device, and so on), currently interacting with the application. It is important to note that the security context information is stored in a `ThreadLocal` object and, thus, it is available to all members running in the current thread. This, essentially, means that the security context information may not need to pass explicitly between different methods executing in the same thread.
- `SecurityContext`: As mentioned earlier, `SecurityContext` is stored within `SecurityContextHolder`, which holds the `Authentication` object and request-specific security information.

- `Authentication`: The `Authentication` object, which represents principal information, can be retrieved from a security context object stored by `SecurityContextHolder`. After user authentication, the `Authentication` object is built using the `UserDetails` object, after which it is stored in the `SecurityContextHolder` component. The following code represents the same:

```
Object principal = SecurityContextHolder.getContext().
    getAuthentication().getPrincipal();
```

- `UserDetails`: This is an interface which represents the user information. It acts as an adapter between an actual application-based user object and what can be stored within `SecurityContextHolder`.

- `UserDetailsService`: This is an interface which when implemented allows to load user-related information from the database. In one of the later sections, we will see the related code sample. The following represents the interface definition:

```
UserDetails loadUserByUsername(String username) throws
    UsernameNotFoundException;
```

- `GrantedAuthority`: Usually loaded by `UserDetailsService`, `GrantedAuthority` is related to the setting application-wide permissions granted to the principal in the form of roles, such as ROLE_ADMINISTRATOR, ROLE_USER, and so on. These roles can be configured for authorizing access to methods/APIs, domain objects, and so on.

Spring Security architecture - authentication

As mentioned earlier, authentication, in Spring Security, represents the principal information. Recall that a principal is an entity such as user, device, or external system interacting with the application. The following approach is commonly adopted for dealing with authentication:

1. Username and password information is retrieved from the incoming request and made into an instance of `UsernamePasswordAuthenticationToken`.
2. The token created in the earlier step is passed to an `AuthenticationManager` instance for validating the principal identity against the one stored in the database.

3. On successful validation, `AuthenticationManager` returns an `Authentication` object populated with the principal details.

4. The authentication object is then populated into the security context by invoking the appropriate method on `SecurityContextHolder`, such as `SecurityContextHolder.getContext.setAuthentication(...)`.

The preceding approach will be illustrated with a code example in one of the later sections related to login authentication.

Spring Security architecture - authorization

Once a user is authenticated, the next step is to decide whether the principal is allowed to access the desired resource. Here, Spring Security provides an `Authroization` component named as `AccessDecisionManager`. The `AccessDecisionManager` component provides an API, which decides what takes arguments, such as the `Authentication` object, a secure object, and a list of security metadata attributes such as one or more roles for taking authorization-related decisions.

Authorization can be achieved using AOP (Spring AOP or AspectJ) advice for deciding whether a method invocation is permitted for the principal having a particular role. Authorization can also be achieved using authorization filters on web requests.

Setting up Spring Security

Spring Security is designed to be a self-contained unit and, thus, could be set up simply by putting appropriate libraries in the classpath. In order to get set up with Spring Security using Maven, the following needs to be put in the Maven `pom.xml` file:

```
<dependencies>
  <!-- ... other dependency elements ... -->
  <dependency>
    <groupId>org.springframework.security</groupId>
    <artifactId>spring-security-web</artifactId>
    <version>4.2.3.RELEASE</version>
  </dependency>
  <dependency>
    <groupId>org.springframework.security</groupId>
    <artifactId>spring-security-config</artifactId>
    <version>4.2.3.RELEASE</version>
  </dependency>
</dependencies>
```

Handling the login authentication

In this section, you will learn about how to use Spring Security for login-based authentication based on the following authentication process related to the Angular app and Spring app running on different servers:

1. The user visits the login page which is part of Angular app. The login page is delivered from the Angular app. Token is grabbed from the server and sent back to the client, and the server expects the same token in each subsequent requests. This token will be added to the header of the subsequent login request submission.

2. On submission of login form details such as username and password, an appropriate Spring Web API such as /account/login is invoked through the HTTP service POST method. The following code represents the Angular code for the login. Pay attention to how the HTTP service is used to invoke Spring RESTful login APIs. Make a note of the withCredentials: true option being set as part of RequestOptions. The XMLHttpRequest.withCredentials property is a Boolean that indicates whether or not cross-site Access-Control requests should be made using credentials such as cookies, authorization headers or TLS client certificates. Setting withCredentials has no effect on same-site requests. However, we have angular and spring app hosted as different apps, this option is required to be set in order to send cookie information in the request headers.

```
import { Injectable } from '@angular/core';
import { Http, RequestOptions } from '@angular/http';
import { Headers } from '@angular/http';
import { Observable } from 'rxjs/Observable';
import 'rxjs/add/observable/of';
import 'rxjs/add/operator/do';
import 'rxjs/add/operator/delay';
import {Login, LoginStatus, NewUser, SignupStatus} from './login';
import {Observer} from 'rxjs/Observer';
import {Router} from '@angular/router';

@Injectable()
export class AuthService {
  isLoggedIn: Observable<boolean>;
  private observer: Observer<boolean>;
  serverUrl = 'http://localhost:8080';
  headers = new Headers({'Content-Type': 'application/json'});

  constructor(private http: Http) {
    this.isLoggedIn = new Observable(observer =>
```

```
      this.observer = observer
  );
}

login(login: Login): Observable<SignupStatus> {
  const url = `${this.serverUrl}/account/login`;
  let options = new RequestOptions({ headers: this.headers,
  withCredentials: true });

  return this.http.post(url, login, options)
    .map(response => {
        const body = response.json();
        if (body.code === 'USER_LOGIN_SUCCESSFUL') {
          this.changeLoginStatus(true);
        }
        return response.json();
      })
    .catch((error: any) => this.handleError(error));
}

logout(): void {
  this.changeLoginStatus(true);
}

private changeLoginStatus(status: boolean) {
  if (this.observer !== undefined) {
    this.observer.next(status);
  };
}

private handleError (error: Response | any) {
  let errMsg: string;
  if (error instanceof Response) {
    const body = JSON.parse(JSON.stringify(error)) || '';
    const err = body.error || JSON.stringify(body);
    errMsg = `${error.status} - ${error.statusText || ''}
    ${err}`;
  } else {
    errMsg = error.message ? error.message : error.toString();
  }
  return Observable.throw(errMsg);
}
}
```

3. On the server side, there are different techniques which can be followed to process authentication. Here are some of them:

- **Approach 1 - Login credentials processed within the controller**: Process the login submission request in the custom controller. This approach is pretty trivial and straightforward. The following code can be used within the controller for processing a login request using Spring Security:

```
@PostMapping(value="/login")
public ExecutionStatus processLogin(@RequestBody User reqUser,
HttpServletRequest request) {
    Authentication authentication = null;
    UsernamePasswordAuthenticationToken token = new
UsernamePasswordAuthenticationToken(reqUser.getEmail(),
reqUser.getPassword());
        try {
        //
        // Delegate authentication check to a custom
        // Authentication provider
        //
        authentication =
this.authenticationProvider.authenticate(token);
        //
        // Store the authentication object in
        // SecurityContextHolder
SecurityContextHolder.getContext().setAuthentication(authentication);
        User user = (User) authentication.getPrincipal();
        user.setPassword(null);
        return new ExecutionStatus("USER_LOGIN_SUCCESSFUL", "Login
Successful!", user);
        } catch (BadCredentialsException e) {
        return new ExecutionStatus("USER_LOGIN_UNSUCCESSFUL", "Username
or password is incorrect. Please try again!");
        }
    }
```

As mentioned in the earlier code, the authentication task is delegated to a custom authentication provider. The following code represents the same:

```
@Component
public class CustomAuthenticationProvider implements AuthenticationProvider
{

    @Autowired
    private UserService userService;

    public Authentication authenticate(Authentication
```

```
  authentication) throws AuthenticationException {
    String username = authentication.getName();
    String password = (String)
    authentication.getCredentials();

    User user = null;
    try {
      user = userService.doesUserExist(username);
    } catch (UserNotFoundException e) {
    }

    if (user == null || !user.getEmail().equalsIgnoreCase(username)) {
      throw new BadCredentialsException("Username not
      found.");
    }

    if (!password.equals(user.getPassword())) {
      throw new BadCredentialsException("Wrong
      password.");
    }
    Collection<? extends GrantedAuthority> authorities
    = new ArrayList<GrantedAuthority>();
  ;
    return new
    UsernamePasswordAuthenticationToken(user, password,
    authorities);
  }

  @Override
  public boolean supports(Class<?> authentication) {
    return authentication.equals(
      UsernamePasswordAuthenticationToken.class);
  }
}
```

In the preceding code, a custom service, `UserService`, is used to get user information from the database. The following code represents the same:

```
@Service
public class UserServiceImpl implements UserService {

  private UserDAO userDAO;

  @Autowired
  public UserServiceImpl(UserDAO userDAO) {
    this.userDAO = userDAO;
  }
```

```
@Override
public User doesUserExist(String email) throws UserNotFoundException {
    List users = (List) userDAO.findByEmail(email);
    if(users.size() == 0) {
      throw new UserNotFoundException("User does not exist in the
database.");
    }
    return users.get(0);
  }
}
```

- **Approach 2- Login credentials processed using custom UsernamePasswordAuthenticationFilter**: Create a custom UsernamePasswordAuthenticationFilter to intercept the JSON request and extract a username and password. Invoke a custom authentication provider for authenticating the user. The custom authentication provider shown in the preceding example can be reused. Respond appropriately by using appropriate handlers. In this approach, appropriate changes need to be made in the configuration instance. The following is the code for custom UsernamePasswordAuthenticationFilter:

```
@Component
public class CustomAuthenticationFilter extends
UsernamePasswordAuthenticationFilter {
    @Override
    @Autowired
    public void setAuthenticationManager(   AuthenticationManager
authenticationManager) {
        super.setAuthenticationManager(authenticationManager);
    }

    @Override
    public Authentication attemptAuthentication(HttpServletRequest
request, HttpServletResponse response)
    throws AuthenticationException {
        UsernamePasswordAuthenticationToken authRequest = null;
        try {
          authRequest =
this.getUserNamePasswordAuthenticationToken(request);
        } catch (IOException e) {
        }
        setDetails(request, authRequest);
        return
this.getAuthenticationManager().authenticate(authRequest);
    }

    @Override
```

```
        protected void successfulAuthentication( HttpServletRequest
request, HttpServletResponse response, FilterChain chain, Authentication
authResult) throws IOException, ServletException {
            super.successfulAuthentication(request, response, chain,
authResult);
        }
        /**
         * @param request
         * @return
         */
        private UsernamePasswordAuthenticationToken
getUserNamePasswordAuthenticationToken(HttpServletRequest request)
  throws IOException {
            StringBuffer sb = new StringBuffer();
            BufferedReader bufferedReader = null;
            String content = "";
            User sr = null;
            try {
              bufferedReader = request.getReader();
              char[] charBuffer = new char[128];
              int bytesRead;
              while ((bytesRead = bufferedReader.read(charBuffer)) != -1) {
                sb.append(charBuffer, 0, bytesRead);
              }
              content = sb.toString();
              ObjectMapper objectMapper = new ObjectMapper();
              try {
                sr = objectMapper.readValue(content, User.class);
              } catch (Throwable t) {
                throw new IOException(t.getMessage(), t);
              }
            } catch (IOException ex) {
              throw ex;
            } finally {
              if (bufferedReader != null) {
                try {
                  bufferedReader.close();
                } catch (IOException ex) {
                  throw ex;
                }
              }
            }
            return new UsernamePasswordAuthenticationToken(sr.getEmail(),
sr.getPassword());
        }
    }
```

The following code represents the changes which need to be made in
SecurityConfiguration:

```
@Configuration
@EnableWebSecurity
@Order(SecurityProperties.ACCESS_OVERRIDE_ORDER)
public class SecurityConfiguration extends WebSecurityConfigurerAdapter {

    @Autowired
    private RestAuthenticationEntryPoint authenticationEntryPoint;

    @Autowired
    private CustomAuthenticationProvider authenticationProvider;

    @Override
    protected void configure(AuthenticationManagerBuilder auth) throws
Exception {
        auth.authenticationProvider(authenticationProvider);
    }

    @Bean
    CustomAuthenticationFilter customAuthenticationFilter() throws Exception
{
        CustomAuthenticationFilter filter = new CustomAuthenticationFilter();
    filter.setAuthenticationManager(authenticationManagerBean());
        filter.setRequiresAuthenticationRequestMatcher(new
AntPathRequestMatcher("/account/login", "POST"));
        return filter;
    }

    @Override
    protected void configure(HttpSecurity http) throws Exception {
        http.addFilterBefore(customAuthenticationFilter(),
UsernamePasswordAuthenticationFilter.class);
        http.authorizeRequests()
            .antMatchers("/doctors/**", "/account/**").permitAll()
            .anyRequest().authenticated()
            .and()
            .addFilterAfter(new XSRFTokenFilter(), CsrfFilter.class)
            .csrf()
            .csrfTokenRepository(csrfTokenRepository());
    http.exceptionHandling().authenticationEntryPoint(authenticationEntryPoint)
;
    }

    private CsrfTokenRepository csrfTokenRepository() {
        HttpSessionCsrfTokenRepository repository = new
HttpSessionCsrfTokenRepository();
```

```
        repository.setHeaderName("X-XSRF-TOKEN");
        return repository;
    }
}
```

Pay attention to some of the following in preceding code example:

- CSRF support is added by invoking `csrf()` method on `HttpSecurity` instance.
- Custom `CsrfTokenRepository` implementation, `HttpSessionCsrfTokenRepository`, is used for storing CSRF token in the `HttpSession`. Notice the fact that `X-XSRF-TOKEN` is set as header name using which CSRF token would appear as part of incoming request.
- Custom `XSRFTokenFilter` is provided as `CsrfFilter` to be invoked once per request. Details in relation with same has been discussed in the next section.

CSRF protection for API requests

In this section, you will learn about different aspects of cross-site request forgery (CSRF or XSRF) attack protection, which need to be taken care in both the Angular app and Spring app. Before getting into details, lets quickly understand what CSRF is.

CSRF is an attack in which attackers lure authenticated users to unknowingly perform undesired action on the website. For example, an attacker can log in as the user, and without the user's knowledge, transfer money from his account to the attacker's account. The following is a typical use-case scenario of a CSRF attack:

1. The user logs into the actual website which will later be compromised using the CSRF attack. Once logged in, the website sends token information assigned to a cookie as part of the response.
2. While the user is logged in, the attacker lures the user to visit attacker's web page from where the CSRF attack would take place. One such example is the attacker luring the user to click on a link in an email or on related webpages.
3. Once the attacker's page loads as part of the users' visit, the attacker's page invokes one or more APIs on the actual website. The request is sent with the cookie information which was sent earlier as a server response as a result of the users' visit. This can lead to the attacker achieving an undesired change to user's data such as transferring money, changing the user's profiles and so on.

The following are some of the ways in which CSRF attack can be prevented:

- Enforce the same origin policy
- Apply a per-session or pre-request token strategy to filter the requests coming as a CSRF attack

In order to prevent a CSRF attack given that Angular and Spring apps are running on different servers and, as a result, would have different origins, different approaches are recommended to be adopted for both the Angular and Spring apps.

CSRF prevention technique for the Angular app

Angular, by default, takes the following approach for handling the CSRF token:

1. Read the value of the cookie named as XSRF-TOKEN in the server response.
2. In case the cookie with XSRF-TOKEN is found, assign the cookie value to the X-XSRF-TOKEN header and send it with the subsequent requests.

In case there is a need to customize the preceding approach with different cookie and header names, Angular recommends providing a custom XSRF strategy as part of module definition. The following code represents the same:

```
@NgModule({
    imports:       [ BrowserModule, FormsModule, DocModule, AuthModule,
AppRoutingModule, HttpModule, JsonpModule],
    declarations: [ AppComponent, PageNotFoundComponent, HomeComponent,
SecurityBypass],
    providers: [
       {
         provide: XSRFStrategy,
         useValue: new CookieXSRFStrategy('myCookieName', 'myHeaderName')
       }],
    bootstrap:     [ AppComponent ]
})
export class AppModule { }
```

With the preceding code in place, Angular would look for a cookie with the key as myCookieName in the server response and send the value of this cookie by assigning it to the header, myHeaderName, in subsequent requests.

CSRF prevention technique for the Spring app

As described earlier, Angular looks out for a cookie, namely, XSRF-TOKEN, which needs to be sent as part of the server response. This is, in fact, taken care of by Spring Security based on the following strategy:

1. **Create a custom CSRF filter** which looks for a cookie, namely, XSRF-TOKEN, in the HTTP request. If the said cookie is not found, create a cookie, XSRF-TOKEN, assign it a token value and add the cookie to the server response. The following code represents a custom CSRF filter:

```
public class XSRFTokenFilter extends OncePerRequestFilter {
    @Override
    protected void doFilterInternal(HttpServletRequest request,
HttpServletResponse response, FilterChain filterChain)
    throws ServletException, IOException {
        CsrfToken csrf = (CsrfToken)
        request.getAttribute(CsrfToken.class.getName());
        if (csrf != null) {
            Cookie cookie = WebUtils.getCookie(request, "XSRF-
            TOKEN");
            String token = csrf.getToken();
            if (cookie==null || token!=null &&
            !token.equals(cookie.getValue())) {
                cookie = new Cookie("XSRF-TOKEN", token);
                cookie.setPath("/");
                response.addCookie(cookie);
            }
        }
        filterChain.doFilter(request, response);
    }
}
```

- **Configure the CSRF token repository.** Do this to include a header such as X-XSRF-TOKEN. The following code represents the same:

```
private CsrfTokenRepository xsrfTokenRepository() {
    HttpSessionCsrfTokenRepository repository = new
    HttpSessionCsrfTokenRepository();
    repository.setHeaderName("X-XSRF-TOKEN");
    return repository;
}
```

- **Configure the filter and CSRF token repository appropriately** when configuring the `HttpSecurity` instance. The following code represents the same:

```
@Override
protected void configure(HttpSecurity http) throws Exception {
    http.authorizeRequests()
    .antMatchers("/doctors/**", "/account/**").permitAll()
    .anyRequest().authenticated()
    .and()
    .addFilterAfter(new XSRFTokenFilter(), CsrfFilter.class)
    .csrf()
    .csrfTokenRepository(xsrfTokenRepository());
}
```

Handling the logout request

When the user clicks on logout, the Angular app invokes a logout API which, primarily, invalidates the HTTP session and removes the authentication object from the `SecurityContextHolder` object. Recall the `SecurityContextHolder` object is used to store the `SecurityContext` object, which holds on to the `Authentication` object. The following represents the code in the Spring app which invokes the logout API on the `SecurityContextLogoutHandler` instance:

```
@GetMapping(value="/logout")
public ExecutionStatus logout (HttpServletRequest request,
HttpServletResponse response) {
    Authentication auth =
SecurityContextHolder.getContext().getAuthentication();
    if (auth != null){
        new SecurityContextLogoutHandler().logout(request, response, auth);
    }
    return new ExecutionStatus("USER_LOGOUT_SUCCESSFUL", "User is logged
out");
}
```

OAuth2 for authentication/authorization

In the preceding sections, you learnt about how to use Spring Security for authentication. In this section, you will learn about the basic fundamentals in relation to OAuth2-based authentication in relation to Spring Security and how to use it with your Angular app. The following topics will be covered:

- Introduction to OAuth2-based authentication and authorization
- Spring Security and OAuth2 authentication/authorization

Introduction to OAuth2-based authentication & authorization

OAuth2 is an authorization framework, which is used to enable third-party applications to get limited access to HTTP services such as Facebook, LinkedIn, Twitter, and so on. OAuth-based authentication and authorization enables consumer applications and service providers to interact with each other in a secure manner. In order to access user's protected data from one or more service providers, such as Facebook, LinkedIn, and so on, consumer or client applications such as web or mobile apps take the user through following workflow:

1. **The users taken to the authorization server**: Take the user, who is also termed as **resource owner** (owner of his data), to the service provider server (such as Facebook), where user has his account. In OAuth terminology, the service provider server is also called a **resource** or **authorization server**. For large applications, authorization and resource servers reside on different hosts.

2. **The user is asked to give permission for accessing the resource**: The service provider's authorization server asks the user whether the consumer app should be permitted to access his data and related operations such as read or write, or both.

3. **The authorization server sends the access token to the consumer app**: If allowed, the authorization server sends the access token along with grant permissions to the consumer app.

4. **The consumer app accesses the users' protected data from the resource server**: Subsequently, the consumer app sends the access token to the resource server and accesses the protected resource.

The following are some of the key concepts, which need to be understood prior to starting OAuth2 implementation:

- **OAuth2 roles**: OAuth2 implementation defines four different roles:
  - **Client**: The is the consumer app which seeks permission (on behalf of resource owner) from the resource server to provide an access to the protected resource which is owned by the resource owner
  - **Resource owner**: This is an entity which owns the resource and grants the permission for accessing the protected resource
  - **Authorization server**: This is the server which issues the access token after authenticating the user (resource owner)
  - **Resource server**: This is the server which actually hosts the protected resources (resource owned by the resource owner) and provides an access to it based on the access token
- **OAuth2 grant types**: These are, primarily, methods using which a client application can acquire an access token. In order to make Angular and Spring apps work, one can simply use the resource owner credential grant type to acquire the access token based on sharing the user's credentials. The following are different types of grants:
  - Authorization code grant
  - Implicit grant
  - Resource owner credentials grant
  - Client credentials grant
  - Refresh token grant
- **OAuth2 tokens**: There are two different kinds of tokens--access and refresh tokens. The access token is one which is provided by the authorization server based on user authentication. The client app gets an access to the resource owner's information (resources) by sharing the access token to the resource server. The refresh token is the one which can be used to acquire a new access token when the original one expires.

Spring Security and OAuth2 authentication

In this section, you will learn about how to implement a **single sign-on** (SSO) using Spring Security OAuth2-based implementation. The following use case scenario for authentication will be dealt with:

1. The client app (Angular app) sends the request on behalf the of end user to the resource server (Spring app) to get an access to the protected resource.

2. The user access token validity is checked against the authorization server (Spring app).

3. With valid access token, user is given access to the resource if he has sufficient privileges.

4. For invalid access token, users are redirected to the login page. Users submit the login credentials.

5. User credentials are checked and an access token is sent back with response based on the valid login credentials.

6. The access token will then be sent to resource server and the data will be retrieved appropriately based on the access token scope.

Above can be implemented using two different strategies:

- Authorization server is different from resource server.
- Authorization and resource server is implemented on the same server.

This book deals with implementation of both authorization and resource server as one server. In the following sections, the OAuth2 implementation is exemplified with concepts and related code to be written for both Angular and Spring app.

OAuth2 Implementation for Spring Web App

The following are some of the key building blocks of the OAuth2 implementation on Spring web app:

- **CorsFilter**: First and foremost, it will be required to configure CORS filter to allow Authorization to be passed in header. Following code represents the same:

```
@Component
@Order(Ordered.HIGHEST_PRECEDENCE)
public class CorsFilter implements Filter {

    @Override
    public void doFilter(ServletRequest req, ServletResponse res,
FilterChain chain) throws IOException, ServletException {
        final HttpServletResponse response = (HttpServletResponse) res;
        response.setHeader("Access-Control-Allow-Origin", "*");
        response.setHeader("Access-Control-Allow-Methods", "POST, PUT,
GET, OPTIONS, DELETE");
        response.setHeader("Access-Control-Allow-Headers",
"Authorization, Content-Type");
        response.setHeader("Access-Control-Max-Age", "3600");
        if ("OPTIONS".equalsIgnoreCase(((HttpServletRequest)
```

```
req).getMethod())) {
            response.setStatus(HttpServletResponse.SC_OK);
        } else {
            chain.doFilter(req, res);
        }
    }

    @Override
    public void destroy() {
    }
    @Override
    public void init(FilterConfig config) throws ServletException {
    }
}
```

- **Resource server**: As described in one of the preceding sections, the resource server actually hosts the resource. In other words, the resource server provides an access to the protected resource. In the code given here, resources for rx and doctors are defined to be located at the URL, /rx/ and /doctor/, respectively. Pay attention to the @EnableResourceServer annotation, which is used to enable a Spring Security filter to authenticate the requests via an incoming OAuth2 token. It requires @EnableWebSecurity to be used somewhere in the application, if not used with the same class, which is annotated with @EnableResourceServer. It may be good idea to use this annotation with the security configuration class. The following code represents the resources related to doctors and patients for the sample health app:

```
@Configuration
@EnableResourceServer
public class ResourceServerConfig extends
ResourceServerConfigurerAdapter {

    @Autowired
    private TokenStore tokenStore;

    @Override
    public void configure(HttpSecurity http) throws Exception {
    http.requestMatchers().antMatchers("/doctor/**", "/rx/**",
"/account/**")
        .and()
        .authorizeRequests()
        .antMatchers
(HttpMethod.GET, "/doctor/**").access("#oauth2.hasScope('doctor') and
#oauth2.hasScope('read')")
        .antMatchers
(HttpMethod.POST, "/doctor/**").access("#oauth2.hasScope('doctor') and
```

```
#oauth2.hasScope('write')")
        .antMatchers
(HttpMethod.GET,"/rx/**").access("#oauth2.hasScope('doctor') and
#oauth2.hasScope('read')")
        .antMatchers
(HttpMethod.POST,"/rx/**").access("#oauth2.hasScope('doctor') and
#oauth2.hasScope('write')")
        .antMatchers("/account/**").permitAll()
        .and()
        .exceptionHandling().accessDeniedHandler(new
OAuth2AccessDeniedHandler())
        .and()
        .csrf().disable();
            }

        @Override
        public void configure(final ResourceServerSecurityConfigurer
config) {
            final DefaultTokenServices defaultTokenServices = new
DefaultTokenServices();
            defaultTokenServices.setTokenStore(this.tokenStore);
            config.tokenServices(defaultTokenServices);
            }
        }
```

In addition to configuring resource server, it will also be required to enable method security using GlobalMethodSecurityConfiguration and @EnableGlobalMethodSecurity annotation. By using @EnableGlobalMethodSecurity annotation, methods can be secured with Java configuration. Following code represents the same:

```
@Configuration
@EnableGlobalMethodSecurity(prePostEnabled = true)
public class GlobalMethodSecurityConfig extends
GlobalMethodSecurityConfiguration {

  @Override
  protected MethodSecurityExpressionHandler createExpressionHandler() {
    return new OAuth2MethodSecurityExpressionHandler();
  }
}
```

- **Authorization server**: It is the authorization server that provides access token to the users based on the valid user credentials, which are, then, used to access the protected resources on the resource server. In case the credentials are verified, the authorization server sends back the access token in the response along with information such a user roles which can be used by client appropriately. Pay to the usage of the annotation @EnableAuthorizationServer annotation. The @EnableAuthorizationServer annotation is a convenience annotation used for enabling an authorization server whose key building blocks are AuthorizationEndpoint and TokenEndpoint.

```java
@Configuration
@EnableAuthorizationServer
public class AuthServerOAuth2Config extends
AuthorizationServerConfigurerAdapter {

    @Autowired
    @Qualifier("authenticationManagerBean")
    private AuthenticationManager authenticationManager;

    @Autowired
    private DataSource dataSource;

    @Override
    public void configure(final AuthorizationServerSecurityConfigurer
oauthServer) throws Exception {
        oauthServer
          .tokenKeyAccess("permitAll()")
          .checkTokenAccess("isAuthenticated()");
    }

    @Override
    public void configure(final ClientDetailsServiceConfigurer
clients) throws Exception {
        clients.jdbc(this.dataSource);
    }

    @Override
    public void configure(final
AuthorizationServerEndpointsConfigurer endpoints) throws Exception {
        final TokenEnhancerChain tokenEnhancerChain = new
TokenEnhancerChain();
        tokenEnhancerChain.setTokenEnhancers
(Arrays.asList(tokenEnhancer()));
        endpoints.tokenStore(tokenStore())
.tokenEnhancer(tokenEnhancerChain).authenticationManager
(authenticationManager);
```

```
        }

        @Bean
        @Primary
        public DefaultTokenServices tokenServices() {
            final DefaultTokenServices defaultTokenServices = new
    DefaultTokenServices();
            defaultTokenServices.setTokenStore(tokenStore());
            defaultTokenServices.setSupportRefreshToken(true);
            return defaultTokenServices;
        }

        @Bean
        public TokenEnhancer tokenEnhancer() {
            return new CustomTokenEnhancer();
        }

        @Bean(name="tokenStore")
        public TokenStore tokenStore() {
            return new JdbcTokenStore(this.dataSource);
        }
    }
```

Pay attention to some of the following in the preceding code:

- **TokenEnhancer**: Custom `TokenEnhancer` implements the interface
  `TokenEnhancer` method, *enhance,* for augmenting the response (consisting of
  access token) with additional information such as user role etc. The
  `TokenEnhancer` is called after the access and refresh tokens have been generated
  but before they are stored by an
  `AuhorizationServerTokenServices` implementation. Following code
  represents implementation of `TokenEnhancer` interface,
  `CustomTokenEnhancer`, which is used to add user role information to the
  response sent back to client.

```
    public class CustomTokenEnhancer implements TokenEnhancer {
        @Override
        public OAuth2AccessToken enhance(OAuth2AccessToken accessToken,
    OAuth2Authentication authentication) {
            final Map<String, Object> additionalInfo = new HashMap<>();
            Collection<GrantedAuthority> authorities =
    authentication.getAuthorities();
            Object[] ga = authorities.toArray();
            SimpleGrantedAuthority sga = (SimpleGrantedAuthority)
    ga[0];
            String role = sga.getAuthority();
```

```
        additionalInfo.put("role", role);
        ((DefaultOAuth2AccessToken)
accessToken).setAdditionalInformation(additionalInfo);
        return accessToken;
    }
}
```

- **DefaultTokenServices**: `DefaulTokenServices` is used for handling of token processing strategies such as setting appropriate token store for persisting the tokens, providing support for refresh access token, setting token enhancer etc.
- **TokenStore**: `TokenStore` represents the storage mechanism to store the access token. Spring supports different kind of token store such as `InMemoryTokenStore`, `JDBCTokenStore`, `JwtTokenStore`, and so on. In preceding code sample, `JDBCTokenStore` is used for storing access tokens.
- **AuthorizationServerEndpointsConfigurer:** `AuthorizationServerEndpoints Configurer` instance is used to configure properties such as authentication manager, token store, token enhancer etc., of authorization server endpoints.
  - **Security configuration**: Following represents code for configuring http web security in addition to defining authentication provider. Pay attention to the usage of `@EnableWebSecurity` annotation. `@EnableWebSecurity` and `WebSecurityConfigurerAdapter` works together to provide web based security. `HttpSecurity` can as well be configured within `WebSecurityConfigurerAdapter` implementation. With `WebSecurityConfigurerAdapter`, Spring Boot application creates a filter chain at order = 0, and protects all resources unless provided with one or more request matchers. With `ResourceServerConfigurerAdapter` and `@EnableResourceServer`, a filter is added at order = 3 and, it acts as a catch-all fallback for `WebSecurityConfigurerAdapter` at order = 0. Thus, `HttpSecurity` configuration which has been configured in class `ResourceServerConfig` in preceding code example could as be defined with `SecurityConfiguration` class which extends `WebSecurityConfigurerAdapter` as shown in the following code example.

```
@Configuration
@EnableWebSecurity
public class SecurityConfiguration extends
WebSecurityConfigurerAdapter {
        @Autowired
        private CustomAuthenticationProvider authProvider;
```

```
        @Override
        @Bean
        public AuthenticationManager authenticationManagerBean() throws
Exception {
            return super.authenticationManagerBean();
        }

        @Override
        protected void configure(AuthenticationManagerBuilder
authBuilder) {
            authBuilder.authenticationProvider(this.authProvider);
        }
    }
```

OAuth2 Implementation for Angular App

In this section, you will learn about what needs to be done in order to have Angular app make use of OAuth2 based authentication/authorization. Following are the key aspects of the OAuth2 implementation in Angular app:

- Acquiring access token
- Accessing resources using access token

Acquiring access token

In this section, you will learn some of the following aspects in relation with acquiring access token from the authorization server.

- **Acquire access token from the auth server**: Pay attention to login(login: Login) function which invokes /oauth/token API on authorization server. Notice the parameters passed using URLSearchParams object. These parameters are username and password (login credentials entered by the user), grant_type and client_id. Parameter grant_type is set as *password*. This represents the grant type such as **Resource owner password credentials grant.** The resource owner password credentials grant type is suitable in cases where the resource owner has a trust relationship with the client, such as the device operating system or a highly privileged application. This grant type is considered suitable for clients capable of obtaining the resource owner's credentials (username and password, typically using an interactive form as like in our case). Also, notice the fact that client_id along with client secret password is sent to server for acquiring the access token. This is required to establish trust on the client (apps/devices) from where users are sending the request.

- **Save token and related information**: Once access token is acquired from the authorization server, it is stored using Cookie class. Cookie class (from ng2-cookies npm package) provides implementation for storing access token and related information such a user role.

- **Delete token and related information**: This is done when user clicks **logout** link which leads to invocation of `logout()` function. Pay attention to code within `logout()` function in the code given ahead.

- **Cookie data structure**: Using Cookie data structure (from ng2-cookies NPM package) to store the information in relation to the access token.

```
@Injectable()
export class AuthService {
    isLoggedIn: Observable<boolean>;
    private observer: Observer<boolean>;

    redirectUrl: string;
    serverUrl = 'http://localhost:8080';

    constructor(private http: Http, private router: Router) {
      this.isLoggedIn = new Observable(observer =>
        this.observer = observer
      );
    }


    login(login: Login): Observable<LoginStatus> {
      let params = new URLSearchParams();
      params.append('username', login.email);
      params.append('password', login.password);
      params.append('grant_type', 'password');
      params.append('client_id', 'healthapp');
      let headers = new Headers({'Content-type': 'application/x-www-
form-urlencoded; charset=utf-8', 'Authorization': 'Basic ' +
btoa('healthapp:HeAltH@!23')});
      let options = new RequestOptions({ headers: headers });

      return this.http.post('http://localhost:8080/oauth/token',
params.toString(), options)
          .map(res => {
            this.saveToken(res.json());
            return new LoginStatus('SUCCESS', 'Login Successful');
          })
          .catch((error: any) => {
            return Observable.of(new LoginStatus('FAILURE', 'Username
or password is incorrect. Please try again!'));
          });
```

```
        }

    saveToken(token: any) {
        let expireDate = new Date().getTime() + (1000 *
token.expires_in);
        Cookie.set('access_token', token.access_token, expireDate);
        Cookie.set('role', token.role);
        this.changeLoginStatus(true);
        if (token.role === 'ROLE_DOCTOR') {
          this.router.navigate(['rx']);
        } else {
          this.router.navigate(['patient/home']);
        }
    }

    checkCredentials() {
        if (!Cookie.check('access_token')) {
          this.router.navigate(['/login']);
        }
    }

    logout() {
        Cookie.delete('access_token');
        Cookie.delete('role');
        this.changeLoginStatus(false);
    }

    changeLoginStatus(status: boolean) {
        if (this.observer !== undefined) {
          this.observer.next(status);
        };
    }
}
```

Accessing resources using access token

Once access token is acquired and stored in the cookie store, next step is to send request to resource server for accessing one or more resources. Pay attention to the fact that OAuth2 authorization (access token) information needs to be passed in the header in order to get an access (getRx function) to the protected resource or create/update (createdRx function) the protected resource.

```
import {Http, Headers, RequestOptions} from '@angular/http';
import {Injectable} from '@angular/core';
import {Rx} from './rx';
import {Observable} from 'rxjs/Observable';
import {Cookie} from 'ng2-cookies';
```

```
@Injectable()
export class RxService {
  private rxUrl = 'http://localhost:8080/rx';
  private newRxUrl = 'http://localhost:8080/rx/new';

  constructor(private http: Http) {
  }

  getRx(): Observable<Rx[]> {
    let headers = new Headers({
      'Content-type': 'application/json',
      'Authorization': 'Bearer ' + Cookie.get('access_token')
    });

    return this.http.get(this.rxUrl, {headers: headers})
      .map(res => res.json())
      .catch(err => {
        return Observable.throw(err.json().error || 'Server error');
      });
  }

  createRx(rx: Rx): Observable<Rx> {
    let headers = new Headers();
    headers.append('Content-Type', 'application/json');
    headers.append('Authorization', 'bearer ' +
Cookie.get('access_token'));
    let options = new RequestOptions({ headers: headers });

    return this.http.post(this.newRxUrl, rx, options)
      .map(res => res.json())
      .catch(err => {
        return Observable.throw('Server Error');
      });
  }
}
```

Summary

In this chapter, you learned about how Spring Security can enhance the overall security of apps developed using the Angular and Spring web framework. Some of the details we went over are using Spring Security and OAuth2 based implementation for authentication and authorization while taking appropriate steps to ensure security with the Angular app.

6
Getting Started with Angular

Angular is a JavaScript framework designed and developed for the purpose of developing an app once, and building and developing it for deployment targets such as the web, native mobile, and native desktop. In this chapter, we will learn about some of the following in relation to Angular 4:

- Introduction to Angular
- How Angular is different from AngularJS
- Setup Angular development environment
- TypeScript fundamentals
- Forms
- Pipes
- Directives
- Server communication
- Bootstrapping Angular app
- Best practices

Introduction to Angular

The current version of Angular follows a major migration releases of Angular such as AngularJS 1.x, that took the **single page app (SPA)** development by storm. In this section, we will look into how Angular 2.x onward and how is it significantly different than AngularJS 1.x.

The following are some of the key architectural building blocks of Angular:

- **Template**: A template is used to represent static/dynamic content, with zero or more form elements using HTML syntax in addition to the Angular template syntax. Templates, in Angular, only exists with an associated component and never standalone. The following code represents a sample template which prints a list of tasks and the task details for the selected tasks.

```
<h2>Tasks List</h2>
<ul>
 <li *ngFor="tasks" (click)="selectTask(task)">
 {{task.name}}
 </li>
</ul>

<task-detail *ngIf="selectedTask" [task]="selectedTask"></task-detail>
```

- In the preceding code, the Angular template syntax includes `ngFor`, `(click)`, `[task]`, and `<task-detail>`.
- **Component:** Components are the most fundamental building block of an Angular UI application. A component represents a view on the web page. While a template is defined solely using HTML and Angular syntax, as shown earlier, a component is defined using the template and the related application logic which is used to process the data within the template. A web page can consist of one or more components. The application logic required to process the data in the view is defined within the class that is defined within the component. The application logic defined within the class is analogous to the controller code in AngularJS 1.x. As a best practice, the business logic resides in the services, and components delegate tasks to the services.

The components are represented using a decorator function (`@Component`). The `@Component` decorator allows one to mark a class as an Angular component and provide metadata that determines how the component should be instantiated, processed, and used at the runtime. A component begins with defining the `@Component` decorator which takes a metadata object as an argument. The most fundamental attributes of the metadata object are `selector` and `template` or `templateUrl` which are used to provide a unique name for the component, and, define the template respectively.

The following is a sample code (Hello World) representing a trivial component, which defines a template that prints the message Hello Calvin Hobbes, Welcome to Angular World!:

```
import { Component } from '@angular/core';

@Component({
  selector: 'my-app',
  template: `<h1>Hello {{name}}, {{message}}</h1>`,
})
export class AppComponent {
  name = 'Calvin Hobbes';
  message = 'Welcome to Angular World!';
}
```

Note the following points in the preceding code:

- **Template**: The template comprises HTML code and data elements surrounded by double curly braces, which are called **Angular interpolation binding** expression. These data elements with the double curly braces are replaced with the components' related property (such as name and message) at runtime. The template is represented using the template attribute, and looks like this:

  ```
  <h1>Hello {{name}}, {{message}}</h1>
  ```

- **Component**: The component decorator function is passed a metadata object (in JSON format) with the selector attribute assigned with the value such as my-app and a template attribute assigned with value such as HTML/Angular syntax which would be displayed on the page when component is rendered. The Component class comprises application logic for processing the data elements.

- **Service**: The application logic is often written as one or more reusable services, and these services are injected in the component classes as appropriate and needed. Simply speaking, a service is just an another class that provides a functionality using one or more methods that can be invoked from external classes such as components. The following represents a sample service, UserService, which, once injected into one or more components, can be invoked appropriately to provide the required functionality. Note the @Injectable annotation which is used to mark the class as available to Injector for creation:

  ```
  @Injectable
  export class UserService {
      private userId: string;
  ```

```
        constructor(userDAO: UserDAO, logger: Logger) {
            ...
        }

        getProfile() {
            ...
        }
    }
```

- **Module**: A module can consist of one or more components and related services. An Angular app has to have at least one angular module, which is also called **root module**. A complex angular app, however, can comprise of multiple modules, each one representing one or more feature. An angular module is represented using @NgModule. The @NgModule decorator function takes the following as the metadata object:

```
@NgModule({
    imports: [...]
    exports: [...]
    declerations: [...]
    providers: [...]
    bootstrap: [...]
})
export class UserModule {
    ...
}
```

- **Directives**: Directives are, primarily, classes with the @Directive decorator. Technically speaking, a component can also be called a directive with additional template-oriented features. Simply speaking, if there is a need to display some information on the page, components are used. On the other hand, if there is a need is to process one or more HTML elements in a specific manner, then, directives are used. For example, if you need to display a div element having textual information with red background, a directive will be used. Directives are of two types--structural and attribute:
  - **Attribute directives**: Change the appearance or behavior of an existing element
  - **Structural directives**: Change layout by adding, removing, and replacing the DOM elements

- **Dependency injection (DI)**: Angular, like AngularJS, uses dependency injection to provide the components with an instance of the dependencies they need. With this, components are not required to instantiate their own copies of dependent classes within the constructor. Instead, they receive the instances of class using the Angular DI system. Following are three critical pieces of DI in Angular:

  - **Dependency**: The dependency is the type of which object needs to be created and injected. The following code represents the component, UserRegistrationComponent, declaring its dependency as AuthService:

```
@Component({
    selector: 'register',
    templateUrl: './user-registration.component.html'
})
export class UserRegistrationComponent {
    constructor(private authService: AuthService) {}
}
```

  - **Provider**: The injector identifies the dependency, tries to create the instance of the dependency, and inject it. In order to do this, it needs to know how to create the instance of this dependency. This is where the Provider comes into picture. Following code represents the provider of AuthService dependency:

```
@NgModule({
    imports: [ BrowserModule,
               FormsModule,
               AuthRoutingModule ],
    declarations: [ UserRegistrationComponent,...],
    providers: [ {provide: AuthService,
                  useClass: AuthService}]
})
export class AuthModule { }
```

  - **Injector**: The injector exposes a set of APIs that can be used to create instances of dependencies.

- **Data binding**: Data binding, in Angular, boils down to property and event binding between a component and its template. Two-way data binding results in data changes flowing from the components to user inputs and vice versa. The following diagram represents this:

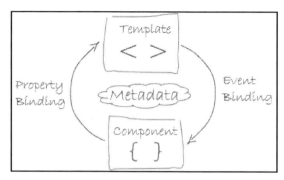

Figure 1. Component data binding (courtesy: angular.io)

Out of the box, Angular supports two-way data binding using directives such as ngModel. The following code represents the usage of ngModel. Typing in the input field will display the name within <p> element:

```
<input type="text" [(ngModel)]="username">

<p>Hello, {{username}}!</p>
```

However, one can achieve the goal of two-way data binding without using ngModel directive with code such as following. In the following code, the value of username expression is bound to the input's value property:

```
<input type="text" [value]="username" (input)="username =
    $event.target.value">

<p>Hello, {{username}}!</p>
```

How is Angular different from AngularJS?

Angular is worlds apart from AngularJS in terms of the architectural building blocks, and, the manner in which apps are developed using them. Let us take both Angular and AngularJS in reverse chronological order, and understand the evolution of the AngularJS framework for developing and delivering an app for different deployment targets.

AngularJS - The MVC way of building UI apps

AngularJS, as a term, is popularly used for Angular version 1.x and prior releases. Information about AngularJS can be found on this website: `https://angularjs.org/`. AngularJS was meant to be used for building single page apps (SPAs) in a simple, quick, and easy manner.

AngularJS introduced several concepts, such as the **Model-View-Controller** (**MVC**) architectural style, Dependency Injection, two-way data binding, templates, directives, and so on, related to building UI apps in an organized manner. It should be noted that concepts such as MVC and dependency injection used to be popularly associated with building server-side apps with programming languages such as Java. The following are some of the key features/concepts found in AngularJS:

- **The MVC architectural style**: This is how the MVC concept is applied to AngularJS UI apps:
  - **Model** represents the data that is either displayed on the UI (view) after being retrieved from the server, or manipulated using one or more UI input elements.
  - **View** represents the UI. The AngularJS UI is formed using a template comprising of HTML and Angular custom syntaxes
  - **Controller** represents the application logic which processes the data (model) arriving from server or UI events (view)
- **Two-way data binding**: AngularJS supports two-way data binding in such a way that any change in the data (model) is propagated to the UI (view), and any change in the data on the UI side leads to a change in the related data (model).
- **Dependency injection**: Dependency injection is a software design pattern that is related to the way components handle their dependencies. A dependency injection system frees the components from concerns related with creating and managing their dependencies' lifecycle. On similar lines, the AngularJS dependency injection system creates components, resolve their dependencies, and inject them into other components as appropriate. Components such as services, filters, directives, and controllers can be injected into providers created using `service` and `value` functions as dependencies. Following code sample represents a service provider created using `service`, which is, later, injected into a controller:

```
angular.module('healthapp',[])
.service('doctorService', function () {
    this.title = 'Doctor Service';
})
.controller('DoctorController', function (doctorService) {
```

```
    expect(doctorService.title).toEqual('Doctor Service');
});
```

The following example represents Dependency Injection with a service provider such as `userService`. Note that, in the following code, the directive and service are defined using the `factory` method:

```
angular.module('registration', [])
.controller('userRegistrationController', ['$scope', function($scope) {
    //...
    $scope.registerUser = function() {
        //...
    }
    //...
}])
.factory('userRegistration', ['userService', function(userService)
{
    // ...
}])
.directive('user-profile', ['userService', function(userService) {
    // ...
}]);
```

- **Services**: A service is an abstract used to represent code that is used to deliver a cohesive set of functionalities. One or more services are wired together using dependency injection, as shown in the preceding code sample. Services are singletons, which basically, means that at any point, only one instance of the service exists and what is injected into controllers, directives, filter, another service, and so on, is reference to that service. The following code represents a service being registered to a module:

```
var userModule = angular.module('userModule', []);
userModule.service('userService', function() {
    return new UserService();
});
```

- **Directives**: One of the most striking features of AngularJS is directives. Directives are explained as follows on the AngularJS page at `https://docs.angularjs.org/guide/directive`:

"Directives are markers on a DOM element (such as an attribute, element name, comment or CSS class) that tell AngularJS's HTML compiler ($compile) to attach a specified behavior to that DOM element (for example, via event listeners), or even to transform the DOM element and its children."

AngularJS comes with **predefined directives** such as `ng-repeat`, `ng-app`, and `ng-model`. Similar to controllers, directives are registered with a module. The following code represents the definition of directives, and how they are defined on the HTML page:

```
angular.module('userModule', [])
.controller('UserController', ['$scope', function($scope) {
    $scope.user = {
        fullname: 'Calvin Hobbes',
        nickname: 'Calvin',
        address: 'San Francisco, CA'
    };
}])
.directive('userDetails', function() {
    return {
        template: 'Name: {{user.fullname}}
        Nickname: {{user.nickname}}
        Address: {{user.address}}'
    };
});
```

The following is the HTML code for the preceding directive:

```
<div ng-controller="UserController">
    <div user-details></div>
</div>
```

To summarize this, AngularJS enabled UI developers to design/visualize an HTML page as a set of **views** consisting of static and dynamic data (`model`), which are processed using **controllers**. The views on the page can have one or more AngularJS predefined **directives** or user-defined directives.

Angular - The Component Way of Building Web Apps

Angular dropped some of the key architectural building blocks of AngularJS, such as MVC and related concepts such as `$scope`, and `$rootScope`. Angular can be considered as a complete rewrite of AngularJS, and one can create Angular apps using JavaScript (both ES5 and ES6), TypeScript, and Dart. However, it is recommended to use the TypeScript to develop Angular apps due to various reasons such as type checking, the tooling it provides (advanced autocompletion, navigation, refactoring). A quick introduction to the TypeScript programming concepts is provided later in this chapter.

Angular enables UI developers to design/visualize a web page as a set of components which represent UI templates and application logic to process events and data associated with these UI templates. The current version of Angular can be said to be an extension of Angular 2, unlike Angular 2 versus AngularJS (1.x) were fundamentally different.

Setting up the Angular development environment

Before getting started with setting up the local development environment for Angular apps, one should install NodeJS and NPM. One can go to the NodeJS website (`https://nodejs.org/en/`), download the appropriate installer for NodeJS/NPM, and install the tool. In order to confirm that NodeJS and NPM are set up correctly, the following command can be executed to print their versions:

```
// Prints NodeJS version
node -v

// Print NPM version
npm -v
```

The next step is to install Angular CLI globally. Angular CLI is command-line interface for Angular. It provides commands for creating a boilerplate app right out of the box based on the best practices, generating components, routes, services, and so on. Also, running/testing the app locally while developing. It provide for an error-free setup, it is recommended to execute the following command as an administrator. On Linux/macOS, `sudo` can be used with the following command. On Windows, one can right click on **Command Prompt** and select the **Run as as administrator** option from the list.

```
npm install -g @angular/cli
```

The next step is to create a new project (say, `healthapp`) using the following command:

```
ng new healthapp
```

Executing the preceding command creates a new directory, namely, `healthapp`. The setup would look like the following image:

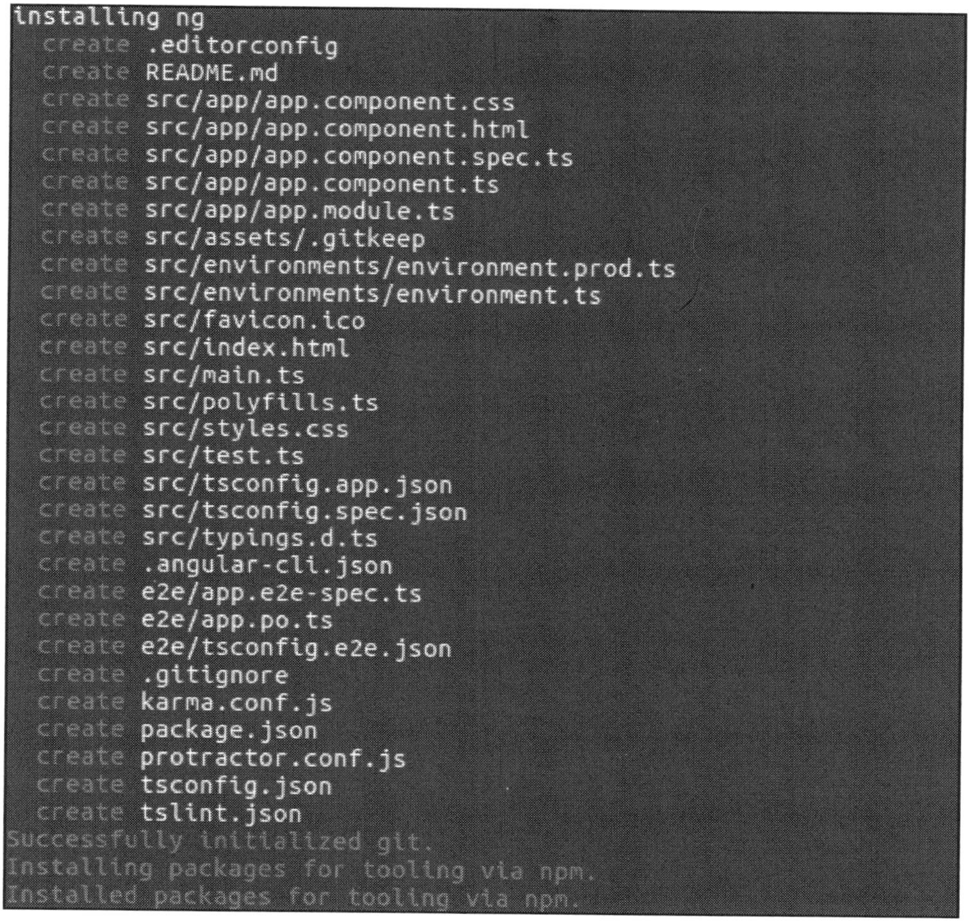

```
installing ng
  create .editorconfig
  create README.md
  create src/app/app.component.css
  create src/app/app.component.html
  create src/app/app.component.spec.ts
  create src/app/app.component.ts
  create src/app/app.module.ts
  create src/assets/.gitkeep
  create src/environments/environment.prod.ts
  create src/environments/environment.ts
  create src/favicon.ico
  create src/index.html
  create src/main.ts
  create src/polyfills.ts
  create src/styles.css
  create src/test.ts
  create src/tsconfig.app.json
  create src/tsconfig.spec.json
  create src/typings.d.ts
  create .angular-cli.json
  create e2e/app.e2e-spec.ts
  create e2e/app.po.ts
  create e2e/tsconfig.e2e.json
  create .gitignore
  create karma.conf.js
  create package.json
  create protractor.conf.js
  create tsconfig.json
  create tslint.json
Successfully initialized git.
Installing packages for tooling via npm.
Installed packages for tooling via npm.
```

Figure 2: Angular app setup

Go to the `healthapp` folder, and start the server using the following commands:

```
cd health
ng serve
```

The preceding commands do the following:

- Launch the server, watch the files, and rebuild the project whenever one or more changes are made.
- Open the app in the browser at `http://localhost:4200`. The page will look something like this:

Figure 3: First Angular App

TypeScript fundamentals

According to its website, `https://www.typescriptlang.org/`, *TypeScript is a typed superset of JavaScript that compiles to plain JavaScript, any browser, any host, any OS--open source*. TypeScript is a typed superset of ES6 JavaScript. It can be noted that ES6 JavaScript is a superset of ES5 JavaScript that runs native in all modern browsers.

You can get the set up and start programming in TypeScript using the following command:

```
npm install -g typescript
```

The following are some salient features of the TypeScript:

- **Typed language**: It is a typed language. The following data types are supported-- `number`, `string`, `array`, `list`, `null`, and `enum`. The user object is represented by the following code:

```
let firstName: string = "Calvin";
let age: number = 19;
```

```
let gender: string = "male";
let isEnrolled: boolean = false;
let address: [string, string, string] =
    ["Nizampet Road, Kukatpally", "Hyderabad", "India"];
```

- **Variable declarations:** It supports variable declaration using keywords such as let, const, and var. The primary difference between let and const is that const keyword prevents re-assignment to a variable.

- **Interfaces**: TypeScript supports defining contracts using an interface. The following code represents the User interface:

```
interface User {
    firstName: string;
    lastName: string;
    age: number;
    address: string;
    mobile: string;
};
```

The following code represents the function for registering a user based on the previously defined User interface:

```
function registerUser(user: User) {
    console.log("User Name: " + user.firstName + " " +
                user.lastName);
    ...
}
```

- **Classes**: With TypeScript, developers can build applications using the object-oriented class-based approach. It should be noted that, traditionally, functions and protoype-based inheritance are used in object-based programming in JavaScript. The following represents a class for user registration:

```
import {User} from "./UserModule";

export class UserRegistration {
    constructor(user: User) {
    ...
}
doesUserExist(emailAddress: string) {
    ...
}
}
```

- **Modules**: Modules represent the variables, functions, interfaces, and classes. They are used to deliver one particular functionality. Variables, functions, or classes defined with a module need to be exported for another module to import and use them. Taking the earlier example, there could be a module for user registration which can create classes such as `UserRegistration` and interfaces such as `User` (possibly imported from another common `User` module).

- **Enums**: Like Java, TypeScript also supports enums for defining a set of numeric constants. The following code represents enum type, `UserType`.

```
enum UserType {
    Patient = 1,
    Doctor
}

let userType = UserType.Doctor;
```

- **Decorators**: According to the decorator webpage on the TypeScript website (https://www.typescriptlang.org/docs/handbook/decorators.html), *decorators provide a way to add both annotations and a meta-programming syntax for class declarations and members.* Decorators can be attached to a class, method, accessor, property and method parameters declaration. Simply speaking, they are defined as a function which gets called at runtime with information provided with decorator declaration. The following code represents a sample decorator. Note the `@expression` format used to declare a decorator.

```
function MethodType(param: string) {
    return function(target: any, key: string, descriptor:
PropertyDescriptor) {
        console.log("Method is of type: " + param);
    }
}

class UserService {
    @MethodType("Utility Function")
    sayHello() {
        //...
    }
}
```

In the preceding example, a decorator function, `MethodType`, is a method decorator which can be attached before a method declaration. Invoking method such as `sayHello` on `UserService` instance will invoke the method decorator, `MethodType("Utility Function")`, as a result of which following will be printed: `Method is of type: Utility Function`. In Angular 2, decorators such as `@Component, @Module`, and so on, are used to annotate class definitions.

Forms

Angular 4 supports creating forms using techniques such as template-driven forms, reactive forms (also termed as model-driven forms), and dynamic forms. In this section, we shall quickly go through some of the important aspects of each technique, and when can they be used.

The following are some key aspects of form handling that shall be dealt with while creating forms using different techniques:

- Creating form controls such as input elements such as text fields, dropdowns, and so on
- Binding form controls with the associated data
- Creating appropriate validations rules, and displaying validation message appropriately for one or more form controls based on business rules
- Conditionally enabling or disabling one or more form controls such as input fields
- Interacting with the backend for data processing
- Submitting data to the backend
- Retrieving responses from the backend and displaying them on the UI appropriately

Template-driven forms

Template-driven forms are created using templates based on the Angular template syntax with form-driven directives and techniques. Template-driven forms can be created using `FormsModule`. We will learn about template-driven forms using the Login form, as shown in this screenshot:

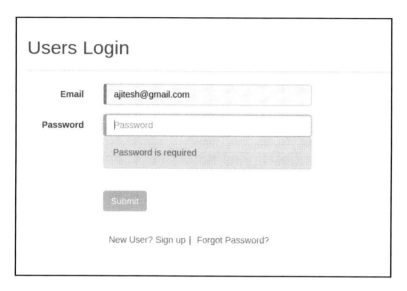

Figure 4. Users Login Form

The following are some of the key aspects that will be learnt in relation with creating template-driven forms:

- **Login component** (`login.component.ts`): Create the `Login` component to process the login user inputs as follows:

```
import { Component } from '@angular/core';

import { Login } from './login';

@Component({
    selector: 'login',
    templateUrl: './login.component.html'
})
export class LoginComponent {
    model = new Login('', '');

    onSubmit() {
```

```
console.log('Email Address: ' + this.model.email + ',
             Password: ' + this.model.password);
    }
  }
```

In the preceding code sample, one can observe the use of `Login` model class. It will be used to capture the changes and update the instance of the model as users enter the form data. Following is the related code sample. This can be defined in a file, namely, `login.ts` and imported appropriately in `login.component.ts` as shown in the preceding code:

```
export class Login {
    constructor(
        public email: string,
        public password: string
    ) {}
}
```

- **Login template** (`login.component.html`): Place the template code in a different file, namely `login.component.html`, and put the file within the same folder as `LoginComponent`. This is what the template code looks like:

```html
<div>
  <h2>Users Login</h2>
  <hr/>
  <form class="form-horizontal" (ngSubmit)="onSubmit()"
  #loginForm="ngForm" novalidate>
  <div class="form-group">
    <label for="email" class="col-sm-2 control-label">Email</label>
      <div class="col-sm-6">
        <input type="email"
          class="form-control"
          id="email"
          placeholder="Email"
          required
          [(ngModel)]="model.email"
          name="email"
          #email="ngModel"
        >
        <div [hidden]="email.valid || email.pristine"
            class="alert alert-danger">
            Email address is required
        </div>
      </div>
    </div>
    <div class="form-group">
      <label for="password" class="col-sm-2 control label">
          Password</label>
```

```
<div class="col-sm-6">
  <input type="password"
    class="form-control"
    id="password"
    placeholder="Password"
    required
    [(ngModel)]="model.password"
    name="password"
    #password="ngModel"
  >
  <div [hidden]="password.valid || password.pristine"
      class="alert alert-danger">
      Password is required
  </div>
  </div>
</div>
<div class="form-group">
  <div class="col-sm-offset-2 col-sm-10">
    <button type="submit" class="btn btn-success"
        [disabled]="!loginForm.form.valid">Submit</button>
  </div>
</div>
<div class="col-sm-offset-2 col-sm-10"
    style="padding-top:20px">
  <span style="padding-right: 5px"><a href="">New User?
      Sign up</a></span>|
  <span style="padding-left: 5px"><a href="">Forgot
      Password?</a></span>
</div>
  </form>
</div>
```

Note some of the following points for the preceding code:

- Binding syntax `[(ngModel)]` is used to bind the user inputs in the form with the model. In the preceding form, `[(ngModel)]` binds input field with name such as email and password with `Login` model property such as email and password respectively.

- The, `name`, found with `<input>` tag needs to be defined when using `[(ngModel)]` in a form.

- `Template variable`, `#loginForm = "ngForm"` is defined with `<form>` element in order to display the data. Note that Angular directive, `ngForm`, supplements the `<form>` element with additional features such as monitoring the input controls created for the input elements with the `ngModel` directive and name attribute.

- **User-input validation**: There may be a requirement for user-input validation, and to display or hide error messages appropriately. The following needs to be done to enable user-input validation:

  - Put validation-related styles in either the existing `styles.css` or a new style file. As a matter of fact, any styles which are common through out the application can be kept in `styles.css` provided its an `Angular-cli` project. For any component specific styles, the following code can put in component specific CSS file, such as `app.component.css`:

```
.ng-valid[required], .ng-valid.required  {
    border-left: 5px solid #42A948; /* green */
}

.ng-invalid:not(form)  {
    border-left: 5px solid #a94442; /* red */
}
```

- Put the following validation code under each input element, as shown in the preceding form, for the `email` and `password` form element. As per the following code, the message is hidden when it is valid or `pristine`, which means that the value has not changed since it was displayed:

```
<!-- Validate Email Field -->
<div [hidden]="email.valid || email.pristine"
    class="alert alert-danger">
    Email address is required
</div>

<!-- Validate Password Field -->
<div [hidden]="password.valid || password.pristine"
    class="alert alert-danger">
    Password is required
</div>
```

- Put a template reference variable in relation to each element. Pay attention to `#email="ngModel"` and `#password="ngModel"` in the input element, which are related to the email and password respectively in the preceding login template code.

- **Two-way Data Binding**: Each of the form controls in the preceding form, including email and password, are bound to the `Login` model using `ngModel` two-way data binding syntax, which makes it easy to bind the form to the model. Take a look, `[(ngModel)]="model.email"`, `[(ngModel)]="model.password"`. The data can then be displayed in the UI using the Angular interpolation syntax such as `{{model.email}}`. In addition to this, the following is also required to be done:
  - Define a template variable for the form. This is defined as `#loginForm="ngForm"` within the `<form>` tag.
  - Create a data model object, such as `Login`, with attributes, email, and password. This is illustrated in the next point.
- **Model (Data)**: Define a model representing the form data, and capturing and updating the instance of the model in the login form shown earlier, the following model is used. The file is named `login.ts` and placed in the same folder as `login.component.ts` and `login.component.html`:

```
export class Login {

    constructor(
        public email: string,
        public password: string
    ) {  }

}
```

- **Changes for handling login**: This includes the login component (represented using `<login> ... </login>`) in the `AppComponent` template so that the login UI shows up as the `AppComponent` bootstraps. The following represents the code for `AppComponent` (`app.componenent.ts`) and the related template, `app.component.html`:

//app.component.ts

```
import { Component } from '@angular/core';

@Component({
    selector: 'my-app',
    templateUrl: './app.component.html',
})
export class AppComponent {
    ...
}
```

```
//app.component.html;
//Pay attention to login component (<login>      </login>)

<div class="container">
  <h1>HealthApp - A Platform for Doctors & Patients</h1>
  <hr/>
  <div>
      This is a platform bringing together Doctors and Patients and
      helping them communicate, collaborate.
  </div>
  <login></login>
</div>
```

The previously mentioned AppComponent, when bootstrapped, ends up loading the following UI:

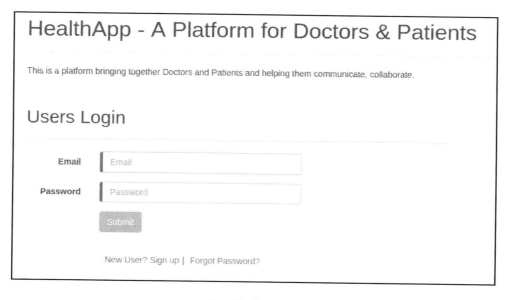

Figure 5: AppComponent bootstraped

- **AppModule Changes**: Change the AppModule code (app.module.ts) appropriately to include FormsModule (within imports array) and LoginComponent within the declarations array. The inclusion of FormsModule in the imports array provides the application with access to all of the template-driven features including ngForm and ngModel:

```
import { NgModule }      from '@angular/core';
import { BrowserModule } from '@angular/platform-browser';
import { FormsModule }   from '@angular/forms';
```

```
import { AppComponent }  from './app.component';
import { LoginComponent } from './login/login.component';

@NgModule({
  imports:      [ BrowserModule, FormsModule ],
  declarations: [ AppComponent, LoginComponent ],
  bootstrap:    [ AppComponent ]
})
export class AppModule { }
```

- **App Folder Structure**: The following represents the folder structure displaying the new folder that was created to manage the Login module. Pay attention to some of the best practices followed in terms of placing the files related to a new feature in a separate folder, login:

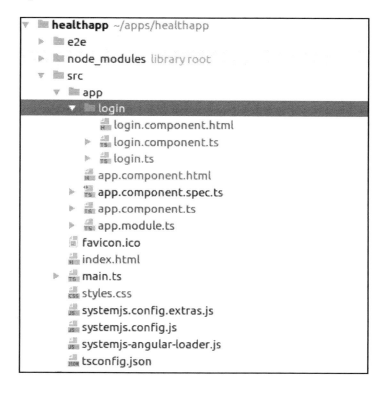

Figure 6: Folder structure representing Login module in different folder

Reactive forms

Angular provides two different techniques to create forms: *reactive* forms and *template-driven* forms. Reactive forms facilitate creating and managing angular forms and the related data in the following manner:

- They enable creating and managing form control objects in the component class, and binding them to the native form control elements in the component template. This is unlike the template-driven forms, where form controls are put into the component template, and bound to the data model properties in the component using directives such as ngModel.

- Data model values are pushed to the UI, and user-made changes are pulled back into the form control objects managed in the component class.

For reactive forms, you need to import ReactiveFormsModule in AppModule, just like template-driven forms that are part of FormsModule.

Before getting into the code related to reactive forms, let's quickly understand the key building blocks of reactive forms.

- AbstractControl: This is an abstract base class for three different control classes, such as FormControl, FormGroup, and FormArray. These are never instantiated directly.

- FormControl: This represents individual UI/HTML input elements. Form control is a class used to capture the values and events generated in the UI inputs. The following code represents a sample FormControl:

```
var email = new FormControl('', Validators.required);
```

- FormGroup: One or more AbstractControl interaces (such as FormControl, FormGroup, and so on) make up an instance of FormGroup. FormGroup is used to track the value and validity status of the AbstractControl interfaces. The following code represents a FormGroup:

```
const loginform = new FormGroup({
    email: new FormControl('', Validators.required),
    password:new FormControl('', Validators.required),
});
```

- FormArray: FormArray is an array of instances of AbstractControl interfaces. It aggregates the values of each child FormControl into an array. It calculates its status by reducing the statuses of its children. For example, if one of the controls in a FormArray is invalid, the entire array becomes invalid. The following represents a FormArray sample code:

- ```
const formArr = new FormArray({
    new FormControl(''),
    new FormControl(''),
});
```

Here are some of the key aspects of creating a reactive form:

- **Login Component**: Components, in reactive forms, need to import components such as FormBuilder, FormGroup, FormControl, and so on. Pay attention to the code within the constructor which invokes the createForm method, which results in the creation of form controls such as email and password using FormBuilder. The following snippet represents the component code when working with reactive forms:

```
import {Component} from '@angular/core';
import { FormBuilder, FormGroup, Validators } from
'@angular/forms';

import { Login } from './login';

@Component({
  selector: 'login',
  templateUrl: './login.component.html'
})
export class LoginComponent {
  formErrors = {
    'email': '',
    'password': ''
  };

  validationMessages = {
    'email': {
      'required': 'Email is required.'
    },
    'password': {
      'required': 'Password is required.'
    }
  };
```
```

```
loginForm: FormGroup;
login = new Login('', '');

constructor(private fb: FormBuilder) {
  this.createForm();
}

onSubmit() {
  console.log('Email Address: ' +
    this.loginForm.get('email').value + ', Password: ' +
    this.loginForm.get('password').value);
  this.login = this.loginForm.value;
  console.log('Email Address: ' + this.login.email + ',
            Password: ' + this.login.password);
}

createForm() {
  this.loginForm = this.fb.group({
    email: [this.login.email, Validators.required],
    password: [this.login.password, Validators.required],
  });

  this.loginForm.valueChanges
    .subscribe(data => this.onValueChanged(data));

  this.onValueChanged();
}

onValueChanged(data?: any) {
  if (!this.loginForm) {
    return;
  }
  const form = this.loginForm;

  for (const field in this.formErrors) {
    // clear previous error message (if any)
    this.formErrors[field] = '';
    const control = form.get(field);

    if (control && control.dirty && !control.valid) {
      const messages = this.validationMessages[field];
      for (const key in control.errors) {
        this.formErrors[field] += messages[key] + ' ';
      }
    }
  }
}
```

- **Login template**: The following code represents the login template. In the following code, the input element requires usage of the attribute `formControlName` for assigning a name to the input element. In cases where `FormGroup` is not used, one is required to use `[formControl]` to assign the name of the element. In addition, pay attention to the attribute, `[formGroup]`, which is required to be defined with a form tag element.

```
<div>
  <h2>Users Login</h2>
  <hr/>
  <form class="form-horizontal" (ngSubmit)="onSubmit()"
[formGroup]="loginForm" novalidate>
      <div class="form-group">
        <label for="email" class="col-sm-2 control-
label">Email</label>
        <div class="col-sm-6">
          <input type="email"
                 class="form-control"
                 id="email"
                 placeholder="Email"
                 formControlName="email"
                 required
          >
          <div *ngIf="formErrors.email" class="alert alert-
              danger">
            {{ formErrors.email }}
          </div>
        </div>
      </div>
      <div class="form-group">
        <label for="password" class="col-sm-2 control-
label">Password</label>
        <div class="col-sm-6">
          <input type="password"
                 class="form-control"
                 id="password"
                 placeholder="Password"
                 formControlName="password"
                 required
          >
          <div *ngIf="formErrors.password" class="alert alert-
              danger">
            {{ formErrors.password }}
          </div>
        </div>
      </div>
      <div class="form-group">
```

```
            <div class="col-sm-offset-2 col-sm-10">
              <button type="submit" class="btn btn-
                success">Submit</button>
            </div>
          </div>
          <div class="col-sm-offset-2 col-sm-10" style="padding-top:
            20px">
            <span><a href="">New User? Sign up</a></span>|
            <span><a href="">Forgot Password?</a></span>
          </div>
        </form>
      </div>
```

- **User-input validation**: For validation, one would need to write validation logic within the component in addition to placing the validation code in the template. This is unlike template-driven forms which are quite straightforward, and one is only required to place the validation logic in the template code. Code such as the following needs to be written within the template code for each UI input element requiring the validation:

```
    <!-- For input validation of email  -->
    <div *ngIf="formErrors.email" class="alert alert-danger">
     {{ formErrors.email }}
    </div>

    <!-- For input validation of password -->
    <div *ngIf="formErrors.password" class="alert alert-danger">
     {{ formErrors.password }}
    </div>
```

The following needs to be coded within the Component class to take care of the validation logic. One needs to define all the fields (formErrors) which need to be validated, validation messages (validationMessages) which need to be displayed in case of validation errors, and application logic which needs to be executed for value changes in the UI input elements (onValueChanged).

```
formErrors = {
 'email': '',
 'password': ''
};

validationMessages = {
 'email': {
   'required': 'Email is required.'
 },
 'password': {
```

```
    'required': 'Password is required.'
  }
};

onValueChanged(data?: any) {
  if (!this.loginForm) {
    return;
  }
  const form = this.loginForm;

  for (const field in this.formErrors) {
      // clear previous error message (if any)
      this.formErrors[field] = '';
      const control = form.get(field);

      if (control && control.dirty && !control.valid) {
        const messages = this.validationMessages[field];
        for (const key in control.errors) {
          this.formErrors[field] += messages[key] + ' ';
        }
      }
    }
  }
}
```

- **Changes to** AppModule: The following code represents the change in AppModule. Pay attention to the import of ReactiveFormsModule. In case of template-driven forms, FormsModule needs to be imported.

```
import { NgModule }         from '@angular/core';
import { BrowserModule } from '@angular/platform-browser';
import { ReactiveFormsModule }    from '@angular/forms';

import { AppComponent }  from './app.component';
import { LoginComponent } from './login/login.component';

@NgModule({
  imports:        [ BrowserModule, ReactiveFormsModule ],
  declarations: [ AppComponent, LoginComponent ],
  bootstrap:      [ AppComponent ]
})
export class AppModule { }
```

Pipes

Angular pipes allow us to transform data retrieved from the server in a format that is easy to read and understand. Pipes are very similar to filter in AngularJS. Pipes help to transfer data to more understandable or custom user-defined types. For instance, data such as date retrieved from the server looks like `Fri Mar 18 2003 00:00:00 GMT-0700 (Pacific Daylight Time)`. For an improved user experience, the date could be transformed to March 18, 2003 using an Angular pipe. The following represents a code sample shows the use of data pipe:

```
{{ creation_date | date }}
```

The following is a list of some of the built-in pipes in Angular:

- `DatePipe`
- `UpperCasePipe`
- `LowerCasePipe`
- `CurrencyPipe`
- `PercentPipe`

Here are some of the key features of pipes:

- **Parameterizing pipes**: A pipe can further be parametrized, based on arguments that are passed, to transform data in to the desired format. Take a look at the following code sample:

  ```
  {{ creation_date | date:"MM/dd/yy" }}
  ```

- **Chaining Pipes**: Pipes can be chained to do a series of data transformation. The following code shows an instance of chaining of pipes:

  ```
  {{ creation_date | date:"MM/dd/yy" | uppercase }}
  ```

- **Custom pipes**: Custom pipes are user-defined pipes. These are classes annotated with the `@Pipe` decorator, which passes the pipe metadata. A custom pipe is required to implement the `transform` method of the `PipeTransform` interface. The following represents the sample code for a custom pipe called **greet** which prints the greeting message to a user whose name is passed to the pipe:

  ```
  import { Pipe, PipeTransform } from '@angular/core';
  /*
   * Print Greeting Message
   * Usage:
  ```

```
 * name | greet
 * Example:
 * {{ "Calvin" | greet}}
 * prints: "Hello Calvin, How are you?"
 */
@Pipe({name: 'greet'})
export class GreetPipe implements PipeTransform {
  transform(name: string): string {
    return "Hello, " + name + "! How are you?";
  }
}
```

Directives

Angular supports three different types of directives. They are as follows:

- **Components**: Components are the most trivial type of directives. As described earlier in this chapter, components are classes annotated with the @Component decorator. They consist of metadata such as selector (name of the directive), the template or templateUrl (for the HTML syntax), and application logic used to process the form data. The following is a sample login directive of the type Component:

```
import {Component} from '@angular/core';

import { Login } from './login';

@Component({
  selector: 'login',
  template: `<div>
<form (ngSubmit)="onSubmit()" #loginForm="ngForm">
<input type="email"
            class="form-control"
            id="email"
            placeholder="Email"
            [(ngModel)]="model.email"
            name="email">
<input type="password"
            class="form-control"
            id="password"
            placeholder="Password"
            [(ngModel)]="model.password"
            name="password">
</form>
</div>`
```

```
  })
  export class LoginComponent {
    model = new Login('', '');
    onSubmit() {
      console.log('Email Address: ' + this.model.email + ', Password:
' + this.model.password);
    }
  }
```

- **Structural directives**: These are directives such as `ngFor` or `ngIf`, which change the structure of the view by changing the HTML layout by adding and removing the DOM elements. The following is a sample structure directive:

```
<p *ngIf="true">This is an example of structure directive. It leads
to inclusion of p in DOM</p>
```

- **Attribute directives**: These are directives which are used as attributes of the elements. They change the appearance or behavior of the elements, components, or other directives. For example, the`NgStyle` directives are attribute directives. The following is a sample code for the `NgStyle` directives:

```
<div [ngStyle]="currentStyles">
    This div is larger or smaller.
</div>
```

Structural directives

Structural directives change the HTML layout or, rather, change the DOM's structure by adding, removing, or manipulating the DOM elements. These directives are applied to the host element, and look like following:

```
<ul>
   <li *ngFor="let member of team">{{member.name}}</li>
</ul>
```

Structural directives are preceded by an asterisk (*). The simplest of the structural directives is `ngIf`. Here is an example:

```
<div *ngIf="true">
    This sentence is in the DOM.
</div>
<div *ngIf="false">
    This sentence is not in the DOM.
</div>
```

Attribute directives

As defined earlier, attribute directives change the appearance or behavior of an element, component, or another directive. The following is an example of a trivial attribute directive setting the custom style for the element:

```
<div myStyle>Hello World!</div>
```

The next code snippet is an example of the aforementioned attribute directive, `myStyle`. Pay attention to the following in the code:

- The Decorator `@Directive` is used.
- `@Directive` is passed metadata with the name of the directive assigned using the selector attribute. Pay attention to [,] used with the name.
- The class consists of logic for the directive.

```
import { Directive, ElementRef, Input } from '@angular/core';

@Directive({ selector: '[myStyle]' })
export class MyStyleDirective {
    constructor(el: ElementRef) {
        el.nativeElement.style.width = '50%';
        el.nativeElement.style.backgroundColor = 'green';
        el.nativeElement.style.border = '1px';
        el.nativeElement.style.borderColor = 'red';
    }
}
```

Server communication

Angular enables communication between the browser and server apps using the HTTP library, which supports both XHR and JSONP APIs. The following steps need to be taken to achieve server communication:

- Import HTTP-related modules/components in `AppModule`, as follows:

```
import { NgModule } from '@angular/core';
import { BrowserModule } from '@angular/platform-browser';
import { ReactiveFormsModule } from '@angular/forms';
import { HttpModule, JsonpModule } from '@angular/http';

import { AppComponent } from './app.component';
import { LoginComponent } from './rlogin/login.component';
```

```
@NgModule({
  imports: [ BrowserModule, ReactiveFormsModule, HttpModule,
JsonpModule ],
    declarations: [ AppComponent, LoginComponent ],
    bootstrap: [ AppComponent ]
})
  export class AppModule { }
```

- Create a service which will be delegated tasks by the components to invoke one or more APIs on the server. As a best practice, components should be injected with the appropriate service, and these services should be delegated with tasks to process the data using server APIs. The following set of code represents these concepts:

```
// LoginService
//
import { Injectable } from '@angular/core';
import { Http, Response } from '@angular/http';

import { Observable } from 'rxjs/Observable';
import 'rxjs/add/operator/catch';
import 'rxjs/add/operator/map';

import { Login } from './login';

@Injectable()
export class LoginService {
  private loginUrl = 'http://localhost:8080/login';
  // URL to web API

  constructor (private http: Http) {}

  login(data: Object): Observable<User> {
    let headers = new Headers({ 'Content-Type':
      'application/json' });
    let options = new RequestOptions({ headers: headers });

    return this.http.post(this.loginUrl, data, options)
                 .map(this.extractData)
                 .catch(this.handleError);
  }

  private extractData(res: Response) {
    let body = res.json();
    return body.data || { };
  }
```

```
      private handleError (error: Response | any) {
        let errMsg: string;
        if (error instanceof Response) {
          const body = error.json() || '';
          const err = body.error || JSON.stringify(body);
          errMsg = `${error.status} - ${error.statusText || ''}
${err}`;
        } else {
          errMsg = error.message ? error.message :
          error.toString();
        }
        console.error(errMsg);
        return Observable.throw(errMsg);
      }
    }
```

The following code demonstrates the injection of service, LoginService, in the component, LoginComponent. Pay attention to how the instance of login Service is delegated with the task of processing users' login attempts:

```
export class LoginComponent {
    constructor (private loginService: LoginService) {}

    login() {
        this.loginService.login(email, password)
                    .subscribe(
                        user => this.user = user,
                        error => this.errorMessage = <any>error);
    }
}
```

- Pay attention to some of the following in the preceding code:
  - Angular Http service is injected into the LoginService constructor:

    ```
    constructor (private http: Http) {}
    ```

  - The post method on the Http service is invoked to send the login data to the server. Other methods supported are get, put, delete, options, and so on.

    ```
    let headers = new Headers({ 'Content-Type': 'application/json' });
    let options = new RequestOptions({ headers: headers });

    this.http.post(this.loginUrl, data, options)
      .map(this.extractData)
    ```

```
.catch(this.handleError);
```

- Conceptually, the method invoked within the `Service` returns Observable objects. Observables are explained in the later chapters. These instances of Observables send out data and events information as they occur. Components wanting to listen to these events need to subscribe to these Observable objects. The following code shows how to subscribe to an Observable:

```
this.loginService.login(email, password)
  .subscribe( user => this.user = user,
              error => this.errorMessage = <any>error);
```

Bootstrapping an Angular app

Every Angular app has, at least, one Angular module which is bootstrapped to launch the application. The module is also called as **root module** and it is placed in the root folder of the app. The root module is used to define all the modules and components which fit in together to build the app. The conventional name for this module is `AppModule`. The following is a sample code for `AppModule`, that is used to bootstrap the app with reactive forms.

```
import { NgModule }        from '@angular/core';
import { BrowserModule } from '@angular/platform-browser';
import { ReactiveFormsModule }   from '@angular/forms';

import { AppComponent }  from './app.component';
import { LoginComponent } from './rlogin/login.component';

@NgModule({
  imports:      [ BrowserModule, ReactiveFormsModule ],
  declarations: [ AppComponent, LoginComponent ],
  bootstrap:    [ AppComponent ]
})
export class AppModule { }
```

Pay attention to some of the following points in the preceding code:

- `@NgModule` decorator: This takes the metadata object, which defines how angular app can be bootstrapped using the following:
    - `imports`: Includes the dependent modules representing the different features which are required to run the app
    - `declarations`: Includes declaration for one or more components which belong to `AppModule`.
- `bootstrap`: Defines the `root` component that Angular creates and inserts in the `index.html` page:
    - `AppModule`: This is the class definition

As mentioned earlier, an Angular app requires a module, decorated with `@NgModule`, to bootstrap. The recommended way to bootstrap is to place following code in a file, namely, main.ts. The code given below creates a browser platform dynamic **Just-in-Time** (**JIT**) compilation and bootstraps the `AppModule`:

```
import { platformBrowserDynamic } from '@angular/platform-browser-
    dynamic';

import { AppModule } from './app/app.module';

platformBrowserDynamic().bootstrapModule(AppModule);
```

Best practices

The following are some of the best practices which one can adopt for developing Angular apps:

- Apply the single responsibility principle:
    - Write one thing such as component, directive, service, and module per file
    - Write small functions with a function doing just one thing
- Naming Convention:
    - Use upper camel case for class names and interfaces. For example, `AppComponent`, `AppModule`.
    - Use lower camel case for naming properties and methods.
    - Avoid using underscore as a prefix for naming methods and properties.

- Match the class names with the file names in the following manner: `AppComponent` - `app.component.ts`, `BigAppComponent` - `big-app.component.ts`, `AppModule` - `app.module.ts`, `AppDirective` - `app.directive.ts`, `AppService` - `app.service.ts`
- Use custom prefixes for components and directives selectors.
- **Bootstraping**: Put bootstraping logic in a file named `main.ts`
  - **Use Data Services**: One should use data services for doing data operations such as making XHR calls, processing data with local storage, and doing remote data operations.

- **Folder structure**
  - All the app's code goes within the top-level `src` folder.
  - Put each component, service, piped directive, and module is in its own file.
  - With tiny apps having not more than five to six files, all files can be put in one folder such as `src/app`.
  - For larger apps, do the following within the `src/app` folder:
    - **A folder per component**: Consider creating a folder per component which consists files related to that component including `*.ts`, `*.html`, `*.css`, `*.spec.ts` files.
    - **A folder per feature module**: Consider creating a folder per module. The module folder will have each of components within its own folders, and files such as module and routing file.
  - **A folder for core feature module**: Consider creating a folder such as `core` for housing components, services, directives, and so on, which are used across different feature modules.
  - **A folder for shared feature module**: Consider creating a folder named `shared` for housing services which are used across different modules.

- Create an angular module, namely, the `root` module within `src/app`.
  - **Components as elements**: Consider creating an element selector for components as opposed to attributes or class selector.
  - **Attributes directives**: Use attributes directives in places where there is only presentation logic involved and no template.
  - Extract templates and styles to their own files.

Summary

In this chapter, we learned about the architectural building blocks of Angular, TypeScript fundamentals, differences between Angular and earlier versions, form handling concepts, pipes concepts, and some of the best practices you need to adopt while developing Angular apps. In the next chapter, we will learn how to create an SPA using Angular.

7
Creating SPA with Angular and Spring 5

Navigating through different pages/views in an effective manner is the most important aspect of creating a single page app (SPA). This is where routing comes into picture. Angular provides different concepts in relation to implementing routing in order to achieve navigation from one view to another. In this chapter, we will learn concepts such as the following to create single page applications (SPAs) using Angular and Spring 5:

- Introduction to routing
- Configuring route definitions
- RouterLink for navigation
- Route Guards for access control
- Routing configuration design patterns
- Creating a single page app
- Debugging Angular app

Introduction to routing

The routing concept in relation to web applications represents the ability to do some of the following:

- Navigate to different pages, for example, from one page to another, or, from one view to another by clicking on a URL
- Navigate back and forward through the history of pages using the back and forward button of the browser

The Angular router helps to achieve the earlier mentioned capability of moving from one view to another while users work through the application. When the browser's URL changes, the **router** looks for a corresponding **route** from which it can determine the component to display. The following are some key aspects which need to be taken care of while working with the Angular router:

- Add a base element in `index.html`. This instructs Angular Router to create navigation URLs for different views. The following code can be found within the `<head>` tag in `index.html`. While moving the app to production, the base href need to be set to appropriate path such as "/" (instead of "./") or any other context path. For example, if angular app is available at path, `http://www.somewebsite.com/my/app/`, the `base href` needs to be set to `/my/app/`.

  ```
  <base href="./">
  ```

- Create route definitions in the appropriate routing module. The route definitions can be created within AppModule, root module, as a separate routing module at the root level, or as a routing module specific to each of the feature modules. The details on different techniques based on which route definitions can be created has been detailed in one of the later sections.
- In case route definitions are defined as a separate module, import the routing module in the *root* module, as appropriate, either in `AppModule` or in the feature module. This is demonstrated in later this chapter.

Configuring Route definitions

Route definitions represent association of one or more URL paths to the respective components. Each of these route definitions can also be termed as a *route*. Route definitions or routes, are stored in an array and loaded using `Router.forRoot` or `Router.forChild` API depending upon whether routes are defined at *root level* or submodule/feature module level. When the users click on the hyperlink (URL), the router looks for the corresponding route, and based on appropriate path matching strategy (prefix by default) determines the component to display. The following are the key steps to configure route definitions:

- Define route definitions in the form of an array of routes. The following code represents route definitions where no parameters are passed (such as new user registration and user login), and one where parameters are passed (such as to get information for doctors, patients, hospitals, and so on).

  Note that the path will have no leading slashes (/). The Router parses each of these route definitions, and creates the final URLs. The `data` attribute in the route definition can be used to store static data such as page title, and so on.

```
const appRoutes: Routes = [

{ path: 'register', component: UserRegistrationComponent, data:
{title: 'New User Registration'} },
{ path: 'forgotpassword', component: ForgotPasswordComponent,
data: {title: 'Forgot Password'} },
{ path: 'login', component: LoginComponent, data: { title:
      'User Login' }   },

{ path: 'doctor/:id', component: DoctorComponent },
{ path: 'patient/:id', component: PatientComponent },
{ path: 'hospital/:id', component: HospitalComponent },

{ path: 'index', component: HomeComponent },
{ path: '', redirectTo: '/index', pathMatch: 'full' },

{ path: '**', component: PageNotFoundComponent }

];
```

Note some of the following points in the preceding code:

- The path has no leading slashes (/). The Router parses each of these route definitions and create final URLs.
- The `data` attribute in the route definition can be used to store static data, such as page title, and so on.

- The order of the route definitions matters. Thus, it is recommended to put more-specific routes up the order than the less-specific routes.
- The `redirectTo` attribute used to redirect the request to the appropriate based route on the path matching strategy used for URL matching. In the preceding example, URL matching technique is defined using another attribute such as `pathMatch`.
- The `pathMatch` attribute can take two values. One is `full` and the other one is `prefix`. By default, the path matching strategy is `prefix`. In the following example, let's learn the aspects of path matching. Given that default path matching strategy is prefix, the router will check the array of routes to find whether route starts with the route's path. Thus, for a path such as `/doctor/prediatrician`, it will check whether the route starts with `doctor`. In the following given case, this turns out to be true. The router, thus, continues matching the path by looking at the child routes. In the following given case, the matching child route `:speciality` is found. Thus, the `DoctorListComponent` component is displayed:

```
const docRoutes: Routes = [
  {
    path: 'doctor',
    component: DocComponent,
    children: [
      {
        path: '',
        children: [
          {
            path: 'home',
            component: DocHomeComponent,
          },
          {
            path: '',
            component: DoctorListComponent,
          },
          {
            path: ':speciality',
            component: DoctorListComponent,
          },
        ],
      }
    ]
  }
];
```

The pathMatch attribute, when set as full, tries to match the path with whatever is left in the URL. Thus, when matching for empty path such as ' ', the pathMatch attribute will look to match full URL such as /. This is important for redirects.

- Given the rules followed in relation to ordering of route definitions, the route with a wildcard is defined in the end such that this route gets selected only when no other routes are matched before it.
- Configure the Router via the RouterModule.forRoot API when defining routing at the root level. The forRoot API creates a module which consists of all the directives, the given routes, and the router service itself. Note that an Angular application has one singleton instance of the Router service. The following code sample represents usage of forRoot API:

```
@NgModule({
  imports: [
    RouterModule.forRoot(appRoutes)
  ],
  exports: [
    RouterModule
  ]
})
export class AppRoutingModule {}
```

- Configure the Router via the RouterModule.forChild API for submodules or lazy-loaded submodules. The forChild API results in the creation of a module which contains all directives and the given routes, but does not include the router service. In the section, *Routing Configuration Design Patterns*, one of the techniques for defining route definitions is to define routing module for each of the feature modules. This is where forChild API will be used. The following is a code sample:

```
@NgModule({
  imports: [
    RouterModule.forChild(docRoutes)
  ],
  exports: [
    RouterModule
  ]
})
export class DocRoutingModule { }
```

- **Router outlet**: Place the `router-outlet` tag appropriately on the page or view where you want the Router to render the component associated with the URL path. The following is the code related to the router outlet, which is placed in the `app.component.html`:

```
<div class="container">
  <h1>HealthApp - A Platform for Doctors & Patients</h1>
  <hr/>
  <div>
    This is a platform bringing together Doctors and Patients
    and helping them communicate, collaborate.
  </div>
  <router-outlet></router-outlet>
</div>
```

RouterLink for navigation

In this section, we will learn about the different techniques used for navigating route definitions having URL paths such as the following:

- Fixed or static navigation paths such as `/doctors` and `/hospitals`
- Dynamic navigation paths such as `/doctors/PEDIATRICIAN` or, rather, `/doctors/:specialitycode`, where the specialty code is the dynamic parameter

The following are the two key concepts which need to be understood in relation to navigating fixed or dynamic navigation paths, as mentioned earlier:

- `RouterLink`
- `ActivatedRoute`

What is RouterLink?

Once the route definitions have been configured, and the router outlet is defined to render the routes, the next requisite step is to determine a way to navigate to these routes. This is where `RouterLink` comes into the picture.

`RouterLink` is a directive which is used with the anchor tag. It helps in navigating to different views based on the route paths (both, fixed and dynamic) configured as part of the route definitions in `AppModule` (`app.module.ts`). The following is a sample code which represents an anchor tag with attribute bindings for `routerLink` representing the route definitions having both fixed (`/login` and `/register`) and dynamic URL paths (`doctors/PHYSICIAN`). Anchor tags are then followed by the `router-outlet` directive, where the components associated with the route definitions are rendered:

```
<a routerLink="/login" routerLinkActive="active">Login</a>
<a routerLink="/register" routerLinkActive="active">Signup</a>
<a routerLink="/doctors/PHYSICAN" routerLinkActive="active">
    Doctors - Physician</a>
<router-outlet></router-outlet>
```

In the preceding code, note the following:

- The `routerLink` directive is assigned a string representing the URL paths in the related route definitions.
- The `routerLinkActive` directive helps distinguish the anchor for the currently selected `active` route. Simply speaking, it basically adds a CSS class for the active route for highlighting purposes.

What is ActivatedRoute?

As one navigates through URLs, the router builds a tree of objects called `ActivatedRoute`. This tree of objects represents the current state of the router, the details of which can be retrieved from the `RouterState` object. In other words, the `RouterState` object representing the current state of navigation consists of a tree of `ActivatedRoute` objects. One could navigate to the parent, child, or sibling routes by invoking methods on this `ActivatedRoute` object. The `RouterState` object can be retrieved using `routerState` property of the router service. Note that the router service is the singleton service that every Angular application has.

`ActivatedRoute` is a router service which, once injected into the component, can be used to retrieve information such as route URL paths, required or optional parameters, static data, resolve data, query parameters, and so on. For route definitions with dynamic navigation paths such as `/doctor/pediatrician` or `/doctor/cardiologist`, this service will be used to obtain the parameters from the navigation path.

The following is required to be done when using the `ActivatedRoute` service for navigating through dynamic paths:

- Import services such as `Router`, `ActivatedRoute`, and `ParamMap` from the router package, as follows:

```
import { Router, ActivatedRoute, ParamMap }    from
'@angular/router';
```

- Import an operator such as `switchMap`, as it will be used to process the observable route parameters, like this:

```
import 'rxjs/add/operator/switchMap';
```

- Inject services such as `Router` and `ActivatedRoute` in the component's constructor, as follows:

```
constructor (private router: Router,
             private route: ActivatedRoute,
             private doctorService: DoctorService) {
}
```

- Within `ngOnInit`, use the `ActivatedRoute` service to get the parameter, and invoke the appropriate delegate service to invoke the remote (server) API. In the following code, note that `DoctorService` instance's `getDoctorsBySpeciality` API is invoked with the specialty code retrieved from `ParamMap`. As `ngOnInit` is instantiated only once, the observable `ParamMap` instance, `paramMap`, is used to detect the change in the parameters and pass the appropriate value to the service API as shown here:

```
ngOnInit() {
    this.route.paramMap.switchMap((params: ParamMap) =>
    this.doctorService.getDoctorsBySpeciality
    (params.get('speciality')))
    .subscribe(doctors => this.doctors = doctors,
    error =>  this.errorMessage = <any>error);
}
```

- The component code will look like the following, taking all of the aforementioned conditions into consideration:

```
import {Component, OnInit} from '@angular/core';
import {Doctor} from './doctor';
import { DoctorService } from './doctor.service';
import { Router, ActivatedRoute, ParamMap }    from
```

```
        '@angular/router';
import 'rxjs/add/operator/switchMap';

@Component({
  selector: 'doctor-list',
  templateUrl: './doctor-list.component.html'
})
export class DoctorListComponent  implements OnInit {

  doctors: Doctor[];
  errorMessage: string;

  constructor (private doctorService: DoctorService, private
    router: Router, private route: ActivatedRoute) {}

  ngOnInit() {
      this.route.paramMap
      .switchMap((params: ParamMap) =>
      this.doctorService.getDoctorsBySpeciality
          (params.get('speciality')))
      .subscribe(doctors => this.doctors = doctors,
      error =>  this.errorMessage = <any>error);
  }
}
```

Route Guards for access control

Route Guards help guard access to one or more server resources (features, functionality, and data). Routes which are guarded will require the user to authenticate and get authorized before he/she can get access to the features/functionality being rendered as one or more components. One or more guards can be applied at any route level. Route Guards are supported using the following interfaces:

- CanActivate: This guards navigation to a route. The CanActivate interface can be used to handle scenarios such as allowing users to access the resources only after login-based authentication or role-based permissions. Users can be blocked or allowed limited access to resources until he/she has a sufficient role, and he/she has been authenticated. Anonymous users will be redirected to the login page if they try to access the access-controlled resources.

- `CanActivateChild`: This guards navigation to a child route. As with the `CanActivate` interface, the `CanActivateChild` interface is also used to handle authentication/authorization-related scenarios. This guard is activated after the parent route has been mediated using the `CanActivate` guard.
- `CanDeactivate`: This mediates navigation away from the route. In the scenarios where the user navigates to different routes, and there is a need to save the data, the `CanDeactivate` interface is used.
- `Resolve`: This processes data retrieval before route activation. In scenarios where one or more datasets need to be prefetched before users navigate to the route, the `Resolve` interface is used. In other words, the rendering of the component can be delayed until all the required data is prefetched.
- `CanLoad`: This guards navigation to a feature module which is loaded asynchronously.

Routing configuration design patterns

Routing configuration can be defined based on different strategies depending upon the complexity of the application. If this is a small application, route definitions can be defined either in root module such as `AppModule` (`app.module.ts`) or another routing module (such as `app-routing.module.ts`) at the root level which is later imported in `AppModule`. If it is a complex or an enterprise app having several features and each of those features has its route definitions, it is recommended to define routing at feature module level.

In this section, we will learn about some of the following techniques for routing:

- Routing within `AppModule`
- Routing as a separate module at the app root level
- Routing within feature modules

Routing within AppModule

The most trivial way of configuring route definitions is to create route definitions within the AppModule file, for example, app.module.ts. This technique may only seem to be OK for learning purposes. When creating complex apps, this is not the recommended way. The following is what needs to be created within app.module.ts:

- Import the routing library such as RouterModule and Routes, as follows:

```
import { RouterModule, Routes }   from '@angular/router';
```

- Create route definitions such as the following. Be sure to include route definitions for handling invalid routes, using components such as PageNotFoundComponent, and the default route to be used when the app launches with an empty path.

```
const appRoutes: Routes = [
    { path: 'register', component: UserRegistrationComponent,
data: {title: 'New User Registration'} },
    { path: 'forgotpassword', component: ForgotPasswordComponent,
data: {title: 'Forgot Password'} },
    { path: 'login', component: LoginComponent, data: {
      title: 'User Login' }   },

    { path: 'doctors', component: DoctorListComponent,     data:
    { title: 'Doctors Information' }   },
    { path: 'doctors/:speciality', component:
    DoctorListComponent, data: { title: 'Doctors Information' }   },

    { path: 'index', component: HomeComponent },
    { path: '', redirectTo: 'index', pathMatch: 'full' },

    { path: '**', component: PageNotFoundComponent }
];
```

- Configure the router module with `RouterModule.forRoot`, as follows:

```
@NgModule({
    imports: [..., RouterModule.forRoot(appRoutes),],
    declarations: [ AppComponent, ...],
    providers: [ DoctorService,...],
    bootstrap:    [ AppComponent ]
})
export class AppModule { }
```

Routing as a separate module at the app root level

As an app starts getting complex, one needs to use routing concepts such as child routes, guards, resolvers, and so on. Defining complex routing definitions in `AppModule` would end up mixing different application concerns. In such scenarios, it is recommended to create a route definition in its own module. This module can be termed as *routing module*. This follows the separation of concerns design pattern in a sense that all the routing related concerns are handled as part of the routing module. The following needs to be done to define a routing module:

- Create a separate file at the root level, for example, `app-routing.module.ts`
- Take out routing-related information such as the following from the `AppModule` file, and place them in `app-routing.module.ts`:
    - Routing library
    - Routing definitions
    - `RouterModule.forRoot` configuration
- The following is the sample code for `app-routing.module.ts` representing the aforementioned data. Make a note of `RouterModule.forRoot` API for registering top-level application routes. Angular mandates `RouterModule.forRoot` to be called in root `AppRoutingModule` or `AppModule` if this is where routes are defined. In any other module, it will `RouterModule.forChild` API which will be called to register the routes specific to feature modules.

```
import { NgModule } from '@angular/core';
import { RouterModule, Routes }  from '@angular/router';

import { HomeComponent }  from './home.component';
import { LoginComponent } from './login/login.component';
```

```
import { UserRegistrationComponent } from './login/user-
       registration.component';
import { ForgotPasswordComponent } from './login/forgot-
       password.component';
import { PageNotFoundComponent } from './utils/page-not-
       found.component';
import { DoctorListComponent } from './doctor/doctor-
       list.component';

const appRoutes: Routes = [
    { path: 'register', component: UserRegistrationComponent,
data: {title: 'New User Registration'} },
    { path: 'forgotpassword', component: ForgotPasswordComponent,
data: {title: 'Forgot Password'} },
    { path: 'login', component: LoginComponent,      data: {
      title: 'User Login' }    },

    { path: 'doctors', component: DoctorListComponent,       data:
    { title: 'Doctors Information' }    },
    { path: 'doctors/:speciality', component:
  DoctorListComponent, data: { title: 'Doctors Information' }    },

    { path: 'index', component: HomeComponent },
    { path: '',    redirectTo: '/index', pathMatch: 'full' },

    { path: '**', component: PageNotFoundComponent }
];

@NgModule({
  imports: [
    RouterModule.forRoot(appRoutes)
  ],
  exports: [
    RouterModule
  ]
})
export class AppRoutingModule {}
```

- Include `AppRoutingModule` in the `AppModule` file, `app.module.ts` by importing it from `app-routing.module.ts`, and, also import it in the `imports` array. The following is the sample code for `AppModule`:

```
import { NgModule } from '@angular/core';
import { BrowserModule } from '@angular/platform-browser';

import { AppComponent } from './app.component';
import { AppRoutingModule } from './app-routing.module';
```

```
import { HomeComponent }  from './home.component';
import { LoginComponent } from './login/login.component';
import { UserRegistrationComponent } from './login/user-
registration.component';
import { ForgotPasswordComponent } from './login/forgot-
password.component';
import { PageNotFoundComponent } from './utils/page-not-
found.component';
import { DoctorListComponent } from './doctor/doctor-
list.component';
import { DoctorService } from './doctor/doctor.service';

@NgModule({
  imports:[ BrowserModule, FormsModule,
    AppRoutingModule, HttpModule, JsonpModule ],
  declarations: [ AppComponent, LoginComponent,
    UserRegistrationComponent, ForgotPasswordComponent,
    PageNotFoundComponent, HomeComponent, DoctorListComponent],
  providers: [ DoctorService ],
  bootstrap: [ AppComponent ]
})
export class AppModule { }
```

Routing within feature modules

For greater modularity, it is often recommended to create modules representing different features. These modules can also be termed as feature modules. A feature module can have its own root component, router outlet, and child routes. The following needs to be done to create a self-contained feature module consisting of its own routing module:

- Create a root module (doc-app.module.ts) just like AppModule. As with AppModule, this module will have a @NgModule decorator with the metadata representing imports, declarations, providers, and so on.

```
import { NgModule }        from '@angular/core';
import { BrowserModule } from '@angular/platform-browser';
import { FormsModule }     from '@angular/forms';
import { HttpModule, JsonpModule } from '@angular/http';

import { DoctorListComponent }    from './doctor-
list.component';
import { DocAppComponent } from './doc-app.component';

import { DoctorService } from './doctor.service';
```

```
import { DocAppRoutingModule } from './doc-app-routing.module';

@NgModule({
  imports: [
    BrowserModule, FormsModule, HttpModule, JsonpModule,
DocAppRoutingModule
  ],
  declarations: [
    DoctorListComponent, DocAppComponent
  ],
  providers: [ DoctorService ]
})
export class DocAppModule {}
```

- Create a root component (doc-app.component.ts) just like AppComponent. This component will act as a shell for feature management. This component will primarily consist of a router-outlet directive used to render the feature components. The following code sample represents the same:

```
import { Component } from '@angular/core';

@Component({
  template: `
    <router-outlet></router-outlet>
  `
})
export class DocAppComponent { }
```

- Create a routing module (doc-app-routing.module.ts) consisting of route definitions. Make a note of RouterModule.forChild API, which is used to register the routes related to the feature modules.

```
import { NgModule }              from '@angular/core';
import { RouterModule, Routes } from '@angular/router';

import { DocAppComponent }        from './doc-app.component';
import { DoctorListComponent }    from './doctor-
  list.component';

const docAppRoutes: Routes = [
  {
    path: 'doctors', component: DocAppComponent,
    children: [
      {
        path: '',
        component: DoctorListComponent,
      },
```

```
        {
          path: ':speciality',
          component: DoctorListComponent,
        }
      ]
    }
];

@NgModule({
  imports: [
    RouterModule.forChild(docAppRoutes)
  ],
  exports: [
    RouterModule
  ]
})
export class DocAppRoutingModule { }
```

- Import the module in `AppModule` (`app.module.ts`). Pay attention to the fact that routing at the app level is extracted in `app-routing.module.ts`, and routing for a feature module is made part of `DocAppModule`. Importing `DocAppModule` will ensure that `DocAppRoutingModule` is appropriately imported and used to navigate the route definitions related to the `Doctor` feature.

```
import { NgModule }       from '@angular/core';
import { BrowserModule } from '@angular/platform-browser';
import { FormsModule }    from '@angular/forms';
import { HttpModule, JsonpModule } from '@angular/http';

import { AppComponent }  from './app.component';
import { AppRoutingModule } from './app-routing.module';

import { HomeComponent }  from './home.component';
import { LoginComponent } from './login/login.component';
import { UserRegistrationComponent } from './login/user-
registration.component';
import { ForgotPasswordComponent } from './login/forgot-
password.component';
import { PageNotFoundComponent } from './utils/page-not-
found.component';

import { DocAppModule } from './doctor/doc-app.module';

@NgModule({
  imports: [ BrowserModule, FormsModule, DocAppModule,
             AppRoutingModule, HttpModule, JsonpModule ],
```

```
  declarations: [ AppComponent, LoginComponent,
                  UserRegistrationComponent,
                  ForgotPasswordComponent,
                  PageNotFoundComponent, HomeComponent],
  bootstrap:     [ AppComponent ]
})
export class AppModule { }
```

Creating a single page app (SPA)

In this section, we will learn about some best practices which can be used to create a single page app. Some of them are listed next:

- Keep the root module and root component as lean as possible. Program routing as a separate module and import the same in AppModule.
- Design and develop features as separate modules.
- Use route guards to provide controlled access to one or more components.

Lean root module

It is recommended to keep the top-level root module, routing module, and the root/shell component as lean as possible. This, essentially, means some of the following:

- The root module should import the root-level routing module, root components, and feature modules. The following code represents the same. Make a note of the feature modules, such as DocModule, AuthModule, and AppRoutingModule:

```
import { NgModule }        from '@angular/core';
import { BrowserModule }  from '@angular/platform-browser';
import { FormsModule }     from '@angular/forms';
import { HttpModule, JsonpModule } from '@angular/http';

import { AppComponent }   from './app.component';
import { AppRoutingModule } from './app-routing.module';

import { HomeComponent }  from './home.component';
import { PageNotFoundComponent } from './utils/page-not-
found.component';

import { DocModule } from './doctor/doc.module';
import { AuthModule } from './auth/auth.module';
```

```
@NgModule({
  imports: [ BrowserModule, FormsModule, DocModule, AuthModule,
             AppRoutingModule, HttpModule, JsonpModule ],
  declarations: [ AppComponent, PageNotFoundComponent,
                  HomeComponent],
  bootstrap:    [ AppComponent ]
})
export class AppModule { }
```

- The root/shell component should primarily be used for bootstrapping the app. It also renders the template consisting of the navigation links to access the feature modules, and the router outlet to render the components specified in the routing module. The following code represents the same:

```
import {Component} from '@angular/core';

@Component({
  selector: 'my-app',
  templateUrl: './app.component.html',
})
export class AppComponent {
}
```

The following is the code sample of `app.component.html`. Make a note of the `<router-outlet>` element:

```
<div class="container">
  <h3><a routerLink="/"
routerLinkActive="active"><strong>+{{appName}}</strong></a></h3>
  <nav class="navbar navbar-default navbar-static-top">
    <div class="container-fluid">
      <div class="navbar-header">
        <button type="button" class="navbar-toggle collapsed" data-
toggle="collapse" data-target="#bs-example-navbar-collapse-1" aria-
expanded="false">
          <span class="sr-only">Toggle navigation</span>
          <span class="icon-bar"></span>
          <span class="icon-bar"></span>
          <span class="icon-bar"></span>
        </button>
      </div>

      <div class="collapse navbar-collapse" id="bs-example-navbar-
collapse-1">
        <ul class="nav navbar-nav">
          <li class="dropdown active">
            <a href="#" class="dropdown-toggle" data-toggle="dropdown"
```

```
role="button" aria-haspopup="true" aria-expanded="false">Services <span
class="caret"></span></a>
                <ul class="dropdown-menu">
                  <li><a  routerLink="/doctor"
routerLinkActive="active">Doctors</a></li>
                  <li role="separator" class="divider"></li>
                  <li><a  routerLink="/hospital"
routerLinkActive="active">Hospitals</a></li>
                </ul>
              </li>
            </ul>
            <form class="navbar-form navbar-left">
              <div class="form-group">
                <input type="text" class="form-control" placeholder="Search
Doctors">
              </div>
              <button type="submit" class="btn btn-info">Go</button>
            </form>
            <ul class="nav navbar-nav navbar-right">
              <li><a routerLink="/auth/login" routerLinkActive="active"
*ngIf="isLoggedIn === false">Login</a></li>
              <li><a routerLink="/auth/register" routerLinkActive="active"
*ngIf="isLoggedIn === false">Signup</a></li>
              <li><a routerLink="/auth/editprofile" routerLinkActive="active"
*ngIf="isLoggedIn === true">My Profile</a></li>
              <li><a routerLink="/auth/logout" routerLinkActive="active"
*ngIf="isLoggedIn === true"  (click)="onLogout()">Logout</a></li>
            </ul>
        </div>
      </div>
    </nav>
  <router-outlet></router-outlet>
</div>
```

- The routing module should, primarily, consist of route definitions for the default page, page not found, and so on. The following code represents the top-level routing module, which is found at the `/src/app` level:

```
import { NgModule }                from '@angular/core';
import { RouterModule, Routes }    from '@angular/router';

import { HomeComponent }  from './home.component';
import { PageNotFoundComponent } from './utils/page-not-
found.component';


const appRoutes: Routes = [
  { path: 'index', component: HomeComponent },
```

```
    { path: '',    redirectTo: '/index', pathMatch: 'full' },
    { path: '**', component: PageNotFoundComponent }
];

@NgModule({
  imports: [
    RouterModule.forRoot(
      appRoutes, { enableTracing: true }
    )
  ],
  exports: [
    RouterModule
  ]
})
export class AppRoutingModule {}
```

Feature-specific functionality should be handled using separate modules, the details of which are provided in the next section.

Features as separate modules

The most important aspect of creating single page apps (SPAs) is architecting and designing different features as different modules. The feature modules will comprise of the following:

- **Root module**: Each feature will have its own module which can also be termed as a root module of the feature. The feature's root module will be used to define the routing module, components, providers, and so on, specific to the features.
- **Root or shell component**: The feature module will comprise the root component. This will be a top-level component, as with the AppComponent in AppModule. It will, primarily, be used to place a router-outlet directive, using which the routes will be rendered.
- **Routing module**: This will define the route configurations and related components, which would be rendered for different routes.
- **Services**: One or more services will be used for delegating tasks to retrieve the data from the server, or write data to the server.
- **Components**: Components represent the view.

Based on earlier recommendations, let's explore how HealthApp can be designed and developed as a single page app. The following two features will be considered:

- The feature related to signup, login, and forgot password. Let's name this `Auth` module.
- The `Doctor` feature, which is related to functionalities such as retrieving doctors' information and creating/updating/deleting one or more doctors. Let's name this `Doctor` module.

Auth module

`Auth` module is used to provide functionality for new user signup, login, and forgot password. This is how the folder structure of this module would look:

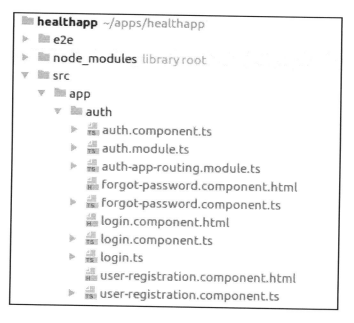

Figure 1. Auth Feature module

The following represent the modules and components of this module:

- **Root module/component**
  - `auth.module.ts`: This represents the root module named `AuthModule`. Note the import of the root component, routing module, and components in the following:

```
import { NgModule }      from '@angular/core';
import { CommonModule } from '@angular/common';
import { FormsModule }   from '@angular/forms';

import { AuthComponent } from './auth.component';

import { LoginComponent } from './login.component';
import { UserRegistrationComponent } from './user-
registration.component';
import { ForgotPasswordComponent } from './forgot-
password.component';

import {  AuthRoutingModule } from './auth-app-routing.module';


@NgModule({
  imports: [ CommonModule, FormsModule, AuthRoutingModule ],
  declarations: [ AuthComponent, LoginComponent,
UserRegistrationComponent, ForgotPasswordComponent, ]
})
export class AuthModule { }
```

  - `auth.component.ts`: This represents the root component named `AuthComponent`. It consists of a `router-outlet` directive for determining navigation within `AuthModule`. Note the fact that there is no selector present in this component.

```
import { Component } from '@angular/core';

@Component({
  template:  `
    <router-outlet></router-outlet>
  `
})
export class AuthComponent { }
```

- **Routing module**
    - `auth-routing.module.ts`: This represents the routing module for this feature. It consists of the route definitions for navigating different pages related to this feature:

```
import { NgModule }                from '@angular/core';
import { RouterModule, Routes } from '@angular/router';

import { AuthComponent }          from './auth.component';
import { LoginComponent } from './login.component';
import { UserRegistrationComponent } from './user-
registration.component';
import { ForgotPasswordComponent } from './forgot-
   password.component';


const authRoutes: Routes = [
  {
    path: 'auth', component: AuthComponent,
    children: [
      {
        path: 'login',
        component: LoginComponent,
      },
      {
        path: 'register',
        component: UserRegistrationComponent,
      },
      {
        path: 'forgotpassword',
        component: ForgotPasswordComponent,
      }
    ]
  }
];

@NgModule({
  imports: [
    RouterModule.forChild(authRoutes)
  ],
  exports: [
    RouterModule
  ]
})
export class AuthRoutingModule { }
```

- **Components**
    - LoginComponent (login.component.ts): This represents the login view, such as the following, and consists of application logic for processing form data. The following view is created using the template login.component.html:

Figure 2. Login Component View

    - The following represents the code for the login component:

```
import {Component} from '@angular/core';
import { Login } from './login';

@Component({
  selector: 'login',
  templateUrl: './login.component.html'
})
export class LoginComponent {
  model = new Login('', '');
  onSubmit() {
  }
}
```

- **Login template**: The following represents the code for the login template:

```
<div class="{{alertStyle}}"
    role="alert" *ngIf="signupStatus.code != ''">
    {{signupStatus.message}}</div>
<div *ngIf="signupStatus.code === '' ||
    signupStatus.code ==='USER_LOGIN_UNSUCCESSFUL'">
  <h2>Users Login</h2>
  <hr/>
  <form class="form-horizontal" (ngSubmit)="onLogin()"
#loginForm="ngForm" novalidate>
    <div class="form-group">
      <label for="email" class="col-sm-2 control-label">
            Email</label>
      <div class="col-sm-6">
        <input type="email"
                class="form-control"
                id="email"
                placeholder="Email"
                required
                [(ngModel)]="model.email"
                name="email"
                #email="ngModel"
          >
        <div [hidden]="email.valid || email.pristine"
            class="alert alert-danger">
          Email address is required
        </div>
      </div>
    </div>
    <div class="form-group">
      <label for="password" class="col-sm-2 control-label">
            Password</label>
      <div class="col-sm-6">
        <input type="password"
                class="form-control"
                id="password"
                placeholder="Password"
                required
                [(ngModel)]="model.password"
                name="password"
                #password="ngModel"
          >
        <div [hidden]="password.valid || password.pristine"
            class="alert alert-danger">
          Password is required
        </div>
      </div>
```

```
      </div>
      <div class="form-group">
        <div class="col-sm-offset-2 col-sm-10">
          <button type="submit" class="btn btn-success"
            [disabled]="!loginForm.form.valid">Submit</button>
        </div>
      </div>
      <div class="col-sm-offset-2 col-sm-10">
        <span><a routerLink="/auth/register"
         routerLinkActive="active">New User? Sign up</a></span>|
        <span><a href="/auth/forgotpassword"
         routerLinkActive="active">Forgot Password?</a></span>
      </div>
    </form>
  </div>
```

- UserRegistrationComponent (user-registration.component.ts): This represents the user registration view, such as the following, and consists of application logic for processing form data. The following view is created using the template user-registration.component.html:

Figure 3. User Registration Component View

- The following represents the code for the user registration component:

```
import { Component } from '@angular/core';
import { NewUser } from './login';

@Component({
  selector: 'register',
  templateUrl: './user-registration.component.html'
})
export class UserRegistrationComponent {

  model = new NewUser('', '', '');
  onSubmit() {
  }
}
```

- **User registration template**: The following represents the code for the user registration template (user-registration.component.html) referenced in UserRegistrationComponent:

```
<div class="{{alertStyle}}" role="alert" *ngIf="signupStatus.code !=
''">{{signupStatus.message}}</div>
<div *ngIf="signupStatus.code === '' || signupStatus.code
==='USER_ACCOUNT_EXISTS'">
  <h2>New User Registration</h2>
  <hr/>
  <form class="form-horizontal" (ngSubmit)="onSubmit()"
#loginForm="ngForm" novalidate>
    <div class="form-group">
      <label for="email" class="col-sm-2 control-label">Email</label>
      <div class="col-sm-6">
        <input type="email"
               class="form-control"
               id="email"
               placeholder="Email"
               required
               [(ngModel)]="model.email"
               name="email"
               #email="ngModel"
        >
        <div [hidden]="email.valid || email.pristine"
             class="alert alert-danger">
          Email address is required
        </div>
      </div>
    </div>
    <div class="form-group">
```

```
        <label for="password" class="col-sm-2 control-label">Password</label>
        <div class="col-sm-6">
          <input type="password"
                 class="form-control"
                 id="password"
                 placeholder="Password"
                 required
                 [(ngModel)]="model.password"
                 name="password"
                 #password="ngModel"
          >
          <div [hidden]="password.valid || password.pristine"
               class="alert alert-danger">
            Password is required
          </div>
        </div>
      </div>
      <div class="form-group">
        <label for="firstname" class="col-sm-2 control-label">First
Name</label>
        <div class="col-sm-6">
          <input type="text"
                 class="form-control"
                 id="firstname"
                 placeholder="First Name"
                 required
                 [(ngModel)]="model.firstname"
                 name="firstname"
                 #firstname="ngModel"
          >
          <div [hidden]="firstname.valid || firstname.pristine"
               class="alert alert-danger">
            First name is required
          </div>
        </div>
      </div>
      <div class="form-group">
        <div class="col-sm-offset-2 col-sm-10">
          <button type="submit" class="btn btn-success"
[disabled]="!loginForm.form.valid">Submit</button>
        </div>
      </div>
    </form>
</div>
```

- ForgotPasswordComponent (forgot-password.component.ts): This represents the forgot password view, such as the following, and consists of the application logic for processing form data. The following view is created using the forgot-password.component.html template:

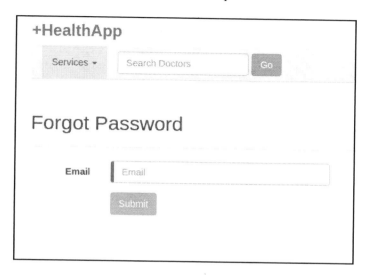

Figure 4. Forgot password component view

- The following represents the code for the forgot password component:

```
import { Component } from '@angular/core';
import { Login } from './login';

@Component({
  selector: 'forgotpassword',
  templateUrl: './forgot-password.component.html'
})
export class ForgotPasswordComponent {
  model = new Login('', '');
  onSubmit() {
  }
}
```

- **Forgot password template**: The following represents code the for the forgot password template (`forgot-password.component.html`), which is referenced in `ForgotPasswordComponent`:

```html
<div>
  <h2>Forgot Password</h2>
  <hr/>
  <form class="form-horizontal" (ngSubmit)="onSubmit()"
        #loginForm="ngForm" novalidate>
    <div class="form-group">
      <label for="email" class="col-sm-2 control-label">
            Email</label>
      <div class="col-sm-6">
        <input type="email"
              class="form-control"
              id="email"
              placeholder="Email"
              required
              [(ngModel)]="model.email"
              name="email"
              #email="ngModel"
        >
        <div [hidden]="email.valid || email.pristine"
            class="alert alert-danger">
            Email address is required
        </div>
      </div>
    </div>
    <div class="form-group">
      <div class="col-sm-offset-2 col-sm-10">
        <button type="submit" class="btn btn-success"
[disabled]="!loginForm.form.valid">Submit</button>
      </div>
    </div>
  </form>
</div>
```

Doctor module

The `Doctor` module provides the functionality related to performing CRUD operations on doctors' information, retrieving the list of doctors, searching for doctors, and so on. This is how the folder structure for this module would look:

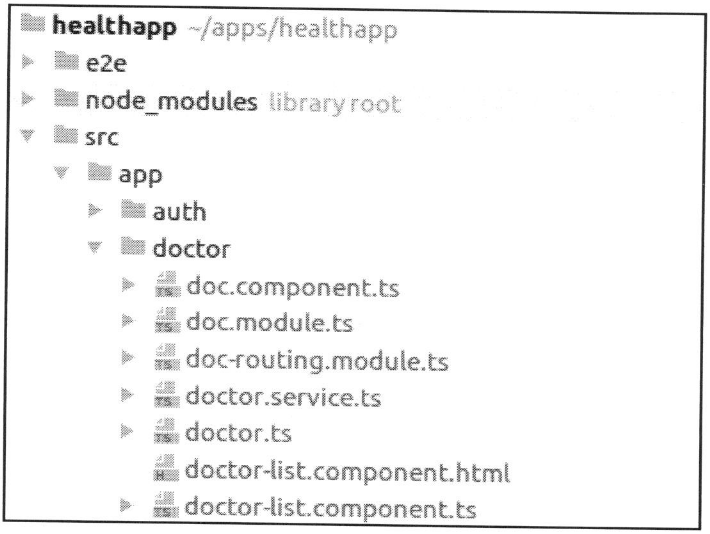

```
healthapp ~/apps/healthapp
▶ e2e
▶ node_modules library root
▼ src
   ▼ app
      ▶ auth
      ▼ doctor
         ▶ doc.component.ts
         ▶ doc.module.ts
         ▶ doc-routing.module.ts
         ▶ doctor.service.ts
         ▶ doctor.ts
           doctor-list.component.html
         ▶ doctor-list.component.ts
```

Figure 5. Doctor Feature module

The following represents the modules and components of this module:

- **Root module/component**
  - `doc.module.ts`: This represents the root module named `DocModule`. Note the import of the root component, routing module, services, and components:

```
import { NgModule }        from '@angular/core';
import { CommonModule } from '@angular/common';
import { FormsModule }     from '@angular/forms';
import { HttpModule, JsonpModule } from '@angular/http';

import { DoctorListComponent }    from './doctor-list.component';
import { DocComponent } from './doc.component';

import { DoctorService } from './doctor.service';
import { DocRoutingModule } from './doc-routing.module';

@NgModule({
```

```
    imports: [
      CommonModule, FormsModule, HttpModule, DocRoutingModule
    ],
    declarations: [
      DoctorListComponent, DocComponent
    ],
    providers: [ DoctorService ]
})
export class DocModule {}
```

- `doc.component.ts`: This represents the root component named `DocComponent`. It consists of a `router-outlet` directive for determining navigation within `DocModule`:

```
import { Component } from '@angular/core';

@Component({
  template:  `
    <router-outlet></router-outlet>
  `
})
export class DocComponent { }
```

- **Routing module**
  - `doc-routing.module.ts`: This represents the routing module `DocRoutingModule`. It consists of the route definitions for navigating the different pages related to the `Doctor` feature.

```
import { NgModule }              from '@angular/core';
import { RouterModule, Routes } from '@angular/router';

import { DocComponent }         from './doc.component';
import { DoctorListComponent }    from './doctor-list.component';


const docRoutes: Routes = [
  {
    path: 'doctors', component: DocComponent,
    children: [
      {
        path: '',
        component: DoctorListComponent,
      },
      {
        path: ':speciality',
        component: DoctorListComponent,
```

```
      }
    ]
  }
];

@NgModule({
  imports: [
    RouterModule.forChild(docRoutes)
  ],
  exports: [
    RouterModule
  ]
})
export class DocRoutingModule { }
```

- **Services**

    - DoctorService: As a best practice, components should delegate the task related to interacting with the backend to one or more services. For retrieving the doctors list, DoctorListComponent delegates the task to the DoctorService instance, the code for which is given as follows. Make a note of the usage of HTTP service, which is used to get the data from the server:

```
import { Injectable } from '@angular/core';
import { Http, Response }  from '@angular/http';

import { Observable } from 'rxjs/Observable';
import 'rxjs/add/operator/catch';
import 'rxjs/add/operator/map';
import 'rxjs/add/observable/throw';

import { Doctor } from './doctor';

@Injectable()
export class DoctorService {
  private doctorsUrl = 'http://localhost:8080/doctors';

  times: number;

  constructor (private http: Http) {}

  getDoctorsBySpeciality(specialityCode: string):
Observable<Doctor[]> {
    let path = '';
    if (specialityCode != null) {
      path = '/' + specialityCode;
    }
```

```
        return this.http.get(this.doctorsUrl + path)
          .map(this.extractData)
          .catch(this.handleError);
      }

      private extractData(res: Response) {
        let body = res.json();
        let doctors = [];
        for (let i = 0; i < body.doctors.length; i++) {
          let doctorInfo = body.doctors[i];
          let doctor = new Doctor(doctorInfo.user.firstname,
doctorInfo.user.lastname, doctorInfo.user.email,
doctorInfo.specialityCode);
          doctors.push(doctor);
        }
        return doctors;
      }

      private handleError (error: Response | any) {
        let errMsg: string;
        if (error instanceof Response) {
          const body = JSON.parse(JSON.stringify(error)) || '';
          const err = body.error || JSON.stringify(body);
          errMsg = `${error.status} - ${error.statusText || ''}
${err}`;
        } else {
          errMsg = error.message ? error.message : error.toString();
        }
        console.error(errMsg);
        return Observable.throw(errMsg);
      }
    }
```

- **Components**
  - `DoctorListComponent`: This represents the view for listing down doctors, as shown in the following screenshot. The component consists of application logic for invoking an instance of `DoctorService` to retrieve data from the server. The view shown next is created using the `doctor-list.component.html` template. The following view represents the route definition, such as `doctors`, and is rendered using `RouterLink`, such as `/doctors`:

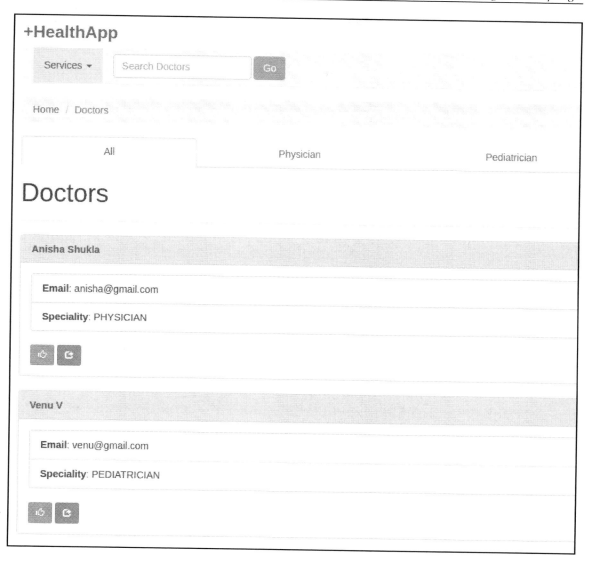

Figure 6: All Doctors List

The following view represents the child route definition, such as `doctors/:speciality`, and is rendered using `RouterLink`, such as `/doctors/PEDIATRICIAN`:

Figure 7. Doctors whose specialty is Pediatrics

- The following represents the code for `DoctorListComponent`, which is used to render the preceding UI:

```
import {Component, OnInit} from '@angular/core';
import {Doctor} from './doctor';
import { DoctorService } from './doctor.service';
import { Router, ActivatedRoute, ParamMap }   from
'@angular/router';
import 'rxjs/add/operator/switchMap';

@Component({
  selector: 'doctor-list',
  providers: [DoctorService],
  templateUrl: './doctor-list.component.html'
})
export class DoctorListComponent   implements OnInit {

  doctors: Doctor[];
  errorMessage: string;


  constructor (private doctorService: DoctorService, private
router: Router, private route: ActivatedRoute) {}

  ngOnInit() {
      this.route.paramMap
      .switchMap((params: ParamMap) =>
        this.doctorService.getDoctorsBySpeciality
(params.get('speciality')))
        .subscribe(doctors => this.doctors = doctors,
          error =>  this.errorMessage = <any>error);
  }
}
```

Route Guards for controlled access

In a real-world application, it is imperative that there is one or more server resources (data, functionality) which will only be available to authenticated and authorized users. This is where route guards come into the picture. As discussed in one of the earlier sections, there are different route guard interfaces, such as `CanActivate`, `CanActivateChild`, `CanDeactivate`, `Resolve`, and so on, which can be used for working with the guards. Let's look into the most common use-case scenario of providing access to server resources, such as `DoctorList`, to only authenticated users.

In this section, two different features modules will be designed. They are as follows:

- `Auth` module for login and signup related features
- `Doctor` module for providing access to doctors' information

Let's use the `Auth` module to enable the guards, as it looks the most appropriate to make this part of this module. In the following example, the `CanActivate` interface will be used. The following needs to be done:

- Create an `AuthGuard` service, as follows:

```
import { Injectable }      from '@angular/core';
import {
  CanActivate, Router,
  ActivatedRouteSnapshot,
  RouterStateSnapshot
}                          from '@angular/router';
import { AuthService }      from './auth.service';

@Injectable()
export class AuthGuardService implements CanActivate {
    constructor(private authService: AuthService, private router:
Router) {}

    canActivate(route: ActivatedRouteSnapshot, state:
RouterStateSnapshot): boolean {
        let url: string = state.url;

        return this.checkLogin(url);
    }

    checkLogin(url: string): boolean {
      if (this.authService.isLoggedIn) { return true; }

      // Store the attempted URL for redirecting
      this.authService.redirectUrl = url;

      // Navigate to the login page with extras
      this.router.navigate(['/auth/login']);
      return false;
    }
}
```

- Create `AuthService`, as shown here:

```
import { Injectable } from '@angular/core';

import { Observable } from 'rxjs/Observable';
import 'rxjs/add/observable/of';
import 'rxjs/add/operator/do';
import 'rxjs/add/operator/delay';

@Injectable()
export class AuthService {
  isLoggedIn = false;

  // store the URL so we can redirect after logging in
  redirectUrl: string;

  login(): Observable<boolean> {
    return Observable.of(true).delay(1000).do(val =>
this.isLoggedIn = true);
  }

  logout(): void {
    this.isLoggedIn = false;
  }
}
```

- Include `AuthGuard` in the `Doctor` module
- Include `AuthGuard` in the `doctor-routing` module

Debugging Angular app

In this section, you will learn how to debug an Angular app using browsers such as Firefox and Chrome and tools such as Augury. Augury is a Google Chrome extension which can be used for debugging Angular apps.

Debugging Angular app using Firefox and Chrome

The following steps need to be taken to debug an app using Firefox:

1. Use *Ctrl + Shift + I* to open the Firefox Developer Tools window. The following screenshot represents the same:

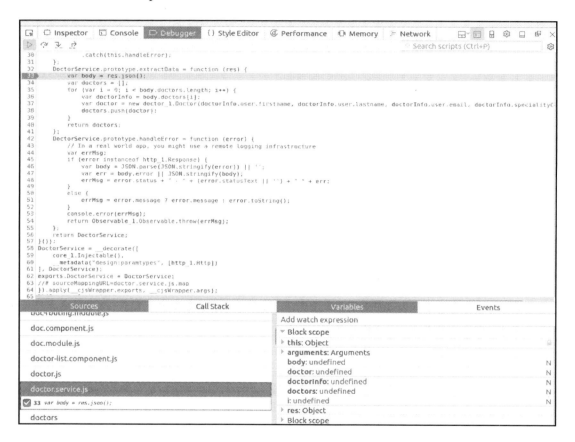

Figure 8. Debugging an Angular app using Firefox

2. Click on **Debugger** to open the code section vis-a-vis the related file in which the code resides.

3. Open up the file where the code which needs to be debugged exists. In the preceding screenshot, `doctor.service.js` is used for debugging data retrieval from the server.

4. Add one or more breakpoints. The green-colored line in the preceding screenshot represents the breakpoint in the `doctor.service.tjs` file.

5. Refresh the page, the rendering of which will involve the component/service which needs to be debugged.

6. As a result of the preceding steps, the execution will stop at the breakpoint. Step in or step over appropriately to debug your application.

The following steps need to be taken to debug the app using Chrome:

1. Use *Ctrl + Shift + I* to open the Chrome Developer Tools window. The following screenshot represents the same:

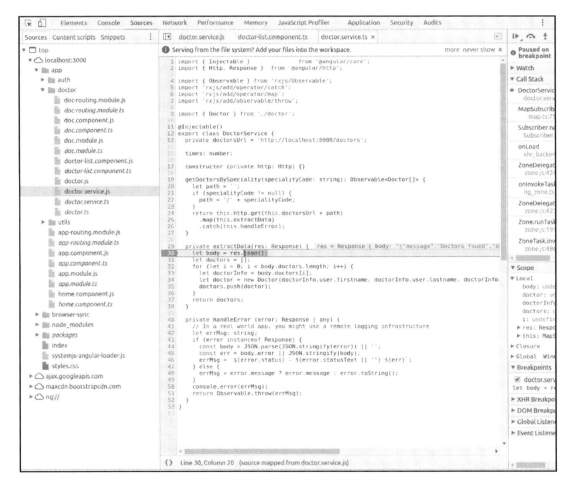

Figure 9. Debugging an Angular app using Chrome

2. Click on **Sources** to open the code section vis-a-vis the related file in which the code resides.

3. Go to the source tree and select the file which needs to be debugged. In the preceding screenshot, `doctor.service.js` is chosen for debugging.

4. Select one or more breakpoints in the file. In the preceding screenshot, the breakpoint is put on the `let body = res.json()` line.

5. Click on the link/URL to open the page to be debugged, or refresh the page to be debugged.

6. As a result of the earlier steps, execution will stop at the breakpoint. Step in or step over appropriately to debug your application.

Debugging Angular app using Augury

Augury is a Google Chrome Dev extension tool which can be used for debugging and profiling Angular apps. It helps in visualizing and inspecting the component tree with different properties of one or more components. In order to get started with Augury, one needs to go to the Augury Chrome extension page (`https://chrome.google.com/webstore/detail/augury/elgalmkoelokbchhkhacckoklkejnhcd`) and click on **ADD TO CHROME** button. Once done with the installation, the following steps need to be taken in order to work with Augury:

- Use *Ctrl + Shift + I* to open the Chrome Developer Tools window.
- Click on **Augury** to open up the tool. It displays menu options such as **Component Tree**, **Router Tree**, and **NgModules**. The following represents a quick snapshot representing **Router Tree**. This view can be used for visualizing purposes. Hovering on any component will display the handler, path, and data for that component:

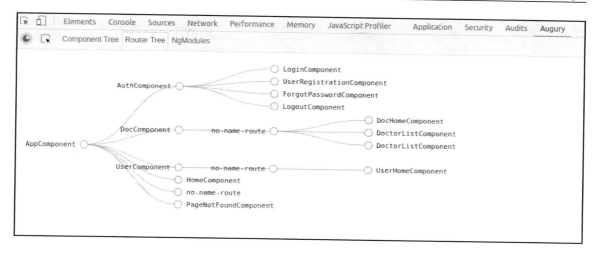

Figure 10. Augury Router Tree

- In a similar manner, one can click on **Component Tree** to see the components and their properties. This can be used for inspection purposes. By clicking on any specific component, one can then view the injector graph shown as follows, or go to the source code and add a breakpoint for debugging purposes. The following is the screenshot:

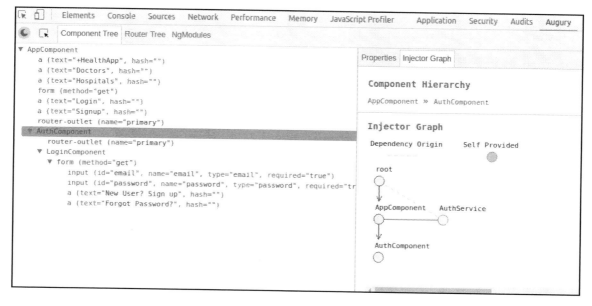

Figure 11. Augury Component Tree

Summary

In this chapter, you learnt the different aspects of routing, design patterns, and how one can create a single page app based on some of the best practices recommended by Angular. In the next chapter, you will learn how to do unit testing on Angular apps.

8
Unit Testing with Angular Apps

Unit testing is all about testing a block of code in isolation. As with any other programming language, unit testing allows developers to create robust and reliable software by designing and developing the software components based on testability principles. Angular provides support for unit testing components, services, and so on, using tools such as Jasmine, Karma, and Protractor, along with in-built testing utilities. In this chapter, you will learn concepts such as the following in relation to creating **single page applications (SPA)** using Angular and Spring 5:

- Introduction to unit testing
- Unit testing tools for Angular apps
- Setting up the testing environment
- Angular unit testing building blocks
- Unit testing strategies
- Unit testing the components
- Unit testing the services

Introduction to unit testing

Unit testing is defined as testing a block of code in isolation. A class can have multiple methods. And, thus, there could be multiple unit tests for a class. The following are some of the best practices that need to be followed when working with unit tests:

- **Refactor code**: A method that is long and complex enough, or rather, does multiple things, or has multiple responsibilities that need to be refactored. In other words, a method with a very high cyclomatic complexity would need to be refactored to small methods that conform to the single responsibility principle (a block of code will have just one reason to change).

- **Using test doubles**: As the unit tests are about testing a block of code in isolation, any dependencies from the code would need to be mocked. In other words, it will be necessary to make use of test doubles instead of actual service or components when writing unit tests. This can be achieved using some of the following concepts related to mocking:
    - **Stub**: When creating a stub for dependencies, the entire service is mocked. This essentially means that the actual service is not invoked during code execution. Rather, the test double or stub is used to return the desired value.
    - **Spy**: When using a spy on the dependencies, the actual service is invoked. But one or more methods on which the spy is created are replaced with a test double returning the desired value.
    - **Stub or spy**: One could make use of both stubs and spies based on the requirements of the unit tests.

Unit testing tools for Angular apps

The following are some of the tools which could be used for writing unit tests for some of the building blocks of Angular apps, such as components, services, and so on.

Jasmine

Jasmine is a behavior-driven test framework for unit testing JavaScript code. It can be accessed on this page: `https://jasmine.github.io/`. It is shipped with an HTML test runner which executes tests in the web browser.

Behavior-driven development (BDD) has emerged from **test-driven development (TDD)**. BDD facilitates greater collaboration and communication between different stakeholders in a team including business analysts, software developers, and testers. In the BDD approach, business analysts specify and describe business behaviors expected from the system and the developers focus on understanding on those behaviors and coding/implementing appropriately rather than focusing on the technical aspect of the implementation. This is where BDD differs from TDD, which focuses on testing the technical implementation rather than the business behaviors. TDD test specs are hard to read by business stakeholders.

The following is a sample unit test written using the Jasmine framework:

```
describe('Hello World', () => {
    it('tests true to be equal to true', () =>
        expect(true).toBe(true));
});
```

The following are some of the key functions in relation to writing unit tests using the Jasmine framework:

- `beforeAll` (function, timeout): This runs the setup code, which is run before the execution of the specs start.
- `beforeEach` (function, timeout): This comprises of the setup code, which is run before the execution of each spec.
- `describe` (description, `listOfSpecs`): This creates a group or list of specs.
- `it` (description, `testFunction`, timeout): This is the most important function that is used to define a single spec. The spec can have one or more expectations.
- `expect`: This is used to match the expectation with the real value.
- `fail` (error): This marks a spec as failed.
- `afterEach` (function, timeout): This runs the shared teardown code, which is run after the execution of each spec.
- `afterAll` (function, timeout): This runs the shared teardown code, which is run after the execution of all specs.
- `spyOn`: This creates a spy on an existing object.

Karma

While unit tests are written using Jasmine, the Karma test runner is used to provide the testing environment and run those tests. The details can be accessed at `https://karma-runner.github.io/`. With the Karma test runner, developers can continue developing the code while getting feedback from test execution. Anyone wanting to do test-driven development would find Karma very useful. In addition, it integrates seamlessly with the continuous integration process, and tools such as Jenkins, Travis, and so on.

Protractor

Protractor is used to write and run end-to-end tests, which can also be termed integration tests.

Angular testing utilities

In addition to the earlier, Angular testing utilities are used to create a test environment that can be used to test Angular code by enabling it to interact with the Angular environment.

Setting up the unit test environment

In this section, we will learn how to set up the test environment, and run the first unit test (written using Jasmine) with the Karma test runner.

The Angular app, when set up using the recommended methods such as those mentioned at https://angular.io/guide/setup, one of which was discussed in the Chapter 6, *Getting Started with Angular*, results in the installation of appropriate npm packages, files, and scripts, which can be used for writing and running unit tests with the Angular testing utilities Jasmine and Karma.

Perform the following steps to get started with running your first unit test:

1. Create a file under the app folder, and name it helloworld.spec.ts.
2. Place the following code in the file:

```
describe('Hello World', () => {
    it('unit tests are good', () => expect(true).toBe(true));
});
```

3. Go to the root folder of the app in Command Prompt.
4. Execute the following command; (it concurrently runs the command npm run build:watch and karma start karma.conf.js):

```
npm test
```

The results can be found or read at both the following places: the console used to run the npm test command and in the browser. The following screenshot represents the same:

```
> angular-quickstart@1.0.0 pretest /home/ajiteshkumar/apps/healthapp
> npm run build

> angular-quickstart@1.0.0 build /home/ajiteshkumar/apps/healthapp
> tsc -p src/

> angular-quickstart@1.0.0 test /home/ajiteshkumar/apps/healthapp
> concurrently "npm run build:watch" "karma start karma.conf.js"

    > angular-quickstart@1.0.0 build:watch /home/ajiteshkumar/apps/healthapp
    > tsc -p src/ -w

06 07 2017 05:46:00.378:WARN [watcher]: Pattern "/home/ajiteshkumar/apps/healthapp/testing/**/*.js" does not match any file.
06 07 2017 05:46:00.405:WARN [watcher]: Pattern "/home/ajiteshkumar/apps/healthapp/testing/**/*.ts" does not match any file.
06 07 2017 05:46:00.486:WARN [watcher]: Pattern "/home/ajiteshkumar/apps/healthapp/testing/**/*.js.map" does not match any file.
06 07 2017 05:46:00.809:WARN [karma]: No captured browser, open http://localhost:9876/
06 07 2017 05:46:00.827:INFO [karma]: Karma v1.7.0 server started at http://0.0.0.0:9876/
06 07 2017 05:45:00.827:INFO [launcher]: Launching browser Chrome with unlimited concurrency
06 07 2017 05:46:00.839:INFO [launcher]: Starting browser Chrome
06 07 2017 05:46:00.276:INFO [Chrome 58.0.3029 (Linux 0.0.0)]: Connected on socket goSSM-t2cvRyFnwkAAAA with id 701180
Chrome 58.0.3029 (Linux 0.0.0): Executed 1 of 1 SUCCESS (0.017 secs / 0.003 secs)
```

Figure 1. npm test command execution result

The screenshot shown next represents the Chrome browser window, which opens up as a result of executing the unit tests using the aforementioned command:

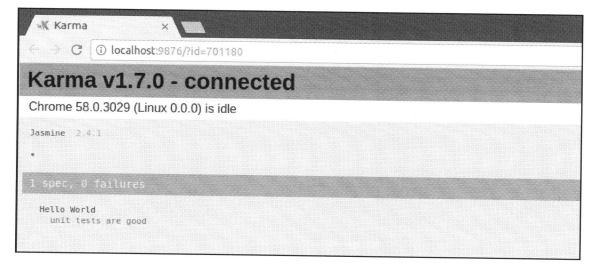

Figure 2: Karma output in the Chrome browser

In order to make sure that the Karma test runner detects the changes and reruns the unit tests, make changes to `helloworld.specs.ts` as follows:

```
describe('Hello World', () => {
    it('unit tests are good', () => expect(true).toBe(false));
});
```

As the expected result is false while the desired result is true, the test would fail. Observe that the Karma test runner refreshes the browser. The following screenshot is how the updated Karma page looks in the browser; note the test failure:

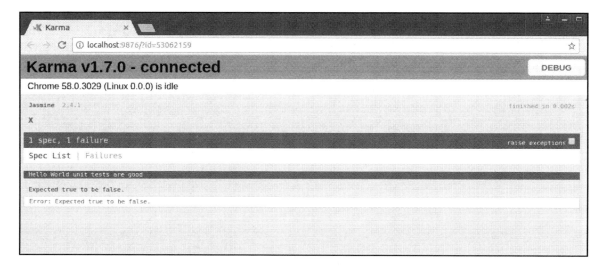

Figure 3: Karma displaying the test failure

Angular unit testing building blocks

The following are some of the key building blocks to be used when writing unit tests for Angular apps:

- `TestBed`: This is the most important building block of Angular testing utilities. `TestBed` is used to create an Angular testing module using the `@NgModule` class, which is configured using the `configureTestingModule` method. Invoking `configureTestingModule` on `TestBed` creates a testing environment for the component to be tested. Essentially, the component to be tested is detached from its own module and reattached to the Angular testing module. A metadata object declaring the components to be tested is passed to the `configureTestingModule` method.

  After configuring the test environment, the next step is to create a component fixture, which is done by invoking the `createComponent` API on `TestBed`. Once the `createComponent` API is invoked, `TestBed` can't be configured any further.

Note that the `configureTestingModule` and `createComponent` methods are invoked within the `beforeEach` method such that the testing environment for the component can be reset before the execution of each of the test specs. The following code shows the usage of `TestBed` to configure the testing module and create the component fixture:

```
foreEach(() => {
    TestBed.configureTestingModule({
        declarations: [ LoginComponent ],
    });

    componentFixture = TestBed.createComponent(LoginComponent);
    ...
});
```

- `componentFixture`: As shown in the preceding code, the component fixture, `componentFixture`, is created by invoking `createComponent` on `TestBed`. `ComponentFbeixture` is a handle to the test environment that has the created component. It is used to access component instances and `DebugElement`. The following code represents the same:

```
beforeEach(() => {
  ...
 // LoginComponent Test Instance
 loginComponent = componentFixture.componentInstance;

 // query for the heading <h2> using CSS element selector
 h2Element = componentFixture.debugElement.query(By.css('h2'))
});
```

- `DebugElement`: This represents the handle on the component's DOM element. It supports APIs such as `query` and `queryAll`, which are used to get information related to one or all DOM elements of the component. The preceding code represents how the `query` API is invoked on the fixture's `debugElement` to get the information related to `h1` element in the component's DOM tree. As a result of the query method invocation, the fixture's entire DOM tree is searched for the matching element and the first match is returned.

Unit testing strategies

Angular supports unit testing with some of the following:

- Components
- Services
- Pipes

Angular supports the following two different unit testing strategies while performing unit tests with the aforementioned building blocks:

- **Isolated unit tests for services and pipes**: Isolated unit tests are about testing the block of code in complete isolation, wherein test doubles are used to replace actual dependencies. As test doubles, test instances are created and injected as constructor parameters. One or more APIs are then invoked on these test instances to continue executing the unit tests. It is recommended to use isolated unit tests for services and pipes.
- **Angular testing utilities for components**: Testing components in an effective manner, however, would require interacting with the Angular environment due to the need for components to interact with templates, or with other components. This is where the Angular testing utilities come into the picture. The following are some of the key building blocks of Angular testing utilities:
  - `TestBed`
  - `ComponentFixture`
  - `DebugElement`

Unit testing the components

Components form the most important building block of any Angular app. Thus, it is of utmost importance to write good unit tests for components, and ensure maximum possible code coverage.

Angular testing utilities will be used for writing unit tests for components. In this regard, concepts discussed earlier such as `TestBed`, `componentFixture`, and `DebugElement` will be used to create the test environment for the components to be tested. In this section, we will take different sample components starting from the most trivial ones to the most complex components, and learn about writing and running unit tests for these components.

Unit testing a component with an external template

As one sets up the Angular app, one can find the most trivial component, `AppComponent`, in the root folder (`src/app`) with an external template used. Note that there are no dependencies, such as services. The following is the code for `AppComponent` saved as the file `app.component.ts`:

```
import {Component} from '@angular/core';

@Component({
  selector: 'my-app',
  templateUrl: './app.component.html',
})
export class AppComponent {
    appName = 'HealthApp';
}
```

In the preceding component, note the usage of a template, `app.component.html`, which consists of HTML and Angular syntaxes. The following is the code for `app.component.html`:

```
<h1>Welcome to {{appName}}</h1>
```

We will write unit tests to test the preceding component. In order to get started, create a file, `app.component.spec.ts`, in the same folder. Make sure that Karma is running (as a result of executing the `npm test` command). Place the following code in the file and save it:

```
import { AppComponent } from './app.component';

import { async, ComponentFixture, TestBed } from
        '@angular/core/testing';

import { By }           from '@angular/platform-browser';
import { DebugElement } from '@angular/core';

describe('AppComponent', function () {
  let de: DebugElement;
  let comp: AppComponent;
  let fixture: ComponentFixture<AppComponent>;

  beforeEach(async(() => {
    TestBed.configureTestingModule({
      declarations: [ AppComponent ]
    })
```

```
            .compileComponents();
    }));

    beforeEach(() => {
      fixture = TestBed.createComponent(AppComponent);
      comp = fixture.componentInstance;
      de = fixture.debugElement.query(By.css('h1'));
    });

    it('should create component', () => expect(comp).toBeDefined() );

    it('should have expected <h1> text', () => {
      fixture.detectChanges();
      // nativeElement is used to represent corresponding DOM element
      const h1 = de.nativeElement;
      expect(h1.innerText).toMatch('Welcome to ' + comp.appName);
    });

    it('should display a different app name', () => {
      comp.appName = 'Test HealthApp';
      fixture.detectChanges();
      const h1 = de.nativeElement;
      expect(h1.innerText).toMatch('Welcome to ' + comp.appName);
    });
  });
```

Go to the browser, and check whether the tests were updated. You should be able to find a new specs entry similar to that shown in the following screenshot; note the AppComponent entry under the spec:

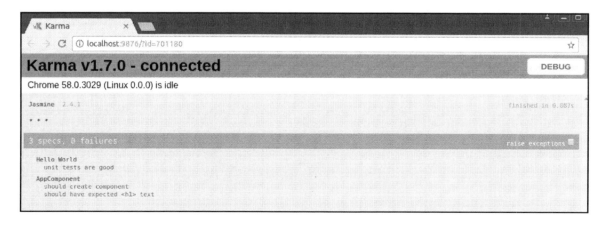

Figure 4: Karma test runner refreshes updating the code changes

Let's go into the details of the preceding code, and understand the different concepts related to writing unit tests for components:

- **Import the component to be tested:** In the earlier code sample, it is `AppComponent` that needs to be tested:

  ```
  import { AppComponent } from './app.component';
  ```

- **Import Angular testing utilities** such as `TestBed`, `ComponentFixture`, `async`, and so on:

  ```
  import { async, ComponentFixture, TestBed } from
          '@angular/core/testing';
  import { By } from '@angular/platform-browser';
  import { DebugElement } from '@angular/core';
  ```

- **Test skeleton setup:** Create a test skeleton to include Jasmine building blocks, such as `describe`, `beforeEach`, `it`, and so on:

  ```
  describe('AppComponent', function () {

      beforeEach(() => {
      });

      it('test 1' () => {
      });
  });
  ```

- **Test environment setup:** Create the testing environment required to test `AppComponent` by attaching `AppComponent` to test `module`. `TestBed`. As as shown in the following code, it is used to create the testing module using `@NgModule`, and to configure the testing module using the `configureTestingModule` method. Essentially, this would lead to `AppComponent` getting detached from its actual module, and getting reattached to the testing module:

  ```
  describe('AppComponent', function () {
      let de: DebugElement;
      let comp: AppComponent;
      let fixture: ComponentFixture<AppComponent>;

      beforeEach(async(() => {
          TestBed.configureTestingModule({
              declarations: [ AppComponent ]
          })
          .compileComponents();
  ```

```
      }));
      ...
   }
```

- **componentFixture Setup**: Create a component fixture using TestBed in order to get a handle to the test environment. An instance of the component fixture would be used to get the instance of the component to be tested, and get access to elements such as DebugElement:

```
describe('AppComponent', function () {
  let de: DebugElement;
  let comp: AppComponent;
  let fixture: ComponentFixture<AppComponent>;

  beforeEach(async(() => {
   TestBed.configureTestingModule({
    declarations: [ AppComponent ]
   })
   .compileComponents();
  }));

  beforeEach(() => {
    fixture = TestBed.createComponent(AppComponent);
    comp = fixture.componentInstance;
    de = fixture.debugElement.query(By.css('h1'));
  });

   ...

}
```

Create one or more tests matching the expected result with the actual result, as follows:

```
describe('AppComponent', function () {

 ...

 it('should create component',
    () => expect(comp).toBeDefined());

 it('should have expected <h1> text',
    () => {
     fixture.detectChanges();
     const h1 = de.nativeElement;
     expect(h1.innerText).toMatch('Welcome to ' + comp.appName);
});

 it('should display a different app name',
```

```
() => {
    comp.appName = 'Test HealthApp';
    fixture.detectChanges();
    const h1 = de.nativeElement;
    expect(h1.innerText).toMatch('Welcome to ' + comp.appName);
});

});
```

The preceding code consists of the following three tests:

- **Spec--should create component**: This is the most trivial unit test and checks whether the component is defined
- **Spec--should have expected <h1> text**: This spec tests whether the expected h1, innerText is displayed as specified in the template
- **Spec--should display a different app name**: This spec tests whether the component property, appName, when changed, leads to display of the changed/modified h1 text.

In order to make sure that changes are detected, and one or more tests result in failure in case of inappropriate changes, modify the h1 inner text to Hello World in the app.component.html file. The code looks like <h1>Hello World</h1>. The spec, should have expected <h1> text would fail.

Observe the updated test results on the Karma page in the browser, which will be as follows:

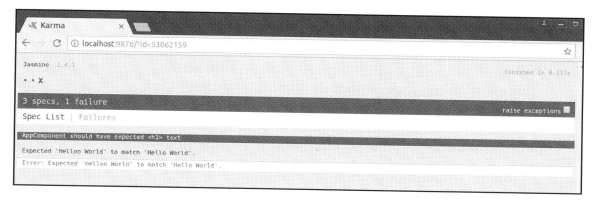

Figure 5: Karma displaying the test failure

The following are some concepts that need to be understood in relation to the preceding code:

- **Change detection within a test**: Note that the detectChanges method is invoked appropriately on the fixture in order to notify Angular about the change detection. However, in production, change detection kicks in automatically when Angular creates a component or an asynchronous operation completes. Angular supports both of the following techniques for change detection:

  - **Manual change detection**: In the specs shown earlier, change detection is manually triggered by invoking detectChanges on the ComponentFixture instance, fixture.

  - **Automatic change detection**: Angular supports automatic change detection. One would be required to use (import) a different ComponentFixture class for this. Note that the method detectChanges is no longer required to be invoked for one of the specs, such as should have expected h1 text. This is mainly because ComponentFixtureAutoDetect only responds to asynchronous activities such as promise resolution, DOM events, and so on. If there is a synchronous update of the DOM property, it would still be required to invoke the detectChanges API on the fixture instance. Thus, as a best practice and to avoid confusion, it may be a good idea to use the detectChanges API for notifying Angular about the updates made to the DOM property. Here is the code for this:

```
. . .
    import { async, ComponentFixtureAutoDetect, TestBed } from
'@angular/core/testing';
    . . .

    describe('AppComponent', function () {
      . . .
      beforeEach(async(() => {
        TestBed.configureTestingModule({
          declarations: [ AppComponent ],
          providers: [ {
            provide: ComponentFixtureAutoDetect,
      useValue: true } ]
        })
        .compileComponents();
    }));
```

```
it('should have expected <h1> text', () => {
    const h1 = de.nativeElement;
    expect(h1.innerText).toMatch('Welcome to ' +
comp.appName);
  });

  it('should display a different app name', () => {
    comp.appName = 'Test HealthApp';
    fixture.detectChanges();
    const h1 = de.nativeElement;
    expect(h1.innerText).toMatch('Welcome to ' +
      comp.appName);
  });
});
```

- **Testing a component with an external template**: In most cases, it would be required to externalize the template code in a different file. In the preceding example, the template code is externalized into the file app.component.html, and the file is then included within app.component.ts using the attribute templateURL as part of the @Component metadata. As the template and other files, such as the style file, would be externalized, it becomes an important first step to read these files before starting to execute the tests. This is where multiple beforeEach method invocations comes into the picture.

  - Asynchronous beforeEach: The external files are compiled and read asynchronously. Notice the async API used as an argument to the beforeEach method. In the following method call, an instance of TestBed is returned as a result of the method invocation, configureTestingModule. The compileComponents *method* is then invoked on this instance of TestBed to compile the external files used in the actual component, such as AppComponent:

```
beforeEach(async(() => {
  TestBed.configureTestingModule({
    declarations: [ AppComponent ]
  })
  .compileComponents();
}));
```

  - Synchronous beforeEach: Once the asynchronous invocation of beforeEach is called, the second invocation of beforeEach is synchronous, and proceeds with the remaining setup related to the component fixture.

Unit testing a component with one or more dependencies

Many of the components in an Angular app, which are required to interact with the server for performing data operations, depend upon the delegate services. As a best practice, Angular recommends that the components should delegate the data processing tasks to the external or delegate services. In this section, we will learn about doing unit tests for such components. In such scenarios, it is recommended to use a *test double* for the dependent service, primarily because the intention is to test the component and not the services.

Let's take a look at a scenario where a component depends upon an authentication service to determine whether a user is logged in or not, and displays an appropriate message on the page. In this example, the component is AppComponent, and the service on which AppComponent depends is AuthService. The following example will use a test double for AuthService:

- **Component under test**: The following is the code for AppComponent (app.component.ts). Pay attention to the usage of the delegate service, AuthService, to be used for determining whether the user is logged in or not. AuthService is imported from the auth feature module, and injected into the AppComponent constructor so that it can be used in one or more methods:

```
import {Component, OnInit} from '@angular/core';
import {AuthService} from './auth/auth.service';

@Component({
  selector: 'my-app',
  templateUrl: './app.component.html',
})
export class AppComponent implements OnInit {
  appName = 'HealthApp';
  userName = '';
  constructor(private authService: AuthService) {
  }

  ngOnInit() {
    this.userName = this.authService.isLoggedIn ?
    this.authService.user.name : 'Guest';
  }
}
```

- **Component dependency (service)**: The following is the code for `AuthService` (`auth.service.ts`). `AuthService` is a part of the `auth` feature module. In the following example, the service consists of simplistic APIs for login and logout operations:

```
import { Injectable } from '@angular/core';

import { Observable } from 'rxjs/Observable';
import 'rxjs/add/observable/of';
import 'rxjs/add/operator/do';
import 'rxjs/add/operator/delay';

@Injectable()
export class AuthService {
  isLoggedIn = false;
  user = {};

  // store the URL so we can redirect after logging in
  redirectUrl: string;

  login(): Observable<boolean> {
    return Observable.of(true).delay(1000).do(val =>
        this.isLoggedIn = true);
  }

  logout(): void {
    this.isLoggedIn = false;
  }
}
```

- **Unit test for components**: The following represents the different aspects of unit tests for components with a dependency on services:
- **Configure the testing module by injecting the service provider (test double)**: Configure the testing module to include the dependent service as part of the testing environment. Pay attention to the providers array wherein `AuthService` is added as a provider. Note that the component under test need not be injected with the real service. Thus, what is injected is a stub (test double), and not the real service:

```
TestBed.configureTestingModule({
    declarations: [ AppComponent ],
    providers: [ {provide: AuthService, useValue:
    authServiceStub } ]
  })
  .compileComponents();
```

- **Define the test double**: Instead of the real service, it is the test double (stub) that is injected into the component under test. The following code represents the stub that is used in place of the real service. This has been specified in the code using the useValue attribute. Alternatively, one can use the spyOn method to prevent the actual API from getting invoked. We will look into an example using spyOn in the next section.

```
authServiceStub = {
  user: {name: 'Micky'}
};
```

- **Get access to the injected service**: Access the injected service (stub or test double). This is achieved by getting the injected service from the injector of the component under test, as follows:

```
authService = fixture.debugElement.injector.get(AuthService);
```

This is the entire code for app.component.spec.ts:

```
import { AppComponent } from './app.component';

import { async, ComponentFixture, TestBed } from '@angular/core/testing';
import { By } from '@angular/platform-browser';
import { DebugElement } from '@angular/core';

import { AuthService } from './auth/auth.service';

describe('AppComponent', function () {
 let de: DebugElement;
 let comp: AppComponent;
 let fixture: ComponentFixture<AppComponent>;
 let authService: AuthService;
 let authServiceStub;

 beforeEach(async(() => {

   authServiceStub = {
     isLoggedIn: false,
     user: {name: 'Micky'}
   };

   TestBed.configureTestingModule({
     declarations: [ AppComponent ],
     providers: [ {provide: AuthService, useValue: authServiceStub } ]
   })
   .compileComponents();
 }));
```

```
beforeEach(() => {
    fixture = TestBed.createComponent(AppComponent);
    comp = fixture.componentInstance;
    de = fixture.debugElement.query(By.css('h1'));
    authService = fixture.debugElement.injector.get(AuthService);
});

it('should display username as Guest for unauthenticated user', () => {
    fixture.detectChanges();
    const h1 = de.nativeElement;
    expect(h1.innerText).toContain('Guest');
});

it('should display actual username for logged in user', () => {
    authService.isLoggedIn = true;
    fixture.detectChanges();
    const h1 = de.nativeElement;
    expect(h1.innerText).toContain('Micky');
});
});
```

Unit testing a component with an async service

In this section, we will learn how to test the components that depend on one or more delegate services that return values asynchronously. These are the services that make one or more requests to the server, and the data is returned asynchronously. We will take up the following for learning the related concepts:

- DoctorListComponent (doctor-list.component.ts)
- DoctorService (doctor.service.ts)
- Unit tests for DoctorListComponent (doctor-list.component.spec.ts)

Component-under-test - DoctorListComponent

`DoctorListComponent` is used to display the list of doctors and the count of the total number of doctors, as shown in the following sample screenshot:

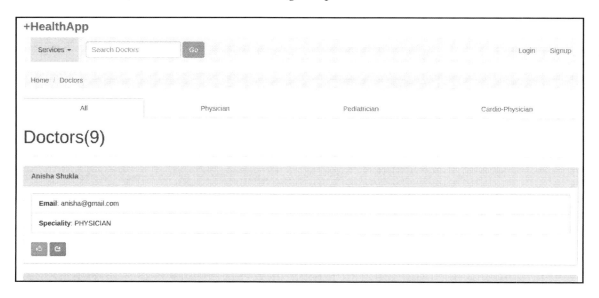

Figure 6: DoctorListComponent

The following is the code for `DoctorListComponent`. Pay attention to some of these points:

- A delegate service, `DoctorService`, is injected into the constructor of `DoctorListComponent`.
- APIs such as `getDoctorsBySpeciality` and `getDoctorsCount` get invoked within the `ngOnInit` method. Later in this section, we will see the mocking of these methods when writing unit tests:

```
import {Component, OnInit} from '@angular/core';
import {Doctor} from './doctor';
import { DoctorService } from './doctor.service';

@Component({
  selector: 'doctor-list',
  providers: [DoctorService],
  templateUrl: './doctor-list.component.html'
})
export class DoctorListComponent  implements OnInit {
```

```
doctors: Doctor[];
doctorsCount: number;
errorMessage: string;
constructor (private doctorService: DoctorService) {}

ngOnInit() {
  this.doctorService.getDoctorsBySpeciality('')
    .subscribe(
      doctors => this.doctors = doctors,
      error =>  this.errorMessage = <any>error);

  this.doctorService.getDoctorsCount()
    .subscribe(
      count => this.doctorsCount = count,
      error =>  this.errorMessage = <any>error);
  }
}
```

External service - DoctorService

As discussed earlier, `DoctorListComponent` depends on `DoctorService`, which returns data asynchronously after making HTTP calls to the server. The following is the code for `DoctorService`. Pay attention to the `getDoctorsBySpeciality` and `getDoctorsCount` APIs, where the HTTP service invokes the `get` method:

```
import { Injectable } from '@angular/core';
import { Http, Response }  from '@angular/http';

import { Observable } from 'rxjs/Observable';
import 'rxjs/add/operator/catch';
import 'rxjs/add/operator/map';
import 'rxjs/add/observable/throw';

import { Doctor } from './doctor';

@Injectable()
export class DoctorService {
  private doctorsUrl = 'http://localhost:8080/doctors';
  public doctorsCount = 0;
  public doctors: Observable<Doctor[]>;

  constructor (private http: Http) {}

  getDoctorsBySpeciality(specialityCode: string): Observable<Doctor[]> {
    let path = '';
    if (specialityCode != null) {
```

```
      path = '/' + specialityCode;
    }
    return this.http.get(this.doctorsUrl + path)
      .map(this.extractData)
      .catch(this.handleError);
  }

  getDoctorsCount() {
    return this.http.get(this.doctorsUrl + '/count')
      .map((res: Response) => res.json().count)
      .catch((error: any) => Observable.throw(error.json().error || 'Server
error'));
  }

  private extractData(res: Response) {
    let body = res.json();
    let doctors = [];
    for (let i = 0; i < body.doctors.length; i++) {
      let doctorInfo = body.doctors[i];
      let doctor = new Doctor(doctorInfo.user.firstname,
doctorInfo.user.lastname, doctorInfo.user.email,
doctorInfo.specialityCode);
      doctors.push(doctor);
      this.doctorsCount++;
    }
    return doctors;
  }
}
```

Unit test for DoctorListComponent

The unit tests illustrated next for DoctorListComponent focus on the following aspects:

- **Use Spy on one or more Service APIs**: Using Spy in place of a fake object, recall that in the previous section, a fake object such as authServiceStub was used in place of AuthService. Also recall that spy allows the invocation of the actual service. However, only the method which is spied on is replaced to return the predefined result. In the following code sample, two APIs, getDoctorsBySpeciality and getDoctorsCount, are spied on. Note the value returned in both the cases. SpyOn, when invoked on getDoctorsBySpeciality, returns an observable on the predefined object (array of doctors) as shown further. SpyOn, when invoked on getDoctorsCount, returns some random value as per the actual doctorService parameter's getDoctorsCount API.

The following is the code sample:

```
spyOn(doctorService, 'getDoctorsBySpeciality')
  .and.returnValue(Observable.of([{
      'firstname': 'Calvin',
      'lastname': 'Hobbes',
      'email': 'ch@gmail.com',
      'specialityCode': 'PHYSICIAN',
  }]));

spyOn(doctorService, 'getDoctorsCount')
  .and.returnValue(Observable.of(5));
```

- **Pass the async function as an** it **argument**: Use Angular testing utilities such as the async function along with the ComponentFixture API such as whenStable. The async function takes a parameterless function, and returns the function that becomes an argument to the Jasmine it call. This function enables the test code to run in what is called a special async test zone, thereby hiding Angular's asynchronous execution mechanisms. The following code represents the usage of the async function in the Jasmine it call:

```
it('should show count after getDoctorsCount method is called',
async(() => {
    fixture.detectChanges();
    fixture.whenStable().then(() => { // wait for async call
      fixture.detectChanges();        // update view with count
      const h1 = de.nativeElement;
      expect(h1.innerText).toContain('Doctors(5)');
    });
}));
```

- **Pass the fakeAsync function as an** *it* **argument**: Use Angular testing utilities such as fakeAsync and tick. Like the async function, fakeAsync takes a parameterless function, thereby returning a function which becomes an argument to the Jasmine it call. This function enables the test code to execute in a special fakeAsync test zone. Instead of whenStable, the tick() method is called. The fakeAsync utility makes the test code more readable and seem synchronous, unlike the async function (due to the use of the whenStable method). The following is the sample code:

```
it('should show count after getDoctorsCount method is called',
fakeAsync(() => {
    fixture.detectChanges();
    tick();                        // wait for async getDoctorsCount
    fixture.detectChanges(); // update view with count
```

```
      const h1 = de.nativeElement;
      expect(h1.innerText).toContain('Doctors(5)');
    }));
```

- **Import one or more modules**: `DoctorListComponent` depends upon modules such as `HttpModule`, as `DoctorService` requires `HttpModule`. Thus, the dependent modules would need to be imported in the testing environment configured using the `TestBed` API such as `configureTestingModule`. The following code shows this:

```
      beforeEach(async(() => {
        TestBed.configureTestingModule({
          imports: [ HttpModule ],
          declarations: [ DoctorListComponent ],
          providers: [ DoctorService ],
        })
        .compileComponents();
      }));
```

The following is the code for the unit test for `DoctorListComponent`:

```
import { DoctorListComponent } from './doctor-list.component';
import { DoctorService } from './doctor.service';

import {async, ComponentFixture, fakeAsync, TestBed, tick} from
'@angular/core/testing';
import { By }          from '@angular/platform-browser';
import { DebugElement } from '@angular/core';

import { HttpModule } from '@angular/http';
import {Observable} from "rxjs/Observable";

describe('DoctorListComponent', function () {
  let de: DebugElement;
  let comp: DoctorListComponent;
  let fixture: ComponentFixture<DoctorListComponent>;
  let doctorService: DoctorService;
  let spy = jasmine.createSpy('');

  beforeEach(async(() => {
    TestBed.configureTestingModule({
      imports: [ HttpModule],
      declarations: [ DoctorListComponent],
      providers:    [ DoctorService ],
    })
      .compileComponents();
  }));
```

```
beforeEach(() => {
  fixture = TestBed.createComponent(DoctorListComponent);
  comp = fixture.componentInstance;
  doctorService = fixture.debugElement.injector.get(DoctorService);

  spy = spyOn(doctorService, 'getDoctorsBySpeciality')
    .and.returnValue(Observable.of([{
        'firstname': 'Calvin',
        'lastname': 'Hobbes',
        'email': 'ch@gmail.com',
        'specialityCode': 'PHYSICIAN',
      }]));

  spy = spyOn(doctorService, 'getDoctorsCount')
    .and.returnValue(Observable.of(5));
  de = fixture.debugElement.query(By.css('h1'));
});

it('should not invoke service methods before OnInit', () => {
  expect(spy.calls.any()).toBe(false, 'service methods not yet called');
});

it('should invoke service methods after component initialized', () => {
  fixture.detectChanges();
  expect(spy.calls.any()).toBe(true, 'service methods called');
});

it('should show count after getDoctorsCount method is called', async(()
  => {
  fixture.detectChanges();
  fixture.whenStable().then(() => { // wait for async call
    fixture.detectChanges();        // update view with count
    const h1 = de.nativeElement;
    expect(h1.innerText).toContain('Doctors(5)');
  });
}));

it('should show count after getDoctorsCount method is called',
  fakeAsync(() => {
  fixture.detectChanges();
  tick();                    // wait for async getDoctorsCount
  fixture.detectChanges(); // update view with count
  const h1 = de.nativeElement;
  expect(h1.innerText).toContain('Doctors(5)');
}));
});
```

Unit testing a routed component

In this section, you will learn how to test a component that injects the `Router` and/or `ActivatedRoute` in order to route to a different address/URL based on the parameters. The following are some of the key aspects related to unit tests for such components:

- Unit tests for a routed component essentially mean testing whether the components navigate with the right address (using the Router `navigateByURL` API), or whether the components retrieve the expected parameters (using the `ActivatedRoute` `paramMap` APIs), and not testing the `Router`/`ActivatedRoute` APIs. The following code represents `DoctorListComponent`, which injects the Router and `ActivateRoute` to handle routes such as `doctors` or `doctors/:speciality`. Notice the `navigateByUrl` API invoked on the Router instance for navigating to a different route definition, and `paramMap.subscribe` invoked on the `ActivatedRoute` instance to retrieve the parameter passed with the route definition's URL:

```
import { Component, OnInit } from '@angular/core';
import { Router, ActivatedRoute, ParamMap } from '@angular/router';

import { DoctorService } from './doctor.service';
import { Doctor } from './doctor';

@Component({
 selector: 'doctor-list',
 providers: [DoctorService],
 templateUrl: './doctor-list.component.html'
})
export class DoctorListComponent implements OnInit {

  constructor ( private doctorService: DoctorService,
       private  router: Router,
       private  route: ActivatedRoute) {}

  ngOnInit() {
    this.route.paramMap.subscribe(
      params => this.doctorService.getDoctorsBySpeciality(
          params.get('speciality'))
          .subscribe(doctors => this.doctors = doctors,
              error => this.errorMessage = <any>error));

    onSelect(speciality: string) {
      this.router.navigateByUrl('doctors/' + speciality);
    }
  }
}
```

- As mentioned earlier, the `Router` or `ActivatedRoute` APIs will not be tested. Thus, in place of `Router` and `ActivatedRoute`, their test doubles will be used.
- The following routes are handled using `DoctorListComponent` and their navigation will be tested. Refer to *Figure 6*, which shows, `DoctorListComponent` displaying the list of doctors by specialty:
    - `/doctors`: Lists all the doctors
    - `/doctor/:speciality`: Lists the doctors by specialty
- The aforementioned routes, when used in a template, would look like the following. Pay attention to the click event, which leads to the `onSelect` method of `DoctorListComponent` being invoked:

```
<ul>
    <li><a routerLink="/doctors"
routerLinkActive="active">All</a></li>
    <li (click)="onSelect('PHYSICIAN')">Physician</li>
    <li (click)="onSelect('PEDIATRICIAN')">Pediatrician</li>
    <li (click)="onSelect('CARDIOPHYSICIAN')">Cardio-Physician</li>
</ul>
```

Test doubles for Router and ActivatedRoute

As mentioned earlier, test doubles will be used in place of actual instances of Router and `ActivatedRoute`. As a best practice, it is recommended to write the test doubles in different files, and place them within the `testing` directory so that they can be reused in unit tests/specs for more than one component. Thus, let's write the test doubles' classes in a file named `src/app/testing/router-stubs.ts`. Pay attention to some of the following in the given code:

- The class `RouterStub` will be used in place of `Router`. It defines `navigateByUrl`, which will be invoked appropriately as a result of the code execution of the component under test.
- The class `ActivatedRouteStub` will be used in place of `ActivatedRoute`. The stub implements two capabilities of `ActivatedRoute`, `params` and `snapshot.params`. Notice how `BehaviorSubject` leads to the creation of the Observable stub for `paramMap`, which returns the same value until it is pushed with the newer parameter.

- The class `BehaviorSubject` is used to subscribe to change of state of the Observable object such as `this.testParamMap`. The `BehaviorSubject` class, being an Observable, is unique in the way it is instantiated (it needs an initial value) and returns the value on subscription (the last value of the subject):

```
import { BehaviorSubject } from 'rxjs/BehaviorSubject';
import { convertToParamMap, ParamMap } from '@angular/router';

export class RouterStub {
  navigateByUrl(url: string) { return url; }
};

export class ActivatedRouteStub {
  // ActivatedRoute.paramMap is Observable
  private subject = new BehaviorSubject(convertToParamMap(
    this.testParamMap));
  paramMap = this.subject.asObservable();

  // Test parameters
  private _testParamMap: ParamMap;
  get testParamMap() { return this._testParamMap; }
  set testParamMap(params: {}) {
    this._testParamMap = convertToParamMap(params);
    this.subject.next(this._testParamMap);
  }

  // ActivatedRoute.snapshot.paramMap
  get snapshot() {
    return { paramMap: this.testParamMap };
  }
}
```

Unit test for a routed component

The following represents the unit test for `DoctorListComponent`, and tests whether the right address is passed when the `onSelect` method is invoked:

```
import { DoctorListComponent } from './doctor-list.component';
import { DoctorService } from './doctor.service';

import {async, ComponentFixture, TestBed, inject} from
'@angular/core/testing';

import { HttpModule } from '@angular/http';
import { Router, ActivatedRoute } from '@angular/router';
import {ActivatedRouteStub, RouterStub} from '../testing/router-stubs';
```

```
describe('DoctorListComponent', function () {
  let comp: DoctorListComponent;
  let fixture: ComponentFixture<DoctorListComponent>;

  beforeEach(async(() => {
    TestBed.configureTestingModule({
        imports: [ HttpModule ],
        declarations: [ DoctorListComponent ],
        providers:    [
            { provide: DoctorService, useClass: {} },
            { provide: Router, useClass: RouterStub },
            { provide: ActivatedRoute, useClass: ActivatedRouteStub },
            ],
    })
        .compileComponents();
  }));

  beforeEach(() => {
    fixture = TestBed.createComponent(DoctorListComponent);
    comp = fixture.componentInstance;
  });

  it('should tell ROUTER to navigate when speciality is clicked',
    inject([Router], (router: Router) => {

        const spy = spyOn(router, 'navigateByUrl');
        comp.onSelect('PHYSICIAN');
        const navArgs = spy.calls.first().args[0];
        expect(navArgs).toBe('doctors/PHYSICIAN');

        comp.onSelect('PEDIATRICIAN');
        navArgs = spy.calls.mostRecent().args[0];
        expect(navArgs).toBe('doctors/PEDIATRICIAN');
    }));

});
```

Make a note of some of the following in the preceding code:

- **Usage of test doubles**: They provide stubs such as RouteStub and AcivatedRouteStub to be used in place of ActivatedRoute and Router:

```
beforeEach(async(() => {
  TestBed.configureTestingModule({
    imports: [ HttpModule ],
    declarations: [ DoctorListComponent ],
    providers: [
      { provide: DoctorService, useClass: {} },
```

```
    { provide: Router, useClass: RouterStub },
    { provide: ActivatedRoute, useClass: ActivatedRouteStub}],
})
```

- **Test the route navigation**: The `inject` function, one of the Angular testing utilities, is used to inject one or more services. One can then use spies on these injected services to alter their behavior. In the following code sample, the *Router* service is injected, and a spy is created on the `navigateByUrl` method:

```
it('should tell ROUTER to navigate when speciality is clicked',
    inject([Router], (router: Router) => {

    const spy = spyOn(router, 'navigateByUrl');
    comp.onSelect('PHYSICIAN');
    const navArgs = spy.calls.first().args[0];
    expect(navArgs).toBe('doctors/PHYSICIAN');

    comp.onSelect('PEDIATRICIAN');
    navArgs = spy.calls.mostRecent().args[0];
    expect(navArgs).toBe('doctors/PEDIATRICIAN');
}));
```

Unit testing the services

In this section, you will learn how to write unit tests for services. Services are meant to be reused in one or more components. There can be different kinds of services, such as those providing utility APIs, reusable business rules/logic, and data processing tasks (also termed data services) such as retrieving data from the server. Components inject these services via the constructor, and later, use one or more APIs of the injected services to perform different tasks such as sending/retrieving data to/from the server. Externalizing the data handling logic in the services helps the components stay lean and easy to unit test, as the services can be mocked.

In this section, we will learn some of the following aspects of unit tests for data services that invoke one or more server APIs for data processing:

- Test double for HTTP
- MockBackend
- BaseRequestOptions

Service under test - DoctorService

For illustration purposes, we will consider `DoctorService`, which has these two APIs:

- `getDoctorsBySpeciality (specialityCode: string)`: This API uses the HTTP service to retrieve doctors' information from the server, based on specialty
- `getDoctorsCount ()`: This API retrieves the total doctors count

The following is the sample code for `DoctorService` representing the aforementioned APIs. We will write a couple of unit tests to test each of the APIs:

```
import { Injectable }         from '@angular/core';
import { Http, Response }  from '@angular/http';

import { Observable } from 'rxjs/Observable';
import 'rxjs/add/operator/catch';
import 'rxjs/add/operator/map';
import 'rxjs/add/observable/throw';

import { Doctor } from './doctor';

@Injectable()
export class DoctorService {
  private doctorsUrl = 'http://localhost:8080/doctors';

  public doctorsCount = 0;
  public doctors: Observable<Doctor[]>;

  constructor (private http: Http) {}

  getDoctorsBySpeciality(specialityCode: string): Observable<Doctor[]> {
    let path = '';
    if (specialityCode != null) {
      path = '/' + specialityCode;
    }

    this.doctors = this.http.get(this.doctorsUrl + path)
      .map(this.extractData)
      .catch(this.handleError);

    return this.doctors;
  }

  getDoctorsCount() {
    return this.http.get(this.doctorsUrl + '/count')
      .map((res: Response) => res.json().count)
      .catch(this.handleError);
```

```
    }

    private extractData(res: Response) {
      let body = res.json();
      let doctors = [];
      for (let i = 0; i < body.doctors.length; i++) {
        let doctorInfo = body.doctors[i];
        let doctor = new Doctor(doctorInfo.user.firstname,
doctorInfo.user.lastname, doctorInfo.user.email,
doctorInfo.specialityCode);
        doctors.push(doctor);
        this.doctorsCount++;
      }
      return doctors;
    }

    private handleError (error: Response | any) {
      let errMsg: string;
      if (error instanceof Response) {
        const body = JSON.parse(JSON.stringify(error)) || '';
        const err = body.error || JSON.stringify(body);
        errMsg = `${error.status} - ${error.statusText || ''} ${err}`;
      } else {
        errMsg = error.message ? error.message : error.toString();
      }
      console.error(errMsg);
      return Observable.throw(errMsg);
    }
}
```

Unit test for DoctorService

In writing unit tests for DoctorService, the following is required to be done:

- **Test double for HTTP service**: The HTTP service needs to be faked or stubbed. In other words, there is a need to use fake functions/APIs in place of the HTTP service APIs such as GET. This is primarily because what needs to be tested is the code within the DoctorService APIs, and not the external services such as the HTTP service. The following code represents the usage of a factory function that creates an HTTP instance that makes use of MockBackend and BaseRequestOptions.

- **Fake server:** In addition to the fake HTTP service, there is also a need to create a fake backend server. This is where Angular testing utilities such as `MockBackend` come into the picture. `MockBackend` is used to create a fake backend, which helps in tracking HTTP requests from the service. The following code represents the creation of a fake HTTP service using `MockBackend` and `BaseRequestOptions`:

```
TestBed.configureTestingModule({
    providers: [ MockBackend, BaseRequestOptions, DoctorService,
        {
            deps: [ MockBackend, BaseRequestOptions ],
            provide: Http,
            useFactory: (backend: MockBackend, defaultOptions:
BaseRequestOptions) => {
                return new Http(backend, defaultOptions);
            }
        },
    ],
})
```

- **Response from the fake server**: With the preceding steps in place, one last thing that needs to be set is how the fake server responds to the incoming HTTP request. This is where another testing utility such as `MockConnection` comes into the picture. `MockConnection` is used to respond appropriately to the incoming request made to the fake server. To achieve this objective, as with the helper `router-stubs.ts` file (illustrated in the previous section) that consisted of `Router` helper classes, another file is created within the testing folder, `src/app/testing/http-stubs.ts`. This file comprises of a `ConnectionHelper` class that provides the API to establish the connection. In the following code, pay attention to the fact that whenever the backend gets a connection request, the function passed in the `subscribe` method is executed:

```
import {MockBackend, MockConnection} from '@angular/http/testing';
import {Response, ResponseOptions} from '@angular/http';

export class ConnectionHelper {
    setupConnections(mockBackend: MockBackend, options: any) {
        mockBackend.connections.subscribe((connection:
MockConnection) => {
            const responseOptions = new ResponseOptions(options);
            const response = new Response(responseOptions);
            connection.mockRespond(response);
        });
    }
}
```

Based on some of the earlier concepts, the unit tests for `DoctorService` look like the following:

```
import {async, ComponentFixture, TestBed, inject, getTestBed} from
'@angular/core/testing';
import {BaseRequestOptions, Http, HttpModule} from '@angular/http';

import {DoctorService} from './doctor.service';
import {MockBackend} from '@angular/http/testing';
import {ConnectionHelper} from '../testing/http-stubs';
import {Doctor} from "./doctor";


describe('DoctorService', function () {
  let doctorService: DoctorService;
  let mockBackend: MockBackend;
  let connectionHelper: ConnectionHelper;

  beforeEach(async(() => {
    TestBed.configureTestingModule({
      providers:     [
        MockBackend, BaseRequestOptions, DoctorService,
        {
          deps: [ MockBackend, BaseRequestOptions ],
          provide: Http,
          useFactory: (backend: MockBackend, defaultOptions:
BaseRequestOptions) => {
            return new Http(backend, defaultOptions);
          }
        },
      ],
    }).compileComponents().then(() => {
      const testbed = getTestBed();
      mockBackend = testbed.get(MockBackend);
      doctorService = testbed.get(DoctorService);
      connectionHelper = new ConnectionHelper();
    });
  }));

  it('should return the list of doctors by speciality', () => {
    connectionHelper.setupConnections(mockBackend, {
      status: 200,
      body: {
        message: '',
        doctors: [
          {
            user: {
              firstname: 'Calvin',
```

```
            lastname: 'Hobbes',
            email: 'ch@gmail.com',
          },
          specialityCode: 'PHYSICIAN'
        },
        {
          user: {
            firstname: 'Micky',
            lastname: 'Mouse',
            email: 'mm@gmail.com',
          },
          specialityCode: 'PEDIATRICIAN'
        }],
      count: 3
    }
  });

  doctorService.getDoctorsBySpeciality('').subscribe((doctors: Doctor[])
=> {
    expect(doctors.length).toBe(2);
    expect(doctors[0].firstname).toBe('Calvin');
    expect(doctors[0].specialityCode).toBe('PHYSICIAN');
    expect(doctors[1].firstname).toBe('Micky');
    expect(doctors[1].specialityCode).toBe('PEDIATRICIAN');
  });
});

it('should return the doctors count', () => {
  connectionHelper.setupConnections(mockBackend, {
    status: 200,
    body: {
      message: '',
      doctors: [],
      count: 3
    }
  });
  doctorService.getDoctorsCount().subscribe((count: number) => {
    expect(count).toBe(3);
  });
});
});
```

In the preceding code, pay attention to how the fake responses, such as the following, are created within the unit test functions to mock the response. Make a note that the helper class, `ConnectionHelper`, is used to invoke an API such as `setupConnections`, which is used to determine the response from the fake server:

```
connectionHelper.setupConnections(mockBackend, {
  status: 200,
  body: {
    message: '',
    doctors: [
      {
        user: {
          firstname: 'Calvin',
          lastname: 'Hobbes',
          email: 'ch@gmail.com',
        },
        specialityCode: 'PHYSICIAN'
      },
      {
        user: {
          firstname: 'Micky',
          lastname: 'Mouse',
          email: 'mm@gmail.com',
        },
        specialityCode: 'PEDIATRICIAN'
      }],
      count: 3
  }
});
```

Summary

In this chapter, you learned about unit testing fundamentals, unit testing tools for Angular code, and the fundamentals related to unit testing services, along with components that have dependencies, routes, services, and so on. In the next chapter, you will learn about the different aspects of securing an Angular app.

9

Securing an Angular App

In this chapter, you will learn about some of the concepts related to protecting content displayed by an Angular app from common web vulnerabilities and attacks such as **Cross-Site Scripting (XSS)**, and **Cross-Site Request Forgery (CSRF)**.

We will cover the following topics in the chapter:

- Common web application security vulnerabilities
- Securing app from XSS
- Securing app from XSSI
- Securing app from CSRF
- Best practices

Common web application security vulnerabilities

In this section, you will learn about some of the common web application securities as specified by **Open Web Application Security Project (OWASP)** standards (`https://www.owasp.org/`), against which web applications need to be protected. Angular comes with a built-in support for protecting app against following security vulnerabilities:

- Cross-Site Scripting (XSS)
- Cross-Site Script Inclusion (XSSI)
- Cross-Site Request Forgery (CSRF)

What is Cross-Site Scripting (XSS)?

Cross-Site Scripting (XSS) is one of the most common web application security vulnerabilities found in web applications. Using Cross-Site Scripting, attackers inject the the data or malicious code such as HTML/JavaScript code into web pages by sending untrusted data to the server. The attacker-injected data is not handled properly using one or more mechanisms such as content (HTML/JavaScript) escaping, leading to some of the following outcomes, which can all be called **XSS attack**:

- Deface the web page
- Steal cookie information
- Steal users' data
- Redirect to different web pages
- Hijack users' browsers
- Perform actions to impersonate other users

The following are the two types of XSS attacks:

- **Server-side XSS**: Server-side XSS attacks happen when user-supplied untrusted data is included in the server-generated HTTP response. The user-supplied data can arrive from a database or the incoming HTTP request. If the source of the data is a database, it is called **Stored Server XSS**. In case, the source of data is HTTP request, it is called **Reflected Server XSS**.
- **Client-side XSS**: Client-side XSS attacks happen when user-supplied data such as JavaScript calls is used to change the DOM tree. Such JavaScript calls (script) which could be updated into DOM, are considered unsafe. These scripts could come from sources such as a HTTP response generated from the server or DOM. If the source of data is a stored location such as server or client storage, it is called **Stored Client XSS**. If the source of data is HTTP request itself, it is called **Reflected Client XSS**.

The following are some of the ways in which **Stored or Reflected XSS** attacks can happen:

- Reflected XSS
    - Clicking a URL executes a JavaScript code snippet
- Stored XSS
    - Store a script into the database and serve this script as response to one or more users. Such scripts could hijack the users sessions or deface the website.
    - Inject a script into the HTML request, which can result in the insertion of values in HTML attributes.

XSS exploits the users trust on the website. In a later section, you will learn about how website's (or server's) trust in users can be exploited, resulting in Cross-Site Request Forgery (CSRF) attacks.

What is Cross-Site Script Inclusion (XSSI)?

Cross-Site Script Inclusion (XSSI) is a web application security vulnerability which exploits the exception or relaxation provided to same-origin-policy in relation to script inclusion from different websites. In this relation, recall that a browser, when it loads a website from its hosted server, ends up loading several scripts, such as Bootstrap, JQuery, Angular, and so on, from different servers such as Google **CDN** (**Content Delivery Network**). This flexibility acts as a security vulnerability for an XSSI attack.

XSSI attack can happen in the following two ways:

- **Attacker's website invokes JSON API using a script tag**: Users log into the actual website, which results in the website setting cookie information for further interaction. Users are, then, lured to open attacker's website. As the page loads, the browser invokes the JSON API of the actual website by sending users' cookie information. This JSON API is embedded within script tag. The actual website sends back JSON data and this results in an XSSI attack. Note, that this attack works on older browsers by overriding native JS object constructors and including JSON API as part of a script tag.
- **Attackers website accesses dynamically generated JavaScript files**: Often, it is seen that one or more JavaScript files are generated dynamically based on users' session state and sent back to client as the page loads. The dynamic generation of the scripts from the website based on user session/cookie information results in the leakage of user related information such as user profile data (such as user ID, email), CSRF or auth tokens, and so on, as part of the script data.

The following figure represents how attackers carry out XSSI attacks:

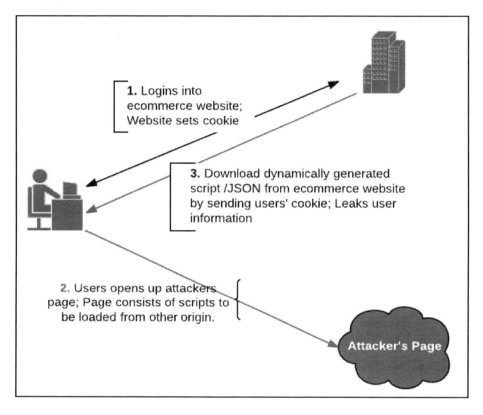

Figure 1. Cross-Site Request Inclusion

Here is how it happens:

1. Users log into the website, which results in the website setting cookies for further message exchanges between user's browser and the website.
2. Attackers lure the users to visit their website through techniques such as clicking a URL in an email, and so on.
3. User visit the attackers' website.
4. Attacker's website loads the script/JSON from original website by sending users' cookie information.
5. As the script/JSON is dynamically generated based on users' cookie information, this results in leakage of users' information to the attacker's website.

What is Cross-Site Request Forgery (CSRF/XSRF)?

Cross-Site Request Forgery (CSRF or XSRF) is a security vulnerability which can lead to trusted users sending forged or unsafe commands to a server which, when executed, lead to undesired outcomes for the end user. For example, a logged-in user (and, thus trusted), unknowingly transferring money from his/her bank account to attackers account or, users making purchases from e-commerce websites or, users changing his/her profile. It can be said that CSRF attacks exploit the server's or website's trust in users.

The following figure represents an example of a CSRF attack:

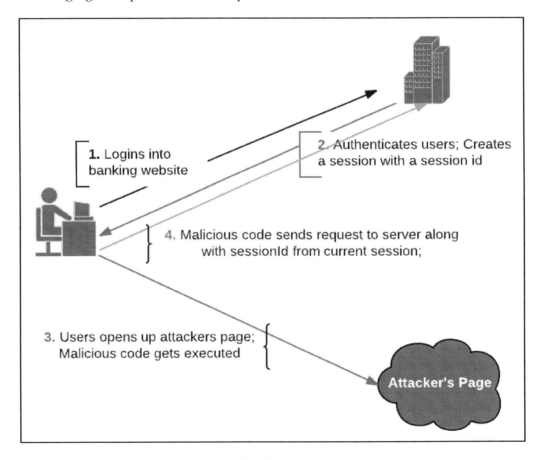

Figure 2. Cross-Site Request Forgery

- Consider that the following REST API is used to transfer money from one's account to another account provided that the request is sent by an authenticated user:

```
http://some.website.com/a/tf?a=2500&da=34526787654
```

- Consider the following being executed as a result of the image tag being executed while the page is loaded due to the fact that logged-in users clicked a URL from his email account or logged-in users opened up a malicious page. It represents the CSRF attack:

```
<img class="image-border"
src="<b>http://some.website.com/a/tf?a=2500&da=attackersAcc
t</b>" width="0" height="0" />
```

The following is how CSRF attack is carried out:

1. Attackers create a forged or unsafe requests/commands such as transfer money from users' account to attackers account.
2. Trick the trusted (logged-in) users to submit those request to the website via one of the following mechanisms:
    - Have the users click a URL sent in an email by the attacker; this leads to the attacker's page getting opened as a result of which malicious code is executed to send a forged request to the actual website.
    - Malicious code execution can happen via image loading as a page is loaded.
    - iFrames
    - XSS
3. Due to lack of CSRF protection, website may not be able to identify the website from which the request is generated.

Securing an app from XSS

As discussed in one of the earlier sections, XSS attacks happen when attackers are able to inject malicious code (JavaScript) into the HTTP request/response or store them in database. Thereby, updating the DOM tree as the malicious code gets executed as part of page getting loaded. Execution of malicious code may result in scenarios such as users' data getting stolen or session being hijacked, and so on. In order to prevent XSS attacks, the key is to prevent attackers from injecting malicious code into the DOM tree. The following is an Angular security model for preventing XSS attacks:

- **By default, Angular sanitizes all data**: All values are treated as unsafe by Angular. That essentially means that all values before getting updated to DOM tree are sanitized and escaped appropriately.
- **Avoid dynamic generation of template code**: Template code such as HTML, attributes, and binding expressions are considered to be trusted data by Angular. Thus, as a recommended practice, one should avoid generating the template code based on the users' state or input, as an attacker could exploit this fact thereby generating malicious template code which can result in undesired updates of DOM tree.
- **Offline template code compiler**: It is recommended to use offline template compiler in order to avoid use of related security vulnerability and inject template code, thereby updating the DOM tree.
- **Security context for data sanitization**: The following is the security context which defines different scenarios when the following data type will not be sanitized by Angular and displayed as it is except for removing JavaScript script tags.

All HTML codes are escaped or sanitized except those which are bound to attribute, inner HTML, as shown in the given example given, sighted in the following code sample:

```
import {Component} from '@angular/core';

@Component({
  template: `
      <p>{{unsanitizedHTML}}</p>
      <p [innerHtml]="unsanitizedHTML"></p>
    `
})
export class HomeComponent {
  unsanitizedHTML= '<script>console.log("hello
world!");</script> Hello, <strong>How are
you?</strong>';
}
```

- Code such as `<p>{{unsanitizedHTML}}</p>` results in Angular escaping the HTML data and displaying it thereafter. The following is what gets displayed on the UI:

```
<script>console.log("hello world!");</script> Hello,
<strong>How are you?</strong>
```

- Code such as `<p [innerHTML]="unsanitizedHTML"></p>` represents the usage of `innerHTML` attribute to bind safe HTML, thereby asking Angular to trust and display the data as it is meant to be. In the following example, Angular escapes unsafe values such as `script` tag and let the safe content such as HTML to be interpreted and displayed on the page appropriately:

```
console.log("hello world!"); Hello, How are you?
```

- Style-related code are sanitized except for the case when they are bound to style property
- URLs are sanitized except for the case when they are bound to href property
- Resource URL (such as `<script src>`) is not sanitized as they can consist of arbitrary code

- **Apply a content-security policy**: Defining a content-security policy as part of a `meta` tag is another technique which ensures the aspect related with where the resources can be loaded from. This, in turn, prevents browser from loading data from any other location, thereby making it harder for attackers to inject malicious code into the website.

The server should return an appropriate content-security-policy header when returning the response. Note that a content security policy allows creation of whitelist of sources of trusted content. Based on this information, browsers only execute or render resources from the whitelisted sources. The following is the sample code representing a content-security policy which can be returned as part of the server response when accessing the website. The following code represents the fact that JavaScript files can be downloaded from the path such as `https://www.somewebsite.com/js/`.

```
<meta http-equiv="Content-Security-Policy" content="script-src
'self' https://www.somewebsite.com/js/"/>
```

- **Implement server-side XSS protection**: All values reaching to server should be escaped appropriately to prevent XSS vulnerabilities on the server.

Displaying trusted HTML values

Apart from the above XSS prevention techniques, it is also required to understand the mechanisms using which Angular can be asked to trust the HTML, style, URL, script, or ResourceURL data and, not sanitize all data for XSS prevention. This is because, many a times, there is a business requirement to do some of the following:

- Execute HTML code rather than escaping them
- Display an iFrame from some URL
- Open up an unsafe URL
- Execute script

In order to bypass Angular's built-in sanitization for the value passed in, Angular provides a class such as DomSanitizer. It provides a set of APIs starting with prefix bypassSecurityTrust which are used to mark the data such as HTML, style, URL, and so on, as trusted or safe. These APIs need to be passed the value which needs to bypass the Angular built-in sanitization and the return value needs to be bound appropriately to some property in the template in the format such as [property]=binding. The following needs to be done in order to avoid Angular's built-in santization:

- Inject DomSanitizer into the constructor:

```
constructor(private sanitizer: DomSanitizer) {}
```

- Invoke one or more of the following APIs to bypass Angular's built-in sanitization against HTML, style, URL, script, and ResourceURL.
    - bypassSecurityTrustHtml: It is recommended to use this API when bound HTML is unsafe (consists of <script> tag) and HTML code needs to be executed. The following example demonstrates the usage of this API:

```
export class SomeComponent {
  constructor(private sanitizer: DomSanitizer) {
    this.trustedHTML = sanitizer.
bypassSecurityTrustHtml(this.unsanitizedHTML);
  }
}
```

Later, in the template, the trustedHTML value needs to be bound to the innerHTML property. Trying to access the value of trustedHTML in an interpolated expression will result in an error such as SafeValue must use [property]=binding.

```
<p [innerHTML]="trustedHTML"></p>
```

- bypassSecurityTrustStyle: In order to avoid Angular sanitize the style, API such as bypassSecurityTrustStyle can be used. The following code represents usage of the API:

```
export class SomeComponent {
  constructor(private sanitizer: DomSanitizer) {
    this.trustedStyle = sanitizer.
    bypassSecurityTrustStyle('color: red;');
  }
}
```

Later in the template, the trustedStyle value needs to be bound to the style property, as shown in the following code:

```
<p [style]="trustedStyle">Hello World</p>
```

- bypassSecurityTrustScript: This API can be used to avoid Angular sanitize script.
- bypassSecurityTrustUrl: In order to avoid Angular sanitize URL, bypassSecurityTrustUrl API can be used. The following code demonstrates the API usage:

```
export class SomeComponent {
  this.unsafeURL = 'JavaScript:alert("Hello World! How are you?")';

  constructor(private sanitizer: DomSanitizer) {
    this.trustedURL =
sanitizer.bypassSecurityTrustUrl(this.unsafeURL);
  }
}
```

- Later, in the template, trustedURL needs to be bound to anchor's href property.

```
<a [href]="trustedUrl">Click Me</a>
```

- bypassSecurityTrustResourceUrl: It helps bypass security and trust the resource URL from where the content or script can be loaded using iframe (`<iframe src="http://...">></iframe>`) or script tag (`<script src="http://...">></script>`).

```
constructor(private sanitizer: DomSanitizer) {
    this.trustedUrl = sanitizer.bypassSecurityTrustResourceUrl(
    '<iframe width="560" height="315"
    src="https://www.youtube.com/embed/xxxxxyyyyy"></iframe>');
}
```

Later, in the template, the trustedURL can be bound to the innerHTML property:

```
<div [innerHTML]="trustedUrl"></div>
```

The Custom SecurityBypass pipe

Instead of using individual APIs for bypassing Angular built-in sanitization, one could create a reusable custom pipe such as the following, save it in file such as app/pipes/security-bypass.pipe.ts, import the pipe in root module such as AppModule, and, use them in one or more components across different modules.

```
import {Pipe, PipeTransform} from '@angular/core';
import {DomSanitizer, SafeHtml, SafeResourceUrl, SafeScript, SafeStyle,
SafeUrl} from "@angular/platform-browser";

@Pipe({
  name: 'trusted'
})
export class SecurityBypass   implements PipeTransform {

  constructor(private sanitizer: DomSanitizer) {}

  public transform(value: string, type: string): SafeHtml | SafeStyle |
    SafeScript | SafeUrl | SafeResourceUrl {
    switch (type) {
      case 'html':
        return this.sanitizer.bypassSecurityTrustHtml(value);
      case 'style':
        return this.sanitizer.bypassSecurityTrustStyle(value);
      case 'script':
        return this.sanitizer.bypassSecurityTrustScript(value);
      case 'url':
        return this.sanitizer.bypassSecurityTrustUrl(value);
```

```
    case 'resourceUrl':
      return this.sanitizer.bypassSecurityTrustResourceUrl(value);
    default:
      throw new Error(`Unable to bypass security for unsupported
        type: ${type}`);
    }
  }
}
```

The preceding pipe can then be used in one or more components shown as follows:

```
import {Component} from '@angular/core';

@Component({
    template: `
    <p [innerHtml]="unsanitizedHTML | trusted: 'html'"></p>
    <p [style]="'color: red;' | trusted: 'style'">Hello world!</p>
    `,})

export class SomeComponent {
    unsanitizedHTML= '<script>console.log("hello world!");</script>
                      Hello, <strong>How are you?</strong>';
}
```

Securing an app from XSSI

The following are the different ways in which an XSSI attack can be prevented:

- All JSON responses are prefixed with string such as)]}', \n. This makes the JSON response non-executable.
- Angular recognizes the previously mentioned string and strips it prior to parsing the response.
- The server should avoid embedding user related information in dynamically generated JavaScript files.

Securing app from CSRF/XSRF

In order to provide protection against CSRF attacks, the following techniques are recommended by OWASP:

- The application needs to make sure that the request is generated from the real application, and not from another website. In order to achieve this, it needs to be verified that origin or referer header consists of a hostname matching the target origin hosting the real application. If both origin and referrer header is missing in HTTP request headers, it is recommended that requests are blocked. This technique is very effective, as all browsers implement the same origin policy.

- Another mechanism is to verify the correctness and validity of what is termed as the CSRF or XSRF token. A challenge random token is generated by the server and associated with the current user session by sending the token as a part of response header or, making it as a hidden parameter of one or more generated forms. This token is, then, sent with every subsequent sensitive operations or form submission performed by the users. The server, then, verifies the correctness and validity of this token and, appropriately, allows operations to proceed. The following are the two different types of CSRF tokens an application can adopt:

  - **Per-session token**: The token can be generated once per session. With each request, the token is sent. Server verifies the correctness of the token and validity in terms of whether the token is expired or not. If the token does not match with actual generated token or, token got expired, server can block the operation and choose to redirect user to login or re-authenticate.

  - **Per-request token**: The token can be generated for each request and later verified and validated. However, there are downsides of this strategy such as users clicking back button on the browser and getting logged out as previous page is associated with different token.

Angular has built-in support for CSRF attack prevention in form of Angular's HTTP service, by default, turning on `CookieXSRFStrategy`. It can be noted that `CookieXSRFStrategy` is an implementation of the `XSRFStrategy` interface. As part of `CookieXSRFStrategy`, Angular does following with each request:

- Angular looks for a cookie namely, XSRF-TOKEN in the server response.
- Angular then sets a header named as X-XSRF-TOKEN and set its value as value of XSRF-TOKEN before sending the request to the server.
- The server must look for both, XSRF-TOKEN and X-XSRF-TOKEN and match their values.

- Alternatively, different cookie names (in place of XSRF-TOKEN) can be used by the server. Accordingly, Angular can customize the cookie names appropriately by creating `CookieXSRFStrategy` with different cookie names. The following is the sample code:

```
{provide: XSRFStrategy, useValue: new
CookieXSRFStrategy('custom-cookie', 'custom-headername')}
```

- The custom `CookieXSRFSTrategy`, as mentioned previously, can be defined in the root module, such as `AppModule`. The following code represents the same:

```
@NgModule({
  imports:  [ CommonModule, FormsModule, AuthModule, ...,
             AppRoutingModule, ],
  declarations: [ AppComponent, PageNotFoundComponent,
                  HomeComponent, SecurityBypass],
  providers: [
          {provide: XSRFStrategy, useValue: new
           CookieXSRFStrategy('custom-cookie',
           'custom-headername')},]
  bootstrap:     [ AppComponent ]
})
export class AppModule { }
```

Best practices

The following are some of the best practices recommended by Angular in order to enhance web security:

- Use the most up-to-date Angular libraries in the app. Attackers do exploit the security vulnerabilities present in previous versions. This is in line with one of the OWASP top 10 security vulnerabilities such as "*Using Components with Known Vulnerabilities*".
- Avoid modifying the copy of Angular libraries. Doing so would lead to one getting stuck with that particular version of Angular, thus preventing one to update the Angular to latest version.
- Use `DomSanitizer` APIs such as `bypassSecurityTrust` methods with utmost care.
- Avoid making use of Angular APIs which are marked as *Security Risk* in the documentation.

Summary

In this chapter, you learnt about securing Angular app against security vulnerabilities such as XSS, CSRF, XSSI, and so on. You also learnt about the best practices in relation with displaying trusted HTML content apart from general best practices. In the next chapter, you will learn about different aspects of integrating Angular app with Spring app.

10
Integrating Angular App with Spring Web APIs

Since we have learned the different aspects of building Angular and Spring apps, it may be worthwhile to understand some of the key concepts in relation to integrating of Angular and Spring apps along with relevant code examples. Some of these concepts include the Angular `Http/HttpClient` service for interacting with Spring endpoints, Spring annotations such as `@RestController`, `@Controller`, and `@ResponseBody` for exposing RESTful APIs, and so on. In this chapter, you will learn about the different aspects of integrating Angular apps with Spring web APIs based on the REST protocol. The following are some of them:

- Building RESTful Spring web APIs
- Configuring Spring app for CORS
- Key aspects of Angular data services
- Building Angular services for RESTful integration
- Examples of consuming RESTful Spring APIs

Building RESTful Spring web APIs

In this section, you will learn about some of the aspects of building RESTful web APIs using Spring. Recall, in `Chapter 1`, *Introduction to Spring Web Framework*, you learned how `DispatcherServlet` is used to dispatch the incoming HTTP requests to the registered handlers, such as web UI controllers, for processing the request and providing convenient mapping, along with exception handling facilities. These controllers provide one or more methods to process incoming requests based on the handler mappings. It is these controllers that are used to expose REST APIs.

The key difference between a RESTful web service controller and the traditional web UI controller is the manner in which the HTTP response body is created and returned as a response. A traditional MVC controller depends upon the `ViewResolvers` to perform server-side rendering of the response data to HTML. RESTful web API controllers return a domain object representing the resource instead of a view. These domain objects are written to the HTTP response as JSON. The following are some of the key steps:

- **Create a RESTful controller**: There are two different ways to create a controller that can act as a RESTful controller, thereby exposing one or more APIs as RESTful web APIs:
    - Annotate controller classes with `@RestController`:

```
@RestController
  public class DoctorSearchController {
}
```

    - Annotate controller classes with `@Controller` and `@ResponseBody`. **Note**, `@RestController` is a shorthand for these annotations.

```
@Controller
@ResponseBody
public class DoctorSearchController {
    ...
  }
```

- **Create a class representing the resource:** The instance of this class will be populated with response data and returned as JSON. In the following example, the `DoctorInfo` class is used to return the list of doctors, the total doctor count, and success or error messages:

```
package com.book.healthapp.helpers;

import java.util.List;
import com.book.healthapp.domain.Doctor;

public class DoctorInfo {
  private String message;
  private List<Doctor> doctors;
  private int count;

  public DoctorInfo(){ }

  public DoctorInfo(String message, List<Doctor> doctors) {
    this.setDoctors(doctors);
```

```
      this.setMessage(message);
   }

   public DoctorInfo(String message, int count) {
      this.setCount(count);
      this.setMessage(message);
   }
}
```

- **Define handler methods for API mappings**: For this, create one or more handler methods within the controller and provide appropriate mappings such as RequestMapping or a set of specific mappings such as GetMapping, PostMapping, and so on:

```
@GetMapping(value="/doctors/count")
public DoctorInfo getDoctorsCount(ModelMap model) {
   int count = docService.findCount();
   return new DoctorInfo("All doctors count", count);
}

@RequestMapping(value="/doctors/{code}",
               method=RequestMethod.GET)
public DoctorInfo getBySpecialityCode(ModelMap model,
@PathVariable("code") String code) {
   List<Doctor> doctors = docService.findBySpeciality(code);
   if(doctors == null) {
      return new DoctorInfo("No Doctors found!", null);
   }
   return new DoctorInfo("Doctors found", doctors);
}
```

- **Create delegate services for processing business logic**: Create one or more delegate services which will be invoked from within the controllers. In the preceding example, docService is an instance of the delegate service DoctorService, whose code looks like this:

```
@Service
public class DoctorServiceImpl implements DoctorService {

   private DoctorDAO doctorDAO;

   @Autowired
   public  DoctorServiceImpl(DoctorDAO doctorDAO) {
      this.doctorDAO = doctorDAO;
   }

   @Override
```

```
  public List<Doctor> findBySpeciality(String specialityCode) {
    return doctorDAO.findBySpecialityCode(specialityCode);
  }
  @Override
  public int findCount() {
    return doctorDAO.findAllCount();
  }
}
```

- **Create data access components for data handling**: Finally, create data access components, which are used to interact with backend databases such as MySQL. In the preceding example, doctorDAO is an instance of the DoctorDAO data access class. The following is the related code sample:

```
@Repository
@Transactional
public class DoctorDAOImpl implements DoctorDAO {

  private SessionFactory sessionFactory;

  @Autowired
  public DoctorDAOImpl(SessionFactory sessionFactory) {
    this.sessionFactory = sessionFactory;
  }

  @Override
  public List<Doctor> findBySpecialityCode(String code) {
    Session session = this.sessionFactory.getCurrentSession();
    TypedQuery<Doctor> query =
      session.getNamedQuery("findBySpeciality");
    query.setParameter("specialityCode", code);
    List<Doctor> doctors = query.getResultList();
    return doctors;
  }
  @Override
  public int findAllCount() {
    Session session = this.sessionFactory.getCurrentSession();
    TypedQuery<Number> query =
      session.getNamedQuery("findAllCount");
    int count = ((Number)query.getSingleResult()).intValue();
    return count;
  }
}
```

Configure Spring app for CORS

In this section, you will learn about appropriate configuration that needs to be done in order to have Angular app invoke Spring RESTful APIs.

In the previous chapters, you learned how to run Angular and Spring apps on different servers which can be accessed using different URLs. An Angular app, when started with the `ng serve --open` command, runs on port `4200` and can be accessed using a URL such as `http://localhost:4200`. On the other hand, a Spring web app runs on a different port such as `8080` and can be accessed using a URL such as `http://localhost:8080`. These apps, therefore, have different origins. Note that *origin* is combination of protocol, hostname, and the port number. As per the same origin policy, web browsers block **XML HTTP Request (XHR)** calls to a remote server whose origin is different from the origin of the web page. Due to this, any attempt to access Spring web/RESTful APIs from Angular apps would result in an error such as `Access-Control-Allow-Origin`, which is a problem related to **Cross-Origin Resource Sharing (CORS)**. In simpler words, this error occurs when one tries to access a resource from one domain to other domain.

Modern web browsers, however, do allow the XHR request across cross-origins if the server supports the CORS protocol. Spring supports the CORS protocol using annotations such as `@CrossOrigin`. The following represents different techniques, based on which, CORS can be enabled:

- **Enabling CORS on specific methods**: CORS can be enabled for one or more specific methods by annotating methods with `@CrossOrigin`:

```
@CrossOrigin(origins = "http://localhost:4200")
@GetMapping(value="/doctors/{code}",
            produces="application/json")
public @ResponseBody DoctorInfo getBySpecialityCode(ModelMap
        model, @PathVariable("code") String code) {
  List<Doctor> doctors = docService.findBySpeciality(code);
  if(doctors == null) {
    return new DoctorInfo("No Doctors found!", null);
  }
  return new DoctorInfo("Doctors found", doctors);
}
```

- **Enabling CORS at class (controller) level**: CORS can be supported at class level by annotating classes with @CrossOrigin. The following is the sample code representing an annotation of the controller with @CrossOrigin. The @CrossOrigin annotation allows requests originating from the domain, localhost:

```
@CrossOrigin(origins = "http://localhost:4200")
@RestController
public class DoctorSearchController {
  ...
}
```

- **Enabling CORS using configuration**: CORS can also be enabled for one or more controllers by defining CORS as a part of the class annotated with the @Configuration annotation. The following code represents enabling CORS support for access to all the resources for requests originating from an Angular app domain, such as http://localhost:4200:

```
@Configuration
@EnableWebMvc
public class AppConfig {
  @Bean
  public WebMvcConfigurer corsConfigurer() {
    return new WebMvcConfigurerAdapter() {
      @Override
      public void addCorsMappings(CorsRegistry registry) {
        registry.addMapping("/**").
        allowedOrigins("http://localhost:4200");
      }
    };
  }
}
```

- **Creating a CORS filter**: CORS can be handled using a CorsFillter class such as the following:

```
@Component
@Order(Ordered.HIGHEST_PRECEDENCE)
public class CorsFilter implements Filter {

  @Override
  public void doFilter(ServletRequest req, ServletResponse res,
FilterChain chain) throws IOException, ServletException {
    final HttpServletResponse response = (HttpServletResponse) res;
    response.setHeader("Access-Control-Allow-Origin", "*");
    response.setHeader("Access-Control-Allow-Methods", "POST, PUT,
```

```
GET, OPTIONS, DELETE");
            response.setHeader("Access-Control-Allow-Headers",
"Authorization, Content-Type");
            response.setHeader("Access-Control-Max-Age", "3600");
            if ("OPTIONS".equalsIgnoreCase(((HttpServletRequest)
req).getMethod())) {
                response.setStatus(HttpServletResponse.SC_OK);
            } else {
                chain.doFilter(req, res);
            }
        }

        @Override
        public void destroy() {
        }
        @Override
        public void init(FilterConfig config) throws ServletException
        {
        }
    }
```

Key aspects of Angular data services

In Chapter 6, *Getting Started with Angular*, you learned that Angular recommends components to delegate tasks related to server communication to one or more services. These services can also be called **data services**. Some of the key aspects of creating data services which can invoke server APIs such as Spring RESTful APIs are:

- **Dependency injection**: Inject the HTTP service as appropriate in the constructor of the service class
- **HTTP APIs invocation**: Invoke the appropriate APIs on the HTTP or the HttpClient service which sends requests to the server APIs for performing CRUD (create, retrieve, update, delete) operations on business entities
- **Response processing**: Process server responses in the form of parsing the JSON data and converting it to JavaScript objects, or handle the exception as appropriate
- **Returns response**: Return Observable to the caller component or service

Before and looking into examples related to building Angular services for RESTful integration, let's understand the concepts related to Observable and Promise. Both Promise and Observable objects can be returned from service APIs and the caller component/service needs to process data appropriately based on the return type. Thus, it is of the utmost importance to understand the basic concepts in relation to Promise and Observable.

Promise and Observable responses

JavaScript supports asynchronous behavior using both Promise and RxJS Observable libraries. Angular supports both Promise and RxJS Observable as return objects from the invocation of service APIs. Invoking one or more APIs on the HTTP or `HttpClient` service, returns an Observable response. Observable is a design pattern used for managing asynchronous data exchange between Angular components and services.

When working with RxJS Observable, it is required to import the related RxJS operators such as Promise, map, catch, and so on, which are useful methods for processing response data. Observable can be converted into Promise by using an API such as to Promise. The following demonstrates using both Promise and Observable for interaction between Angular components and services.

Promise for asynchronous data exchange

Before taking a look at how Promise is used in Angular, let's try and understand the concept related to Promise.

In JavaScript, the **Promise** object represents the eventual completion (of failure) of an asynchronous operation and it's resulting value. Promise allows to associate handler functions to process an asynchronous method's return value which can be success or error/failure data. In scenarios where there is a need to process an operation in an asynchronous manner, the operation can be created as a Promise which when executed results in success or failure. Based on the status of completion, the handler methods get invoked appropriately. The following code represents a Promise:

```
let somePromise = new Promise((resolve, reject) => {
  // Operation is performed asynchronously
  if(/* everything worked fine */) {
    resolve("Successful completion!");
  } else {
    reject(Error("Something went wrong!"));
  }
});
```

```
somePromise.then(function(result) {
  console.log(result); // "Successful completion!"
}, function(err) {
  console.log(err); // Error: "Something went wrong!"
});
```

It must be noted, a Promise handles just a single event after the completion of an asynchronous operation. The Promise object can be in one of the following three states.

- **Pending**: Initial state.
- **Fulfilled**: The operation related to promise succeeded. Note the `resolve` function call in the preceding code sample.
- **Rejected**: The operation related to promise failed. Note the `reject` function call in the preceding code sample.

Let's understand the implementation of Promise in Angular. The following code demonstrates the usage of Promise for asynchronous data exchange between a component and service. Note, how the response from the server API call is processed in the `then` callback. In case of errors arising out of HTTP failures or so on, the same is handled in the `catch` callback. As a best practice, you need to provide code in anticipation for unexpected failures such as HTTP failures.

The following represents the code for a service which returns a `Promise` object:

```
@Injectable()
export class DoctorService {
  private doctorsUrl = 'http://localhost:8080/doctors';
  private headers = new Headers({'Content-Type':
                                 'application/json'});

  constructor (private http: Http) {}

  getDoctorsBySpeciality(specialityCode: string):
                         Promise<Doctor[]> {
    let path = '';
    if (specialityCode != null) {
      path = '/' + specialityCode;
    }
    return this.http.get(this.doctorsUrl + path, {headers:
           this.headers})
      .toPromise()
      .then((res: Response) => this.extractData(res))
      .catch(this.handleError);
  }
}
```

The following represents the code for the component that invoked the preceding API. Pay attention to the processing of the `Promise` object returned by the service API call:

```
@Component({
  selector: 'doctor-list',
  templateUrl: './doctor-list.component.html'
})
export class DoctorListComponent  implements OnInit {

  doctors: Doctor[];
  doctorsCount: number;
  errorMessage: string;

  constructor (private doctorService: DoctorService,
               private router: Router,
               private route: ActivatedRoute) {
    this.doctors = new Array();
  }

  ngOnInit() {
    this.route.paramMap.subscribe(params =>
    this.doctorService.getDoctorsBySpeciality
        (params.get('speciality'))
    .then((doctors: Doctor[]) => { this.doctors = doctors; })
    .catch(error => this.errorMessage = <any>error));
  }
}
```

Observable for asynchronous data exchange

Before taking a look at how Promise is used in Angular, let's try and understand the concept related to Observable.

In JavaScript, Observable is an implementation of the Observer design pattern based on which there can be one or more objects which can choose to listen or observe (and hence, called as **Observer**) the change of state of another object (**Observable**). Observable, which is a *stream of events*, allows to pass *multiple events*, and, each of these events can be processed using a callback method. This is unlike Promise in which just a *single event* is processed as a result of an async operation completion status. An Observable is preferred over Promise due to the very fact that multiple events can be handled. In addition, Observable allows for the cancellation of a subscription whereas Promise eventually results in the callback of the success or failure function.

Angular core does provide basic support for Observables, which is further augmented with operators and extensions from the RxJS library.

The following code demonstrates the usage of Observable for asynchronous data exchange between a component and a service in an Angular app. Pay attention to the API, such as map, which is used to process the response returned from, invocation of the server APIs. As with Promise, it is important to process the error response arising out of HTTP failures or so on.

The following code represents the service API, which returns Observable as a return object:

```
@Injectable()
export class DoctorService {
  private doctorsUrl = 'http://localhost:8080/doctors';
  private headers = new Headers({'Content-Type':
                                 'application/json'});

  constructor (private http: Http) {}
  getDoctorsBySpeciality(specialityCode: string):
    Observable<Doctor[]> {
    let path = '';
    if (specialityCode != null) {
      path = '/' + specialityCode;
    }
    this.doctors = this.http.get(this.doctorsUrl + path, {headers:
this.headers})
                      .map(this.extractData)
                      .catch(this.handleError);
    return this.doctors;
  }
  private extractData(res: Response) {
    let body = res.json();
    let doctors = [];
    for (let i = 0; i < body.doctors.length; i++) {
      let doctorInfo = body.doctors[i];
      let doctor = new Doctor(doctorInfo.user.firstname,
                              doctorInfo.user.lastname,
                              doctorInfo.user.email,
                              doctorInfo.specialityCode);
      doctors.push(doctor);
      this.doctorsCount++;
    }
    return doctors;
  }
}
```

The following represents the component's code which processes an Observable response. Pay attention to the usage of the `subscribe` method. This ensures that any change to an Observable object would be captured by the component using the `subscribe` method:

```
export class DoctorListComponent  implements OnInit {

  doctors: Doctor[];
  errorMessage: string;

  constructor (private doctorService: DoctorService,
               private router: Router,
               private route: ActivatedRoute) {
    ...
  }

  ngOnInit() {
    this.route.paramMap.subscribe(params =>
    this.doctorService.getDoctorsBySpeciality
      (params.get('speciality'))
    .subscribe(doctors => this.doctors = doctors,
               error =>  this.errorMessage = <any>error));
  }
}
```

Building Angular services for RESTful integration

In this section, you will learn about different ways in which Angular components can communicate with server APIs, such as Spring RESTful APIs:

- Invoking server APIs using the Angular HTTP service
- Invoking server APIs using the Angular HtClient service

Invoking server APIs using the Angular HTTP service

In this section, you will learn about some of the key aspects related with usage of the Angular HTTP service APIs for having Angular app communicate with server APIs such as Spring RESTful APIs. Note, the HTTP service is part of HttpModule:

1. **Create a data service**: Create a class, namely, DoctorService in a file, namely, doctor.service.ts and annotate it with @Injectable.

2. **Inject the HTTP service** in the constructor of this service class. The following is the sample code:

```
import { Injectable } from '@angular/core';
import { Http } from '@angular/http';

@Injectable()
export class DoctorService {
  //
  // Inject Http Client Service
  //
  constructor (private http: Http) {}
  ...
}
```

- **Create one or more service APIs** which perform some of the following tasks:
  - Execute appropriate business logic prior to invoking the remote APIs (in our case, the Spring web APIs)
  - Invoke appropriate APIs such as GET, PUT, POST, and so on, on the injected HttpClient service, thereby sending an HTTP request to the server APIs
  - Process the response returned from the API invocation and return the appropriate JavaScript object
  - Handle exceptions by catching them and returning an appropriate error message

- **Inject services in the components**: Inject one or more data services, such as the one created earlier, in one or more of components. Angular recommends that the components should delegate server-related tasks to these injected services. In the following code, a service such as `DoctorService` is injected in the `doctor-list.component.ts` component:

```typescript
import { Component, OnInit } from '@angular/core';
import { Doctor } from './doctor';
import { DoctorService } from './doctor.service';
import { Router, ActivatedRoute } from '@angular/router';

@Component({
  selector: 'doctor-list',
  templateUrl: './doctor-list.component.html'
})
export class DoctorListComponent  implements OnInit {
  doctors: Doctor[];
  errorMessage: string;
  //
  // Inject DoctorService
  //
  constructor (private doctorService: DoctorService, private
router: Router, private route: ActivatedRoute) {}
  ngOnInit() {
    //
    // Invoke getDoctorsBySpeciality API on doctorService
    //
    this.route.paramMap.subscribe(params =>
      this.doctorService.getDoctorsBySpeciality
(params.get('speciality'))
        .subscribe(doctors => this.doctors = doctors,
          error => this.errorMessage = <any>error));
    //
    // Invoke getDoctorsCount API on doctorService
    //
    this.doctorService.getDoctorsCount()
        .subscribe(count => this.doctorsCount = count,
          error => this.errorMessage = <any>error);
  }

  onSelect(speciality: string) {
    this.router.navigateByUrl('doctors/' + speciality);
  }
}
```

- **Configure the feature or root module** by importing `HttpModule` and listing the service providers:

```
@NgModule({
  imports: [
    BrowserModule, FormsModule, HttpModule,
DocRoutingModule
  ],
  declarations: [
    DoctorListComponent, DocComponent
  ],
  providers: [ DoctorService, ... ]
})
export class DocModule {}
```

Based on the preceding instructions, one or more Angular data services can be created to perform CRUD operations on different business entities by invoking server APIs such as Spring RESTful APIs. The following are details on a sample data service such as `DoctorService`, that invokes the HTTP GET API for consuming Spring RESTful APIs and invokes POST, PUT, and delete APIs for posting to RESTful APIs.

Consuming RESTful Spring APIs using the HTTP service

In this section, you will learn how to use the HTTP service's GET API to retrieve data from the server. The HTTP GET API takes a URL along with request headers as arguments and invokes the server API. As a result, it returns an Observable of the HTTP response object which is returned back to the caller either as an Observable object or as a Promise object after converting Observable into a Promise object. Both `toPromise/then` and `map` operator functions of the RxJS library can be used to process the Observable response. This shows in following code:

```
getDoctorsCount() {
    const headers = new Headers({'Content-Type':
                                  'application/json'});
    const url = `${this.doctorsUrl}/count`;

    return this.http.get(url, {headers: headers})
      .toPromise()
      .then((res: Response) => res.json().count)
      .catch(this.handleError);
}
```

The following example represents the usage of the RxJS `map` operator function to process the Observable response and return the Observable response:

```
getDoctorsCount() {
    const headers = new Headers({'Content-Type':
                                 'application/json'});
    const url = `${this.doctorsUrl}/count`;

    return this.http.get(url, {headers: headers})
        .map((res: Response) => res.json().count)
        .catch(this.handleError);
}
```

Posting to RESTful Spring APIs using the HTTP service

In this section, you will learn about the different HTTP service APIs which can be used to create, update, and delete one or more server entities by invoking Spring Web APIs.

- **Create new entities**: In order to create one or more newer entities on the server, the HTTP POST API is used:

```
createDoctor(doctor: Doctor): Observable<Doctor> {
    let headers = new Headers();
    headers.append('Content-Type', 'application/json');
    headers.append('Authorization', 'bearer ' +
                    Cookie.get('access_token'));
    let options = new RequestOptions({ headers: headers });
    const url = `${this.doctorsUrl}/new`;

    return this.http.post(url, doctor, options)
      .map(res => res.json())
      .catch(err => {
        return Observable.throw('Server Error');
    });
}
```

- **Update existing entities**: In order to update one or more existing entities on the server, the HTTP PUT API is used:

```
updateDoctor(doctor: Doctor): Observable<Doctor> {
    let headers = new Headers();
    headers.append('Content-Type', 'application/json');
    headers.append('Authorization', 'bearer ' +
                    Cookie.get('access_token'));
    let options = new RequestOptions({ headers: headers });
                const url = `${this.doctorsUrl}/${doctor.id}`;
```

```
            return this.http.put(url, doctor, {headers: headers})
                        .map(res => res.json())
                        .catch(err => {
        return Observable.throw('Server Error');
    });
}
```

- **Remove entities**: In order to delete one or more existing entities on the server, the HTTP DELETE API is used:

```
removeDoctor(doctorId: number): Promise<void> {
    let headers = new Headers();
    headers.append('Content-Type', 'application/json');
    headers.append('Authorization', 'bearer ' +
                    Cookie.get('access_token'));
    let options = new RequestOptions({ headers: headers });
    const url = `${this.doctorsUrl}/${doctor.id}`;

    return this.http.delete(url, {headers: headers})
        .toPromise()
        .then(() => null)
        .catch(this.handleError);
}
```

Invoking server APIs using the Angular HttpClient service

Angular 4.3 came out with another API named as HttpClient which is built on top of the XMLHttpRequest interface supported by modern browsers for making HTTP requests. The HttpClient service is a part of HttpClientModule, which belongs to the @angular/common/http package. In this section, you will learn about some of the following aspects in relation to using HttpClient for invoking Spring RESTful APIs:

- The HttpClient service can be directly used within components, unlike the HTTP service which is made part of a data service. The component, then, uses these data services to delegate server communication tasks. The following code represents the GET API being invoked on an instance of HttpClient. The HttpClient GET API sends an HTTP request to a Rest URL such as http://localhost:8080/doctors and retrieves the list of doctors:

```
import { Component, OnInit } from '@angular/core';
import { HttpClient } from '@angular/common/http';
```

```
import { Doctor } from './doctor';

@Component({
  selector: 'doctor-list',
  templateUrl: './doctor-list.component.html'
})
export class DoctorListComponent  implements OnInit {
  doctors: Doctor[];

  constructor ( private httpClient: HttpClient ) {
    this.doctors = new Array();
  }

  ngOnInit() {
      this.httpClient.get('http://localhost:8080/doctors').
subscribe(data => {
          //
          // Read the result field from the JSON response.
          //
          const results = data['doctors'];
          for (let i = 0; i < results.length; i++) {
            const doctorInfo = results[i];
            const doctor = new Doctor(
doctorInfo.user.firstname, doctorInfo.user.lastname,
doctorInfo.user.email, doctorInfo.specialityCode);
            this.doctors.push(doctor);
          }
      });
  }
}
```

- The module needs to be configured appropriately to import `HttpClientModule`:

```
import { NgModule } from '@angular/core';
import { BrowserModule } from '@angular/platform-browser';
import { FormsModule } from '@angular/forms';

import { HttpClientModule } from '@angular/common/http';

@NgModule({
  imports: [
    BrowserModule, FormsModule, HttpClientModule, ...
  ],
  ...
})
export class DocModule {}
```

Example of consuming RESTful Spring web APIs

In this section, you will learn about the different aspects of consuming Spring web APIs from custom Angular components and services, while demonstrating the user login functionality. The following will be illustrated:

- Spring RESTful API for user login
- Custom Angular component for managing login view
- Custom Angular service for serving login functionality

Spring RESTful API for user login

In order to serve user login functionality from the server end, the following server-side components need to be developed:

- **RESTful controller exposing login API**: The following is the code for @RestController serving the login API. The details around this is explained in one of the earlier sections. The login form, when submitted, are processed within the Angular component, LoginComponent, which invokes an API of a custom Angular data service such as LoginService. The LoginService API sends a POST request to the Spring RESTful API such as http://localhost:8080/account/login. The POST request sent by the custom Angular service, LoginService, is intercepted in the processLogin method, which is marked with the annotation, @PostMapping(value="/login"). Note, the controller is marked with a RequestMapping annotation with the path value as /account/*:

```
@RestController
@RequestMapping("/account/*")
public class UserAccountController {
  //
  // Delegate Service for serving User Login Functionality
  //
  UserService userService;
  @Autowired
  public UserAccountController(UserService userService) {
    this.userService = userService;
  }
  //
  // Method intercepting the request for URL "/account/login"
```

```
//
@PostMapping(value="/login")
public ExecutionStatus processLogin(ModelMap model,
@RequestBody User reqUser) {
    User user = null;
    try {
        user = userService.isValidUser(reqUser.getEmail(),
reqUser.getPassword());
    } catch (UnmatchingUserCredentialsException ex) {
        logger.debug(ex.getMessage(), ex);
    }
    if(user == null) {
        return new ExecutionStatus("USER_LOGIN_UNSUCCESSFUL",
"Username or password is incorrect. Please try again!");
    }
    User userDetails = new User();
    userDetails.setFirstName(user.getFirstname());
    return new ExecutionStatus("USER_LOGIN_SUCCESSFUL", "Login
Successful!", userDetails);
}

}
```

The following can be noted in preceding code:

- The @RestController annotation is used to inform Spring that the controller, UserAccountController, can serve RESTful APIs.
- The delegate service, UserService, is used to check whether user with the given login credentials, exists in the system.
- The returning response object, such as execution status, consists of the login status and appropriate user details.
- The UserService acts as a delegate service which serves the login functionality. Pay attention to UserDAO, data access objects, which is delegated the task of checking the user login credentials with the database:

```
@Service
public class UserServiceImpl implements UserService {
    //
    // UserDAO service
    //
    private UserDAO userDAO;
    @Autowired
    public UserServiceImpl(UserDAO userDAO) {
        this.userDAO = userDAO;
    }
    //
```

```
        // UserDAO service is delegated task of checking where a user
    with given credentials
        // exists in the database.
        //
        @Override
        public User isValidUser(String email, String password) throws
    UnmatchingUserCredentialsException {
            List<User> users = (List<User>)
    userDAO.findByEmailAndPassword(email, password);
            if(users == null || users.size() == 0) {
                throw new UnmatchingUserCredentialsException("User with
    given credentials is not found in the database.");
            }
            return users.get(0);
        }
    }
```

- The DAO service is used for interacting with the database:

```
@Repository
@Transactional
public class UserDAOImpl implements UserDAO {
    private SessionFactory sessionFactory;
    @Autowired
    public UserDAOImpl(SessionFactory sessionFactory) {
        this.sessionFactory = sessionFactory;
    }

    @Override
    public List<User> findByEmailAndPassword(String email,
                        String password) {
        Session session = this.sessionFactory.getCurrentSession();
        TypedQuery<User> query =
session.getNamedQuery("findByEmailAndPassword");
        query.setParameter("email", email);
        query.setParameter("password", password);
        return query.getResultList();
    }
}
```

- The user object representing a persistent object is marked with the annotation @Entity. Pay attention to the typed query definition which is referred in the preceding UserDAO API implementation, findByEmailAndPassword:

```
        @Entity
        @Table(name="user")
        @NamedQueries({
```

```
        @NamedQuery(
          name = "findByEmailAndPassword",
          query = "from User u where u.email= :email and u.password =
    :password"
          ),
        })
        public class User {
          @Id
          @GeneratedValue(strategy=GenerationType.IDENTITY)
          private int id;
          private String email;
          private String password;
          ..
        }
```

Custom Angular component for managing login view

In this section, you will learn about how `LoginComponent` communicates with the server via `LoginService`. Pay attention to some of the following in the code shown next :

- An inject authentication service such as `AuthService` is delegated the task of checking user login credentials. Based on the service response, the user will either be displayed an error message or redirected to different URL.
- An inject router service is used to redirect users to a different URL based upon a successful login.
- Login and logout APIs are used for processing login and logout requests made by end users:

```
@Component({
  selector: 'login',
  templateUrl: './login.component.html'
})
export class LoginComponent {
  alertStyle = '';
  model = new Login('', '');
  loginStatus = new LoginStatus('', '');

  constructor(private authService: AuthService,
              private router: Router) {}

  onLogin() {
    this.initLogin();
    this.authService.login(this.model)
```

```
      .subscribe((status: LoginStatus) => {
        this.loginStatus.code = status;
        if (this.loginStatus.code === 'FAILURE') {
          this.alertStyle = 'alert alert-danger';
        }
      });
  }

  onLogout() {
    this.authService.logout();
  }

  private reset() {
    this.alertStyle = '';
    this.loginStatus.code = '';
    this.loginStatus.message = '';
  }
}
```

Custom Angular service for serving login functionality

In this section, you will take a look at an example of a data service that is used to delegate tasks for communicating with server APIs. The following represents the custom login service whose APIs, such as `login` and logout, are invoked by `LoginComponent`. Pay attention to some of the following:

- The HTTP service from `HttpModule` is injected in the service constructor.
- `AuthService` supports two APIs such as *login* and *logout* to serve login and logout functionality.
- HTTP service's *post* API is used to send a request to the Spring RESTful API with a URL represented by `${this.serverUrl}/account/login`
- The login status is maintained using an `Observable` object so that a change in the value of this object would lead the caller components to do the necessary operations by redirecting to appropriate pages.

```
@Injectable()
export class AuthService {
  isLoggedIn: Observable<boolean>;
  private observer: Observer<boolean>;
  serverUrl = 'http://localhost:8080';
  headers = new Headers({'Content-Type': 'application/json'});
```

```
constructor(private http: Http) {
  this.isLoggedIn = new Observable(observer =>
    this.observer = observer
  );
}

login(login: Login): Observable<SignupStatus> {
  const url = `${this.serverUrl}/account/login`;
  const options = new RequestOptions(this.headers);

  return this.http.post(url, login, options)
    .map(response => {
      const body = response.json();
      if (body.code === 'USER_LOGIN_SUCCESSFUL') {
        this.changeLoginStatus(true);
      }
      return response.json();
    })
    .catch((error: any) => Observable.throw(error.json().error ||
          'Server error'));
}

logout(): void {
  this.changeLoginStatus(true);
}

private changeLoginStatus(status: boolean) {
  if (this.observer !== undefined) {
    this.observer.next(status);
  };
}
}
```

Summary

In this chapter, you learned about concepts related to Angular apps interacting with Spring web endpoints. In the next chapter, you will learn about deploying Angular and Spring web applications.

11
Deploying the Web Application

In this DevOps age, one of the key requirements is to automate the process of build, tests and deployment in a way that the functionality can be delivered to the end customer in shortest possible time. Given this fact, it is very important to learn key aspects of build and deployment automation. In this chapter, you will learn to use **continuous integration** (**CI**) and **continuous delivery** (**CD**) tools to deploy web apps in an automated manner. The following will be dealt with:

- Introduction to CI and CD
- Setting up Jenkins and GitLab
- Configuring GitLab as code repository
- Creating a Jenkins job for CI
- Configuring Jenkins and GitLab for CI/CD
- Configuring Jenkins job for CD
- Deploying Angular app in production

Introduction to CI and CD

CI is the automated process of retrieving application code from one or more code repositories, building the code, and running unit tests. CD is an automated process of delivering/deploying the application build artifacts to one or more environments, such as **quality assurance (QA)**, **user acceptance testing (UAT)**, and production. The CD process begins with the successful completion of the CI process. The following diagram shows both CI and CD processes:

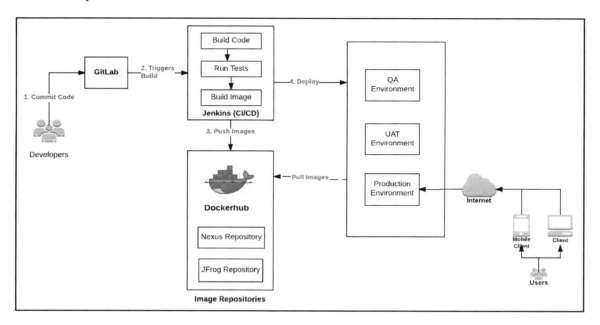

Figure 1: CI/CD Process

These are some of the important aspects of the CI/CD process in the preceding diagram:

- **Developers commit the code**: To start with, one or more developers commits the application code, they have been working upon. This includes both, Angular app and Spring Web app developers.

- **Code repository triggers CI**: As the code changes are pushed into the code repository (GitLab in the preceding diagram), GitLab webhooks triggers the CI builds in CI tool such as Jenkins. The process to achieve the automated trigger of Jenkins builds based upon code changes and push it in to code repository is described later in the chapter.

- **CI build process kicks in**: As the CI build is triggered, the application code is checked out from the code repository (GitLab) and built using appropriate tools. For Spring web apps, the build tool used is **Maven** and for Angular app, the build tool used is **npm**. In case, the build gets successful, unit tests are run. This takes place for both, Angular and Spring web apps.

- **CD process kicks in**: After the successful run of build and unit tests, CD process kicks in. The following happens as a part of the CD process:
  - In non-containerised environments, the build artifacts are uploaded in an appropriate secured local artifactory such as Nexus, or JFrog. Subsequently, **configuration management (CM)** tools such as Ansible, Puppet, or Chef are used to remotely log into one or more environments (QA, UAT, and production) and execute the scripts (cookbook, playbook, and so on) to install and configure appropriate tools and build artifacts and deploy the build using different deployment strategies, such as blue-green and canary deployments.
  - In case of containerized environments, container images (such as Docker images) are built and uploaded in appropriate image repository. Subsequently, CM tool can be used to login remotely in the appropriate environments and deploy the builds.

Setting up Jenkins and GitLab

First, you need to set up a code repository and a CI/CD tool. In this chapter, we will use GitLab as the code repository and Jenkins as CI/CD tool for demonstration purpose. In real world scenario, one may not require to setup these tools and is rather done by the IT team. Both are open source tools, and can thus, be downloaded and set up without any issues.

Setting up Jenkins

In this section, you will learn how to setting up and configure Jenkins and some plugins which will be used to build the Spring project. Jenkins (https://jenkins.io/) is a self-contained Java-based open-source software that is popularly used for continuous integration and continuous delivery of web applications.

- Instructions on installing Jenkins can be found at https://jenkins.io/doc/book/getting-started/installing/. Depending on the development environment OS, you can follow the appropriate instructions and install Jenkins appropriately. In recent times, mostly for development purposes, developers install Jenkins with a Docker image using commands such as following:

```
docker pull jenkins
```

Once the Jenkins Docker image is pulled from the Docker repository, next step is to run Jenkins within the Docker container which can be done using the following command:

```
docker run -dp 18080:8080 --name jenkins -v $PWD/jenkins:/var/jenkins_home
-t jenkins
```

In the preceding command, the Jenkins home directory, /var/jenkins_home, within the Docker container, is mapped to jenkins directory from the current path ($PWD/jenkins) on the host machine. You could access Jenkins from a browser with URL such as http://localhost:18080.

In addition, the container called jenkins can be found running by executing the following command:

```
docker ps -a
```

On initial access of Jenkins from browser, you need to enter a security token that can be obtained from console logs when Jenkins is first run or from the location in the following screenshot. The installation process continues with installation of one or more plugins that user selects:

Unlock Jenkins

To ensure Jenkins is securely set up by the administrator, a password has been written to the log (not sure where to find it?) and this file on the server:

`/var/jenkins_home/secrets/initialAdminPassword`

Please copy the password from either location and paste it below.

Administrator password

Figure 2: Unlocking Jenkins for installation to continue

- **Installing Jenkins Plugins**: Once Jenkins is installed, you are required to install some of the following plugins in order to work with GitLab and Maven jobs. In order to install plugins, you need to log in into Jenkins, visit the page **Jenkins | Manage Jenkins | Manage Plugins**, click on the **Available** tab, and install the following plugins:
  - GitLab
  - Maven integration plugin

After this, you need to install Maven in order to run Java projects using Maven. You can do this by navigating to **Jenkins | Manage Jenkins | Global Tool Configuration.** Assign a name to the Maven installation setup, choose the default option, and save.

Setting up GitLab

GitLab can be installed by following the instructions at `https://about.gitlab.com/installation/`. Alternatively, GitLab can also be installed using a GitLab Docker image by executing the following command:

```
docker pull gitlab/gitlab-ce
```

Once the Docker image has been downloaded and installed, you can install GitLab Docker container using the following command.

```
docker run -d -p 443:443 -p 80:80 -p 2222:22 --name gitlab --restart always
-v /opt/gitlab/config:/etc/gitlab -v /opt/gitlab/logs:/var/log/gitlab -v
/opt/gitlab/data:/var/opt/gitlab gitlab/gitlab-ce
```

Note, this command is valid for GitLab Ubuntu Docker image. It will start GitLab in a Docker container. GitLab can then be accessed using `http://localhost:`

Setting up GitLab and Jenkins using Docker Compose

Instead of setting up GitLab and Jenkins independently, you can run the following code using `docker-compose up` command and, both, Jenkins and GitLab will be installed and started in different containers. Jenkins can be accessed with a URL `http://localhost:18080` and GitLab can be accessed using a URL `http://localhost`. The following code represents a Docker Compose file and can be saved as `docker-compose.yml`:

```
version: '2'

networks:
  prodnetwork:
    driver: bridge

services:
 jenkins:
  image: jenkins
  ports:
    - "18080:8080"
  networks:
    - prodnetwork
  volumes:
    - /var/run/docker.sock:/var/run/docker.sock
    - /usr/bin/docker:/usr/bin/docker
    - /opt/jenkins/:/var/lib/jenkins/
  depends_on:
    - gitlab

 gitlab:
  image: gitlab/gitlab-ce
  restart: always
  networks:
```

```
     - prodnetwork
   environment:
     GITLAB_OMNIBUS_CONFIG: |
       # external_url 'https://gitlab.example.com'
       # Add any other gitlab.rb configuration here, each on its own line
   ports:
     - "80:80"
     - "443:443"
     - "2222:22"
   volumes:
     - /opt/gitlab/config:/etc/gitlab
     - /opt/gitlab/logs:/var/log/gitlab
     - /opt/gitlab/data:/var/opt/gitlab
```

Configuring GitLab as a code repository

In this section, you will learn to setup GitLab as a code repository and start checking in your code in this repository. The following steps must be performed after you have registered itself with a custom user credentials.

- **Create a repository in GitLab**: Once logging in, you can create a project by giving it a project name and selecting the appropriate access permission (choose the default setting such as private). The following screenshot represents the same.

- **Register the existing application folder with GitLab to store code in GitLab**: Go to the application folder and execute the following commands:

```
git init
git remote add origin http://localhost/ajitesh/healthapp.git
git add .
git commit
git push -u origin master
```

Once done, you should be able to commit code in GitLab. Note, the path `http://localhost/ajitesh/healthapp.git`, is project path in GitLab.

- **Some useful commands**: Once a project is configured with GitLab, you can use some of the following commands to commit new changes:

```
git status    // Know the status of code commits
git add .     // Add the newly added files for commits
git commit -am "reason for code commit" // Commit code changes
git push      // Push the code changes to repository
```

Creating Jenkins jobs for CI

In this section, you will learn to create Jenkins jobs for continuous integration builds. This is pretty straightforward. Go to the Jenkins **Dashboard** page and click on **New Item** (**Jenkins | New Item**). Note we need to create two jobs, one for Spring apps and another one for Angular app. For Spring apps, choose **Maven project**, as shown in the following screenshot. For Angular apps, select the **Freestyle project** option, give it a name, to the project and click **Save**. Now you are all set to configure job for the CI build:

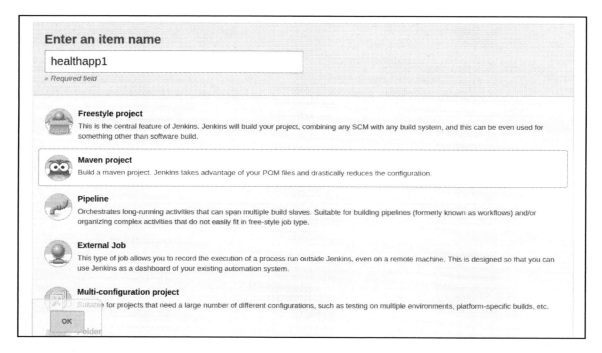

Figure 3: Creating new job in Jenkins

The next step is to configure the job for the CI build. Running a job for a Spring app would do a maven build and run the unit tests, by default.

Angular app would required to be bundled in order to be deployed in production. This can be achieved using browserify (http://browserify.org/). The following are the different steps which can be executed as part of building Angular app for production:

- **Build the app**: The following command can be used to clean up the distribution folder and build the app using the `tsc` command. The `tsc` command is for the Typescript compiler:

```
npm run clean && tsc -p src/
```

- **Bundle the app**: Subsequently, the app needs to be bundled. This can be achieved using the following command. Pay attention to usage of browserify command used for bundling the Angular app.

```
npm run build && browserify -s main dist/main.js > dist/bundle.js
&& npm run minify
```

- **Minify the bundled app**: Lastly, it would be required to minify the `bundle.js` created in preceding step. This is invoked as a part of the preceding code used for bundling the app. Bundling the app can be achieved using the following command. Pay attention to the creation of file, `bundle.min.js`, as part of execution of command shown as following:

```
uglifyjs dist/bundle.js --screw-ie8 --compress --mangle --output
dist/bundle.min.js
```

Configuring Jenkins and GitLab for CI/CD

In this section, you will learn how to configure GitLab webhooks to trigger Jenkins builds as and when the code changes are pushed into GitLab repositories. Note, this aspect of triggering builds based on code changes pushed into repositories is a key aspect of achieving continuous delivery. The following key aspects need to be taken care off, in order to achieve the integration between GitLab and Jenkins:

- Configure webhooks in GitLab for triggering build in Jenkins
- Configure Jenkins for automated build triggers
    - GitLab connectivity
    - Source code management
    - Build triggers

Configuring webhooks in GitLab

To configure webhooks in GitLab, go to the project page and click the **Integrations** link, which can be found in the drop-down menu at the top right of the page. In **URL** field, you need to provide the project link from Jenkins. Note Jenkins running within a Docker container is accessible through the browser `http://10.0.2.119:18080`, where `10.0.2.119`, is the IP address of the host machine. The following screenshot shows the **Integrations** page for configuring the webhook:

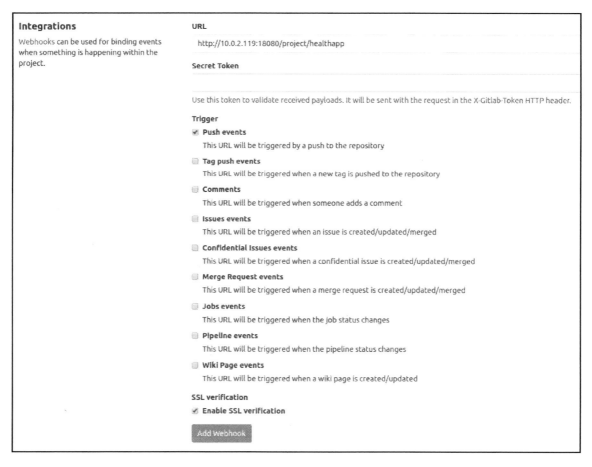

Figure 4: Configure GitLab webhooks

Configuring Jenkins for automated build triggers

Once done setting up webhooks configuration in GitLab, log in to Jenkins and configure the settings in order to enable building triggers as and when code changes are pushed into GitLab.

First, go to **Jenkins** | **Manage Jenkins** | **Configure System** and configure GitLab connectivity by entering appropriate details in the **GitLab host URL** and **Credentials** fields. You need to select **GitLab API token (Gitlab token)** from the list by logging into GitLab, visiting **GitLab** | **Settings** | **Account page**, and getting the private token:

Figure 5: Configure GitLab Connectivity

After configuring GitLab connectivity, configure the source code management so Jenkins knows the details of the code repository from where it will checkout the code for the purpose of building. In order to achieve this, visit the project's **Configure** page and enter the details as follows:

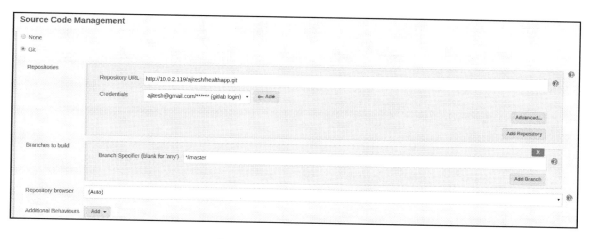

Figure 6. Configure Maven Project for CI Build

Note that the GitLab code repository URL where GitLab is running within a Docker container, can be accessed from the browser at port 80. In addition, you need to add GitLab username/password credentials. You can do this by clicking on **Add** button.

Finally, you need to configure the automated build trigger based on code changes pushed into GitLab. You can do this by entering details in the same page where *source code management* configuration is entered, as shown in the following screenshot:

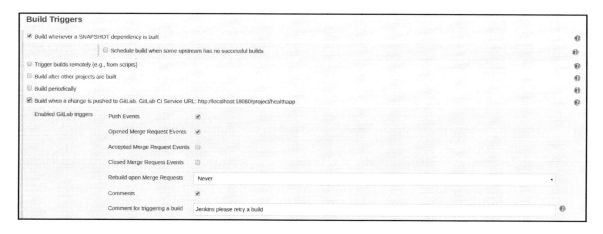

Figure 7: Configuring CI build trigger as a result of code change pushed in GitLab

Configuring Jenkins jobs for CD

So far, you have learned how to achieve continuous integration for both Angular and Spring app. Recall that you can build and run unit tests based on continuous integration of Spring and Angular apps. In this section, you will look into some of the aspects of achieving continuous delivery of apps in QA, UAT, and production environments.

Once build and unit tests are running successfully, you need to perform will some of the following operations:

- **Non-Dockerized deployments**: Traditionally, you can adopt different strategies for delivering/deploying apps to different environments. One of them can be done through using shell script by adding a step *Execute Shell* as a post-build step:
  - Build RPMs for the apps: You would be required to write related RPM scripts and place them along with the project source code.

- Upload RPMs in the code artifacts such as Nexus, JFrog, and so on.
- Use configuration management tool such as Ansible, Chef, and Puppet to run the deployments remotely in different environments. For instance, with Ansible, one would execute playbook which would log into different boxes remotely using SSH. As a result, the RPMs will be downloaded, installed and configured in different environments/boxes.

- **Dockerized deployments**: In Dockerized deployments, the apps will be containerized and deployed. The following code needs to be executed using *Execute Shell* as part of Jenkins build post steps:
  - Build the Docker image
  - Post/upload the Docker image on an image repository, such as Dockerhub. The commands for this with the HealthApp are:

```
# Build the Docker Image
sudo docker build -t ImageName:tag
/var/jenkins_home/workspace/healthapp

# Log into Image repository (Dockerhub) using login credentials
sudo docker login -u="dockerhubLogin" -p="dockerhubPassword"

# Push/upload image into image repository (Dockerhub)
sudo docker push ImageName:tag
```

  - Log in remotely (using SSH) in appropriate environments such as QA, UAT, production, and execute appropriate commands to stop and remove existing Docker containers, pull the new image from the image repository such as Dockerhub and run the container using new image. This would ensure that both, Spring and Angular apps are up and running using fresh builds.

Deploying Angular app in production

This section deals with learning different aspects of deploying an Angular app in production. In one of the preceding section, you have learnt about how, as part of CI build, Angular app can be built, bundled and minified appropriately to create a JS bundle (artifact) which can be referenced within the index.html file.

In this section, you will learn about some of the following aspects in relation with Angular app deployment and related optimization techniques in relation with moving the Angular app to production.

- **Base tag in index.html file**: The HTML tag such as following, as found in `index.htl`, is used for resolving relative URLs to assets such as images, scripts, and style sheets. It can be noted that, during navigation, Angular router uses the `base href` as the base path to component, template, and module files. The following setting works well for development server.

  ```
  <base href="/">
  ```

  On production server, the base `href` path is changed appropriately to context path from where the app is served. If the app is found on URL such `http://www.somewebsite.com/my/healthapp/`, the `base href` path would look like following:

  ```
  <base href="/my/healthapp/">
  ```

- **Changes in main.ts file**: The following (in bold) represents the changes which need to be made in `src/main.ts` file.

  ```
  import { platformBrowserDynamic } from '@angular/platform-browser-
  dynamic';

  import { AppModule } from './app/app.module';
  import {enableProdMode} from '@angular/core';

  // Enable production mode unless running locally
  if (!/localhost/.test(document.location.host)) {
      enableProdMode();
  }

  platformBrowserDynamic().bootstrapModule(AppModule);
  ```

- **Load npm package files from the web**: While deploying using simple technique without adopting bundling/minifying strategy, `index.html` is advised to load npm package files from the internet/web rather than `node_modules` folder. Following file represents the `index.html` used for development. Pay attention to `node_modules` path for loading scripts.

  ```
  <!DOCTYPE html>
  <html>
    <head>
      <title>+HealthApp | Welcome</title>
      <base href="./">
  ```

```
            <meta charset="UTF-8">
            <meta name="viewport" content="width=device-width, initial-
scale=1">
            <link rel="stylesheet" href="styles.css">

            <link rel="stylesheet"
href="https://maxcdn.bootstrapcdn.com/bootstrap/3.3.7/css/bootstrap.min.css
" integrity="sha384-
BVYiiSIFeK1dGmJRAkycuHAHRg32OmUcww7on3RYdg4Va+PmSTsz/K68vbdEjh4u"
crossorigin="anonymous">
            <!-- Latest compiled and minified JavaScript -->
            <script
src="https://ajax.googleapis.com/ajax/libs/jquery/3.2.1/jquery.min.js">
</script>
            <script
src="https://maxcdn.bootstrapcdn.com/bootstrap/3.3.7/js/bootstrap.min.js"
integrity="sha384-
Tc5IQib027qvyjSMfHjOMaLkfuWVxZxUPnCJA712mCWNIpG9mGCD8wGNIcPD7Txa"
crossorigin="anonymous"></script>
            <!-- Polyfill(s) for older browsers -->
            <script src="node_modules/core-js/client/shim.min.js">
</script>

            <script src="node_modules/zone.js/dist/zone.js"></script>
            <script src="node_modules/systemjs/dist/system.src.js">
</script>

            <script src="systemjs.config.js"></script>
            <script>
                System.import('main.js').catch(function(err){
console.error(err); });
            </script>
          </head>

          <body>
            <my-app>Loading...</my-app>
          </body>
        </html>
```

The following is `index.html` changed with recommended technique for deploying it in production:

```
<!DOCTYPE html>
<html>
  <head>
    <title>+HealthApp | Welcome</title>
    <base href="/">
    <meta charset="UTF-8">
```

```
    <meta name="viewport" content="width=device-width, initial-scale=1">
    <link rel="stylesheet" href="styles.css">

    <link rel="stylesheet"
href="https://maxcdn.bootstrapcdn.com/bootstrap/3.3.7/css/bootstrap.min.css
" integrity="sha384-
BVYiiSIFeK1dGmJRAkycuHAHRg32OmUcww7on3RYdg4Va+PmSTsz/K68vbdEjh4u"
crossorigin="anonymous">
    <!-- Latest compiled and minified JavaScript -->
    <script
src="https://ajax.googleapis.com/ajax/libs/jquery/3.2.1/jquery.min.js"></sc
ript>
    <script
src="https://maxcdn.bootstrapcdn.com/bootstrap/3.3.7/js/bootstrap.min.js"
integrity="sha384-
Tc5IQib027qvyjSMfHjOMaLkfuWVxZxUPnCJA7l2mCWNIpG9mGCD8wGNIcPD7Txa"
crossorigin="anonymous"></script>
    <!-- Polyfill(s) for older browsers -->
    <script
src="https://unpkg.com/core-js@2.5.0/client/shim.min.js"></script>
    <script src="https://unpkg.com/zone.js@0.8.16/dist/zone.js"></script>
    <script
src="https://unpkg.com/systemjs@0.20.17/dist/system.src.js"></script>

    <script src="systemjs.config.js"></script>
    <script>
      System.import('main.js').catch(function(err){ console.error(err); });
    </script>
  </head>

  <body>
    <my-app>Loading...</my-app>
  </body>
</html>
```

- **Load Angular and third-party packages from web**: Configure SystemJS to load UMD version of Angular (and other third-party packages) from the web. This would require creation of an alternate file similar to systemjs.config.js and include the same in index.html in place of systemjs.config.js. You may name this file as systemjs.config.prod.js. The following is how the code looks like for systemjs.config.prod.js:

```
(function (global) {
  System.config({
    paths: {
      // paths used in development
      // 'npm:': 'node_modules/'
```

```
            'npm:': 'https://unpkg.com/'
          },
          // map tells the System loader where to look for things
          map: {
            // our app is within the app folder
            'app': 'app',

            // angular bundles
            '@angular/core': 'npm:@angular/core/bundles/core.umd.js',
            '@angular/common':
'npm:@angular/common/bundles/common.umd.js',
            '@angular/compiler':
'npm:@angular/compiler/bundles/compiler.umd.js',
              '@angular/platform-browser': 'npm:@angular/platform-
browser/bundles/platform-browser.umd.js',
              '@angular/platform-browser-dynamic': 'npm:@angular/platform-
browser-dynamic/bundles/platform-browser-dynamic.umd.js',
              '@angular/http': 'npm:@angular/http/bundles/http.umd.js',
              '@angular/router':
'npm:@angular/router/bundles/router.umd.js',
              '@angular/forms': 'npm:@angular/forms/bundles/forms.umd.js',
              '@angular/common/http': 'npm:@angular/common/bundles/common-
http.umd.js',

            // other libraries
            'rxjs':                        'npm:rxjs',
            'angular-in-memory-web-api': 'npm:angular-in-memory-web-
api/bundles/in-memory-web-api.umd.js',
            'tslib': 'node_modules/tslib/tslib.js',
            'ng2-cookies': 'npm:ng2-cookies'
          },
          // packages tells the System loader how to load when no
filename and/or no extension
          packages: {
            app: {
              defaultExtension: 'js',
              meta: {
                './*.js': {
                  loader: 'systemjs-angular-loader.js'
                }
              }
            },
            rxjs: {
              defaultExtension: 'js'
            },
            'tslib': {
              defaultExtension: 'js'
            },
```

```
        'ng2-cookies': {
          main: './index.js',
          defaultExtension: 'js'
        },
      }
    });
  })(this);
```

As with any other app, loading HTML file requires browser making multiple requests to server for downloading individual CSS and JS files. The same can be seen using browser developer tool. Each file download may end up spending a lot of time in communicating with the server and transferring data. In addition, development files are full of comments and whitespace for easy reading and debugging. These are not required for production. All these issues need to be handled appropriately to expedite the page loading time. The following are some of the optimization techniques which can be used for faster page load. Some of these such as bundling, minifying, uglifying, and so on. has been described in one of the previous sections.

- **Ahead-of-Time (AOT) Compilation**: pre-compiles Angular component templates.
- **Bundling**: concatenates modules into a single file (bundle).
- **Inlining**: pulls template html and css into the components.
- **Minification**: removes excess whitespace, comments, and optional tokens.
- **Uglification**: rewrites code to use short, cryptic variable and function names.
- **Dead code elimination**: removes unreferenced modules and unused code.
- **Pruned libraries**: drop unused libraries and pare others down to the features you need.

Angular app can be deployed using the following two strategies:

- Standalone app deployed on a separate server (nodeJS). In this strategy, Spring app is deployed on separate server.
- Angular app deployed on the same server as Spring app.

Angular app deployed on separate server

In this section, you will learn different ways using which Angular app can be deployed in production. The following are some of the techniques:

- As demonstrated earlier in this section, one of the technique which is trivial enough is related with loading npm packages along with Angular and third-party packages from web. However, this would result in page loading very slowly owing to the fact that browser makes multiple requests to server for downloading individual CSS and JS files.
- Alternatively, the following command can be executed to create production bundles and deploy the same on node server. This would be faster enough as all of the files get minified/uglified in 4-5 files.

```
ng build --prod
```

Files such as the following will get created as a result of execution of the preceding command within `dist` folder. These files can be deployed on node server.

- `index.html`
- `inline.xxxxxx.bundle.js`
- `main.xxxxxx.bindle.js`
- `polyfills.xxxxxx.bundle.js`
- `vendor.xxxxxx.bundle.js`
- `styles.xxxxxxx.bundle.css`

Angular app deployed on Spring app server

Angular app can be deployed on the same server as Spring app by placing files created using techniques described in the preceding section within `resources/static` or `resources/public` folder.

Summary

In this chapter, you learned how to setup and configure a code repository with GitLab and Jenkins to achieve continuous integration and continuous delivery. It will help to deliver and deploy, both, Spring and Angular apps in QA, UAT, and production environments as and when the code changes are pushed by the developers in to code repositories.

Index

login functionality, serving 325

D

data binding 174
data retrieval 103
data service 309
data source information
  setting, in application.properties file 93
database tables
  about 97
  user 98
DataSource 94
DataSourceTransactionManager 108
declarative transaction management 111
decorators
  about 182
  reference link 182
dependencies
  components, unit testing 266
  mocking techniques 129
  mocking, Mockito used 128
dependency injection (DI)
  about 9, 173
  dependency 173
  injector 173
  provider 173
Dependency Inversion Principle (DIP) 9
design domain objects 97
development environment
  setting up, Docker compose used 78
  setting up, with Docker compose script 78
directives
  about 172, 177, 198
  attribute directives 172
  attributes directives 200
  reference link 176
  structural directives 172, 199
Dispatcher servlet 18
Docker client 75
Docker compose
  about 76, 78
  development environment, setting up 85
  MySQL, setting up as container service 84
  script, for setting up development environment 78

Tomcat 8.x, setting up as container service 79
  used, for development environment setting up 78
Docker Compose
  used, for setup of GitLab 332
  used, for setup of Jenkins 332
Docker container
  about 69, 74, 75
  and real-world containers, relationship 72
  building blocks 76
  real-world containers, advantages 70
Docker engine 75
Docker host 75
Docker Hub
  about 76
  reference link 117
Docker image 76
Docker Toolbox
  reference link 77
Docker
  about 68
  advantages 68
  Docker container 69
  installing 77
  key building blocks 75
Dockerfile 77
dockerized deployments 339
Doctor module
  components 240
  root module/component 237
  routing module 238
  services 239
DoctorService
  unit testing 282

E

Eclipse IDE
  installing 53
  Maven Project, creating 54
  Maven Project, importing 53
  Spring STS, Setup 20
Eclipse
  Apache Tomcat server, adding 59
  Apache Tomcat server, configuring 59
  URL 53
EhCache 92

Made in the USA
San Bernardino, CA
04 December 2017